Great Private Collections

Great Private

Collections

Edited by **Douglas Cooper**

Introduction by **Kenneth Clark**

The Macmillan Company New York

First published in the United States of America by The Macmillan Company, 1963
Library of Congress Catalog Card Number 63-12758

Designed by Jane Mackay

Printed in Switzerland by Conzett & Huber, Zurich

Contents

Below the name of each collector will be found a brief description
of the types of works of art which form the main body of his collection.
The purpose of this is simply to assist the reader
by providing some indication of what he will find in each section.
These descriptions are not meant to be exhaustive.

Acknowledgements

The editor and publishers wish to thank the owners of the collections for giving permission
for their collections to be described in this book. They also wish to express their appreciation
of the help given by the owners of the collections and the authors of the articles
in assembling the illustrative material.

The publishers are also indebted to the following
for their help and for permission to reproduce photographs:

H M THE KING OF SWEDEN: Dr Bo Gyllensvärd. Photographs by Ekberg, Stockholm.
WALTER C. BAKER: Photographs copyright Walter C. Baker.
GEORGE SPENCER-CHURCHILL: Photographs by Ian Graham, Woodbridge, pp 40, 42, 43, 45 (right top and bottom), 49;
by The Butt Studio, Bourton-on-the-Water 45 (left); by R.E. George, Moreton-in-the-Marsh 44;
by courtesy of The Royal Academy of Arts 46, 47, 48.
LUIGI MARZOLI: Photographs by Federico Arborio Mella, Milan, except pp 51 and 53.
BERNARD BERENSON: Dr Kenneth B. Murdock. Colour photographs by courtesy of Du, Zurich.
Photographs by Bazzechi Foto, Florence p 73 (left); by courtesy of the Uffizi Gallery 67, 70.
ROBERT LEHMAN: Photographs by courtesy of the owner. Colour photograph p 85 by Alec Gregory, New York.
COUNT VITTORIO CINI: Istituto di Storia dell'Arte della Fondazione Giorgio Cini, Venice.
Photographs by Alinari, Venice, pp 91, 94 (centre top, middle and bottom), 95 (top);
by Agencia Fotografica Industriale, Venice 93 (right); by Umberto Rossi, Venice 95 (bottom).
BARON H. H. THYSSEN-BORNEMISZA: All photographs by courtesy of the Galleria Thyssen, Lugano.
JEAN FURSTENBERG: Jaspard, Polus & Cie, Monaco. All photographs by Albert Pik, Paris,
except p 111 by René-Jacques, Paris.
DENIS MAHON: Photographs by courtesy of the owner.
ARTURO LOPEZ-WILLSHAW: Jaspard, Polus & Cie, Monaco. Photographs by Jean Vincent pp 127, 128,
130, 132, 133, 134, 136, 137; by Henri Tabah, Paris 129, 131, 132 (top), 135.
JUDGE IRWIN UNTERMYER: All photographs copyright Collection of Irwin Untermyer, except p 147 by courtesy of the
Metropolitan Museum of Art (gift of Irwin Untermyer). Colour photograph p 146 (top) by Alec Gregory, New York.
FORSYTH WICKES: Photographs by courtesy of the owner. Colour photographs p 157 by
Museum Color Slides Association, Boston. Photographs by Avon Studios, Rhode Island 150, 153.
ARPAD PLESCH: All photographs by M. Atzinger, Avignon.
ELIE DE ROTHSCHILD: Jaspard Polus & Cie, Monaco. Photographs by Henri Tabah, Paris pp 169,
170, 171, 173, 175, 176 (top), 177, 179; by Roland Bonnefoy, Paris 178 (right).
J. PAUL GETTY: All photographs by courtesy of the J. Paul Getty Museum, Malibu.
STAVROS NIARCHOS: Jaspard, Polus & Cie, Monaco. Photographs by Connaissance des Arts p 199;
by R. Guillemot-Connaissance des Arts 200; by M. Knoedler Inc., New York 193;

Foreword

Douglas Cooper

Histories of collecting tend to treat the subject in general terms as though it were relevant only to the history of taste at some given period. I have adopted a different approach, stressing the contributions made by individuals, because I believe that in a culturally benighted, confused and eclectic age like our own, their special sensibility leads to all sorts of valid discoveries and helps to maintain sane standards of judgment. In the present volume, each private collection is treated separately and the illustrations are complemented by a commentary in which the reader will find the essential information concerning the origins of the collection, the history of its development, and the reasons for it being considered important, as well as a discussion of the most important items which it contains.

The conception of this book is thus entirely new, for it sets out to emphasize the connoisseurship and point of view of the informed individual collector as opposed to the vague enthusiasms of the generality, and it also tells the reader why, when and by what means each collector set about making the collection he desired. I hope that in this way the volume will prove useful as a work of reference for art historians, for specialists in many related fields and also for research students. But this volume has not been designed to appeal only to specialist readers. I think that the casual reader too will find much that is fascinating between its covers, and I hope that it will arouse his interest in new aspects of art appreciation and cause him to reflect on the importance to society as a whole of the disinterested cultural activities of true art collectors.

This book is not in any sense a history of collecting in the twentieth century. Indeed it does not pretend to cover more than a very small part of this vast and as yet unstudied subject. But it does provide an authentic account of a few privately owned collections of great artistic and historical importance which have been assembled by some of our more enlightened contemporaries. The list of collectors who appear in this volume owes nothing to chance. Their names were not lightly chosen and this volume is the fruit of much thought and deliberation. For this reason it seems to me not out of place to explain in a few words the principles which have guided me during its compilation.

Generally speaking, private art collections which truly deserve to be described as 'great' belong to one of two basic types. There is the 'historical' type and the 'personal' type. The 'historical' collection is one acquired over the centuries, and without any unifying plan, by a family which has enjoyed spectacular worldly successes in different generations, but of which only a few members have perhaps shown any artistic interests. This type of collection has generally been amassed through marriages, the fortunes of war, the liberality of monarchs or diplomatic and political triumphs. The second – 'personal' – type of collection is a direct result of the creative activity of one, or perhaps two, specially favoured and gifted individuals who set out to build up a library, or a collection of furniture, paintings or objects of a particular kind because they themselves are keenly interested in them.

I decided from the first to rule out all inherited collections of the 'historical' type, because I wanted this book to show the variety of artistic interests which men of culture, scholars and the rich have pursued in the twentieth century. In short, my intention was not that this book should reflect what passes for contemporary taste but that it should reveal the creative contributions made by serious collectors to our cultural heritage and the development of art history. For that reason also I have excluded those haphazard assemblages – nowadays referred to as collections – of a few ill-assorted works by artists currently enjoying a 'great' reputation. These do not deserve to be dignified by calling them collections, for they are dissolved and re-formed by their owners with every fluctuation in market values and smart taste.

Great Private Collections is devoted strictly to collections of a 'personal' kind which have been made, to all intents and purposes, within living memory. And in choosing these collections I have not hesitated to interpret 'greatness' in my own way. So far as I am concerned, a collection of ten thousand postage stamps, stuffed birds or samplers for instance, could not be called a 'great' collection except in the sense that it involves great numbers of things. The fact that such collections contain a few extremely rare items is not a relevant consideration, because that by itself is not enough to constitute 'greatness'. Neither aesthetic sensibility nor a sense of artistic 'quality' has played any part in determining the selection of the objects: collections of that sort are therefore the result of applied methodology and nothing more. The collections in this volume have been chosen on the principle that fine quality, rather than a large quantity, is the element which makes a collection 'great'. Far be it from me to claim that all existing 'great' private collections are described here. On the contrary, I am only too conscious of how much richer this volume would have been if it had proved possible to include as well the private collections belonging to Herr Robert von Hirsch, Dr Frits Lugt and Count Antoine Seilern. But it is not every private collector who will allow the limelight to be focussed upon him, and so omissions of this sort, however regrettable, are inevitable. What is certain, however, is that the collections described and illustrated here represent private collecting during the present century at the highest level of achievement, and also that they represent a very high percentage of those which I ever seriously considered including.

At this point, I should explain that I have interpreted the words 'private collection' in the strictest sense. That is to say, I have included only those collections which are still privately owned and among which their creators, or their immediate heirs, still live. I have ruled out on principle any collection which though still 'private' in a limited sense – such as the Duncan Phillips Collection in Washington – now has museum status and is fully accessible to the public.

Does this book hold any lessons for us? Every reader will want to come to his own conclusions. Yet, speaking for myself, I would like to say this. Collecting on a serious basis and in the grand manner, as it is represented here, has now become – owing to the exigencies of modern society – a luxury in which very few people can even think of indulging. Furthermore, newly-made collections tend to be gobbled up by the State – represented by museums – on the death of their creators. And as this happens there are progressively fewer works of exceptional quality or interest left for private collectors to acquire – unless, that is, they are attracted to the field of strictly contemporary art, which is something of a gamble. All of this works against the formation of new 'great' collections, so collectors as a species are fast disappearing. One need only inquire into the ages of the different collectors represented in this book, for example, to discover that three are dead, the great majority well advanced in years, and none of them under forty. This is not the result of my having excluded younger men: simply they are not there.

Hitherto, those who have benefited from the activities of serious collectors have been legion: the State, the museums, the learned professions, posterity, and in many cases architects and artists who have been commissioned to provide and decorate buildings and rooms to house an ensemble. Today, art-speculators and snobs are favoured at the expense of true *conoscenti*. Is this really a healthy state of affairs, and how will it affect society in the future? The question deserves more careful thought than it has yet received. It takes a trained eye, a special sensibility and love to recognize that essential 'quality' which constitutes 'greatness' in any form of artistic creation. And history teaches us – though the walls of our museums proclaim it no less loudly to those who take the trouble to read – that, irrespective of period, this sense of 'quality', which has inspired all artistic discovery and patronage, has been above all the distinctive attribute of great collectors and (by extension) of their intimate circle. By all means, let us exert ourselves to put art within reach of the masses, because the more that art is brought back into the everyday life of the people the healthier the situation should become for those who are trying to create today. But at least we should be sure that the art which is being sponsored and put into museums is good art. And that will always depend on people with imagination, flair and insight. However, these are just the attributes which will never be developed by the horde of art-administrators into whose hands the power to shape taste has been placed during the last twenty years. For that reason, it is my conviction that any society which genuinely believes in upholding cultural values should show respect for the initiative, powers of aesthetic judgment and devotion to scholarship of men like the great collectors to whom this book is dedicated with the admiration which is their due.

Introduction

Kenneth Clark

Why do men and women collect? As well ask why they fall in love: the reasons are as irrational, the motives as mixed, the original impulse as often discoloured or betrayed. The collector's instinct, if animals and children are any guide, has two roots; the desire to pick up anything bright and shining and the desire to complete a series; and these primitive instincts, under the stress of competition, memory, wealth, and other evolutionary factors, produced the first stages in collecting, the treasury and the cabinet of coins. They are still well to the fore in some of the collections described in this volume; and indeed I should have no confidence in a collector who was wholly without them. Between the rooms full of eighteenth-century masterpieces in Monsieur Groult's house in Paris were cases full of the most exquisite butterflies, and they gave one confidence in his choice of Fragonards. But once the pure delight in the brightness and order of inanimate objects is transferred to those mysterious communications of human experience which we call works of art, our difficulties begin. Not only do they demand a special kind of sympathy, and perhaps a little knowledge; but fashion, self-esteem, commercial speculation and other less reputable impulses all intervene.

The finest collectors look at their possessions with the feelings of an artist and relive, to some extent, the sensuous and imaginative experiences which lie behind each work. Many great collectors have, in fact, been artists, and in the days before photography collected material which could help them in their profession. Such were the antiques collected by Mantegna and the vast accumulation of prints and drawings amassed (together with Roman busts and Japanese armour) by Rembrandt, and imaginatively re-created in his work. Drawings have always been favourites with artist collectors, partly because a drawing is a personal communication, a whisper or hint to a fellow explorer, and partly perhaps because drawings can be put away in boxes, and so are not always staring down at one when one is in the wrong mood for them. The drawings collected by Lely, Richardson, Reynolds, and Lawrence have seldom been equalled, and in more recent times Léon Bonnat's collection of drawings at Bayonne shows a certainty of taste, which, fortunately for him, his rich and fashionable patrons did not possess. Today professional artists of standing do not often collect. Epstein had attics full of negro sculpture (which, in fact, had very little influence on his art), but as a rule painters cannot bear to have anything on their walls but their own works. Degas was one of the last great artists to form a collection, and one remembers also that he was the last great copyist. But the artist's eye remains the surest of all guides. It has been the good fortune of American museums that so many artists like Mrs Chester Dale and Mrs Duncan Phillips, have married rich men, but Mr Phillips is himself a distinguished connoisseur; or were related to rich people, like Mary Cassatt, or were themselves prevented by a fortune from painting professionally, like Mr Stephen Clark and Mr Caroll Tyson. Reading these names, one remembers private collections which had an extra distinction unprocurable by learning, diligence or wealth.

Nevertheless knowledge, when combined with taste, produced that old-fashioned figure to whom I am indebted for some of my happiest hours, the *grand amateur*. The greatest works may be in national institutions, but lesser works bought with love and installed in harmonious surroundings

13

Introduction

retain, in some mysterious way, a touching quality which they inevitably lose in a public gallery. The collection of a *grand amateur* should not be too big or too systematic; it must look completely at home in its surroundings and must be related even to the food and the wine on the sideboard. It must, above all, be personal, an extension of the character of the collector. Raymond Koechlin, who embodied more than any man I have ever known the grace of connoisseurship, spent his life on a catalogue of Gothic ivories, but the things which I remember best in his collection were the Harunobu prints and some pieces of lacquer, worthy of Korin. They were remote in time and place from his special field of study, but they were, so to say, of the same family. The *grand amateur* can spread his net very wide, without loss of consistency, as in the von Hirsch collection in Basle, perhaps the most enviable ensemble I know; but usually the visitor can perceive one department in which the collector's passion has burned with particular intensity. For example, Dr Reinhart at Winterthur has admirable works by early German painters and masterpieces by Van Gogh and Cézanne; but when one comes upon pictures and drawings done between 1820 and 1860 – Delacroix, Corot, Daumier, the early Courbet, even the German romantics – one feels that they gave him a special *frisson* of delight.

No doubt the great collector is wise to limit himself to what comes within his range of feeling; but the limitation must be instinctive, not artificially imposed. In the Stoclet collection, for example, every picture and object had the same degree of magical remoteness from appearances. Any display of realism in that setting would have looked disgusting. But Monsieur and Madame Stoclet seemed quite unaware of their *parti-pris* and knew only that they bought what appealed to them. Also, their limitation was wide enough to give a great range. The collector who adopts narrow limits in hope of achieving completeness falls into another category.

One type of *grand amateur* should perhaps be considered separately, the type which can conveniently (if unhistorically) be named the Epicure. A *grand amateur* like Koechlin may live simply, and collect austere, or even chastening objects. But the Epicure wishes everything that surrounds him to reflect an ideal of richness, and sensual gratification. Of this type the Wallace Collection, both in its strength and weakness, is the supreme example. The strength is a taste for splendour and a devotion to fine craftsmanship, which not only accounts for pictures by Rubens and Watteau, but even led Sir Richard to such unexpected departures as gilt bronzes of the fourteenth century. The weakness lay in a preference for polish and elaboration, which led to a multiplication of Sèvres and snuff boxes, and to a rather uncertain response to contemporary painting. A visit to the store rooms of the Wallace Collection is revealing. Sir Richard does not seem to have recognized that between a silk skirt painted by Watteau and a satin doublet by Meissonier lay the whole secret of art. The epicure collector is also limited by his preference for agreeable subjects; of which the most agreeable of all are a pretty face and a shining bosom. Fortunately Rubens, Boucher and Fragonard felt the same. But Sir Richard's natural inclinations sometimes press too heavily on his taste: there are fifteen Greuzes in his collection, and no Chardins. There are times at Hertford House when I am reminded of Ben Jonson's Sir Epicure Mammon; but I remember that in the threadbare, unheated, half-starved atmosphere of post-war England a visit to the Wallace Collection was better than a hot bath, and it remains a life-enhancing contrast to modern interior decoration. Up to the last war the style of Sir Richard Wallace was still to be seen in private hands in the houses of the Rothschild family. Indeed, if all their collections could have been united they would, I believe, have put the Wallace Collection in the shade. A visit to a Rothschild Collection was always a memorable experience. Hushed, inviolate, almost indistinguishable from one another, they were impressive not only by their size and splendour, but by a sense of the solemnity of wealth which hung about them. In a Rothschild Collection I always found myself whispering, as if I were in church. However, the Rothschild Collection described in these pages is of a much less awe-inspiring kind, and has been humanized by the taste of a *grand amateur*.

This volume also describes one great epicurean collection in New York, that of Robert Lehman. To his parents' early Italian and Flemish panels, chosen with much love and understanding, he has added masterpieces of nineteenth-century painting, of drawing, of Renaissance jewellery, which leave one breathless.

I must now consider the characteristic which is commonly thought to be the basis of collecting, and which must certainly be present to some extent in even the most high-minded collection: the desire to possess. This is a biological function, not unrelated to our physical appetites. It is no accident that the great, greedy collectors, Augustus of Saxony, Catherine of Russia, Caylus, Vivant-Denon, not to mention more recent examples, were also great amorists. There is also some of the miser's instinct, which gives the works collected a kind of totemic value:

> Good morning to the day and next, my gold.
> Open the shrine, that I may see my *Saint*.

Mr Gulbenkian, when asked to show his collection, used to reply, 'Would I admit a stranger to my harem?' And at least two great collectors have solemnly assured me that, like Sardanapalus and his wives, they wished their collections to be burnt on their deaths. Nor is this obsession wholly unsympathetic. Great collections are often made by men who have held high office, and have, in consequence, few illusions about the nature of their fellow men, or women. Pictures become their only reliable friends. There is a famous description of the dying Mazarin, stumbling unobserved through his picture gallery and saying good-bye to Corregio's *Antiope*, Titian's *Venus* and Carracci's '*incomparable Déluge.*' '*Adieu chers tableaux que j'ai tant aimés*'. However, it must be admitted that the lust to possess works of art leads to bizarre excesses. Many collectors – Augustus II, Mr Morgan, Mazarin himself – have bought more pictures than they could unpack, let alone contemplate with enjoyment. Mr Walters of Baltimore, whose collection of early medieval art shows a remarkable discrimination, forgot entirely what he had already bought, so that when the cases in his cellars were opened after his death they were found to contain nine almost identical works by a monotonous fifteenth-century artist known as the pseudo-Pier-Francesco-Fiorentino. These unopened packing cases have become symbolic, and were used with great effect in Orson Welles' film, *Citizen Kane*. But although it may seem irrational to buy something which one will never see, every collector knows that the first tug on the line is the real moment of ecstasy. We do not expect an angler to eat every fish he catches.

Which leads me to observe that the urge to collect is closely allied to the sporting instinct, and just as no one would go out to shoot a cow in a field, so a true collector enjoys the length and difficulty of the stalk and the uncertainties which attend it up to the minute of the kill. This, rather than meanness, leads collectors to take special pleasure in works bought for small sums in unexpected places. The sporting instinct is, of course, open to abuse. Dr Barnes and Sir William Burrell, two of the greatest collectors whom I have known, would tell with relish hair-raising stories of how they had watched at the bedsides of dying widows or paid monthly calls on poor clergymen, in order to get their teeth into some delicate morsel. If the same stories had been told to them with the motive of collecting omitted, they would no doubt have been sincerely shocked. I may add that whereas Gentiles tend to boast of how little they have paid for their prizes, Jewish collectors (in my experience) take the opposite and far more honourable line. Henry Oppenheimer, the most amiable type of Jewish collector, used to show his favourite drawings with the words, 'And when I tell old Lippmann what I paid for it, he says "Mein Gott, Oppenheimer, you are *craissy*".' That argues, surely, a

Introduction

greater love of art than the usual English boast (probably a lie) 'I picked it up for a few coppers'.

Distinguishable from the sporting instinct by its systematic approach is what may be called the stamp-collecting instinct. As I have said, it is one of the fundamental instincts, present in children, and perhaps a youthful passion for stamps and cigarette cards is a necessary foundation for all great collectors. To achieve a complete series of anything requires the same kind of patience and tenacity of purpose that was shown by a Mazarin or a Mariette; and probably the stamp collector, certainly the coin collector, needs to be a judge of quality and scrutinize each purchase with a delicate intensity. But in the end the artistic and human values of the thing collected must be a decisive factor. One can conceive a 'great' collection of Rembrandt's etchings in which the stamp-collecting element, the rare states and wide margins, was admitted only in so far as it affected the beauty of the impression. It becomes less easy to apply the word to a collection of Baxter Prints, and impossible to apply it to a collection of matchboxes.

A stamp-collecting outlook is one of the occupational diseases of museum curators, partly because it can be justified by a display of learning, partly because it has the restful quality of mathematics – it is concerned with *certezze* rather than *opinioni*. This used to be illustrated at a high level by the collections of Mr and Mrs John D. Rockefeller Jr. in Park Avenue. Mrs Rockefeller's apartment was a triumph of taste, in which panels by Duccio hung above Louis XVI furniture with perfect harmony. I can think of few rooms which had achieved more expensively the *douceur de vivre*. But it was touch and go, and had clearly caused Mrs Rockefeller much anxiety. Across the lobby (or was it on the next floor?) Mr Rockefeller kept his collection of *famille noire* porcelain. Seen *en masse*, these large lustrous black objects made a gloomy, not to say funereal, impression, and had on me the reverse effect of Mrs Rockefeller's golden treasury. But they seemed to make Mr Rockefeller very happy, happier, I fancied, than anything else; and each time he could add one more of these rare monsters, differing, perhaps, from the others in the pattern of the hawthorn blooms, his mind could celebrate the triumph of certainty.

I come now to a group of motives for collecting which are usually thought of as discreditable, although in other fields they are accepted without difficulty: I mean the motives associated with conquest, power and self-assertion. From the earliest times conquerors have marked their triumphs by carrying off works of art, not simply because they are important symbols, but because this was a way in which the conqueror could extend his power from the material to the spiritual world. It reflected, in the public sphere, an imperative need for the body to rape the soul. No conqueror has ever looted on so grand a scale as Napoleon who, with the help of Vivant-Denon, took to the Louvre the three-star objects of art from every town in Europe. The allied determination to return these to their original positions after Waterloo caused more resentment in the French people than any other consequence of their defeat. No privations or material humiliations seemed equal to the loss of the Laocoon and the Apollo Belvedere; and the Duke of Wellington, with the help of a Highland Regiment, had personally to supervise the removal of the Raphaels. What Napoleon achieved by force of arms, other collectors achieved by money; Mr Pierpont Morgan's triumphant progresses throughout Italy were like those of a conquering general. As soon as it was known that *il Bobo Morgo* (for it was in this ogreish form that his name was current) was approaching, every impoverished nobleman in the district searched his attics and ransacked his chests, and brought his offerings on bended knee, as subjugated peoples do on old tapestries. But with luck he was paid, and the object, instead of mouldering invisibly, is now preserved and beautifully displayed in the Metropolitan. So that money, as an instrument of conquest, although less romantic, was in every way preferable to the sword.

It is often asked whether the robber barons of the last sixty years purchased works of art because they liked them or because a collection gave them a sense of power and social standing. The answer, of course, varies with each individual. Some of them were men of exceptional insight. Van Horne, who had started as a navvy on the Canadian Pacific Railway, bought his El Grecos and Japanese pots when the directors of the Louvre and National Gallery would not have thought of doing so. And, as is well known, collectors in Chicago bought the Impressionists when the fine flower of French culture was doing its best to stop the Caillebotte Collection from entering the Luxembourg. The two greatest buccaneer collectors of the age, Mr Frick and Mr Morgan, present an insoluble problem. Those who knew Mr Frick do not describe him as a man of marked sensibility; yet his collection has a sober harmony which must surely reflect his personal taste. Mr Morgan's gigantic appetite made him gobble up some things that did not suit him. Yet for the sculpture, enamel and goldsmith's work of the early Middle Ages he had a remarkable instinct, and every visit to the Metropolitan leaves one with an increased admiration for his formidable eye. A collection put together by a dealer or an expert for a client with no particular interest in art may be stuffed full of masterpieces, like those which Duveen reserved for Mr Mellon, and yet lack character and consistency. A possible exception is that of Mrs Gardner, who,

brilliant woman though she was, seems to have had little natural feeling for art. Bernard Berenson used to say that each one of her purchases was like a surgical operation, in which the patient had first of all to be anaesthetized. However, her personality was so strong and his persuasive force so great that the Gardner Collection is certainly not lacking in character.

The deadness of dealer-made collections is not due solely to the natural law by which we all tend to take advantage of those who have more money than understanding; but rather to the fact, mentioned earlier, that a great collection must reflect a strong personal preference. The dealer, who has to satisfy a multiplicity of clients, cannot usually afford a preference (there have been exceptions, of course, like Vollard and Brummer), and one can reasonably argue that a series of pictures certified as authentic by established experts should automatically produce a good collection. In fact most dealers know this to be untrue because they know too much about experts. From about 1900 to 1930 many of the pictures certified as authentic works by great artists were so feeble, or so hopelessly damaged by restoration, that when one meets them today in the cellars of public galleries one can hardly believe one's eyes. The men who signed these certificates of authenticity were not poor, venal hacks, but art-historians of international reputation; and the men who accepted them were the smartest operators on Wall Street, who could have smelt a false prospectus a mile away: a tribute to the hypnotic power of art. This extraordinary situation came to an end with the 1930 slump, and although the experts were never formally exposed and died in the odour of sanctity (I think only one is still with us), collectors began to shy away from certified old masters and turn their attention to late nineteenth-century and modern painting where the possibilities of fraud were much reduced.

Before leaving the less admirable aspects of collecting, I may consider the allegation that rich men collect out of snobbery or the desire to advance their social status. I think it cannot be denied that an outstanding collection of works of art will help forward social ambitions, when other forms of generous display, yachts, polo, lavish entertaining, et cetera, have failed. This is particularly true of America. In England a famous garden or a racing stable would be more effective. But to make a collection which will compel people to overcome their social prejudices cannot be achieved by money alone: so that we are back at our original statement, that a great collection is never the result of a pure motive, not even pure snobbery.

People often ask whether it is possible to make a great collection without being immensely rich. The answer is that it has been done. Chocquet, whom Renoir considered the

Introduction

greatest collector he knew, lived on the tiny income of a government official. Herbert Horne had about £600 a year, on which he managed to make a distinguished collection of early Tuscan art, buy a Renaissance palace and leave it to the town of Florence. When a friend suggested that he should have a photograph of a picture that was a pair to one of his, he replied that it was cheaper to buy originals. The Goncourts had no more than a modest independence, and great collectors of drawings, from Mariette onwards, have not all been rich men by modern standards. Alas, one must admit, that nearly all the great collectors of history have either been very rich, like Mazarin and Mr Morgan, or acted as if they were very rich, like Charles I and George IV; and it has now grown extremely hard to form even a modest collection without a comfortable bank balance. Until quite recently it was possible for a man of moderate wealth to collect a school or an epoch which was out of fashion; and of this the present volume contains an extraordinary example in the collection of *seicento* Italian pictures put together with single-minded devotion and immense learning by Mr Denis Mahon. But today even this opening is closed. A wider diffusion of knowledge has made it almost impossible to discover the underrated or the overlooked; and reports of the enormous prices paid at auctions have spread the notion that *all* works of art must be immensely valuable.

There remains only the possibility of buying the work of contemporary artists before they become famous. This is undoubtedly the most hazardous of all forms of collecting. It offers the maximum of excitement, partly because it must always be something of a gamble, partly because the art of our time affects us more strongly than that of the past. This hazardous element has increased in the last fifty years because modern art depends for its effect on its immediate impact, and the collector can no longer use his learning to 'read' a painting, as Cassiano del Pozzo could 'read' a Poussin. Modern painting speaks with a loud emphatic voice, too loud, we may sometimes feel, for daily companionship; and the *amateur* who wants his collections to be a background to his life, comforting, orderly and discreet, will be well advised to avoid it. A great collection of contemporary art can be formed only by someone who is passionately involved.

This brings me to a final question which would not have occurred to me naturally, but which would certainly be asked by a television interviewer, and so may be in people's minds. Has a single individual the right to possess and keep for his own enjoyment works of art which are part of the cultural heritage of mankind? The fact that I cannot phrase this question without employing clichés, suggests that it has about it an element of humbug. I doubt whether those who object to the privacy of private collections pay many visits to the Dulwich Gallery, Hampton Court, the Wellington Museum or other once private collections which are now open to them. Even the Courtauld Gallery in Woburn Square, full of masterpieces by the school of painting now most fashionable, has only about twenty visitors a day. The question has this much truth in it: that if certain supremely great works of art, say the Elgin marbles or Titian's *Entombment*, were in private hands, and more or less inaccessible, we should feel frustrated, and even indignant. But the number of great works of art which are really inaccessible to the general public must now be very small; even the Michelangelo carving in the dining room of the Royal Academy can be seen on application, although the humble art-student, for whose instruction it was bequeathed to the Academy, may not feel prepared to accost it in such portentous surroundings.

When all is said, the world owes private collectors an enormous debt. Without them many of the greatest works of art would have been lost or destroyed. Our public collections are, to a far larger extent than anyone realizes, private collections which have been accumulated and combined. In fact the more a national or municipal gallery rests on the basis of a private collection, like the Prado or the Mauritshius, the finer it is, and the more it is the creation of museum officials, the drearier. Even Bode, with his encyclopedic knowledge, genuine love of art, and ruthless methods of acquisition, could not make the Kaiser Friedrich Museum anything but cold and museological. It is not town councils or trades unions, or any other emanations of the popular will, which have saved works of art for the people, but a number of exceptional individuals. Ruthless, greedy, tyrannical, disreputable in a dozen ways, they have had one principle worth all the rest, the principle of delight. Each purchase is the record of a vivid experience, either a long pursuit or a struggle in which mounting desire has conquered prudence and economy. It has been brought home in triumph, unpacked with trembling hands, and placed, after many experiments, in the right company and the right light. It is true that after a few months have gone by the collector will forget all about it for days on end. But each time a sympathetic visitor looks at one of his precious pets, something of his first rapture returns; it becomes once more a friend, toy, fetish and familiar and there is re-established that complex human relationship which gives the private collection its life.

HM The King of Sweden

Chinese bronzes, jade and ceramics

BY SOVEREIGN RIGHT, kings and princes formerly enjoyed unique opportunities as patrons of art, and their collections were frequently conceived on the grandest scale. These functions are now shared more and more with public institutions and private individuals. However, in relinquishing some part of this official burden, ruling monarchs of our day enjoy increased freedom to follow their own personal interests and taste. The private collection of His Majesty King Gustaf VI Adolf of Sweden might well be regarded as a model of such an untrammelled royal taste. The collection is housed in the private apartments of the Kungliga Slottet in Stockholm; and, unlike the historic contents of the State Apartments of the Palace, or those of the delightful residences at Drottningholm and Ulriksdal, it is at no time directly accessible to the general public. It is therefore as a rare privilege that we welcome His Majesty's gracious permission to show a selection of his treasures in this book.

The collection reveals interests somewhat unusual, perhaps, among present day sovereigns, although they are those which the King has pursued ardently throughout his life. When Crown Prince, he engaged in a wide range of cultural activities, both in Sweden and abroad; best known has been his deep interest in archaeology, and in the various researches into the history of civilisations in which archaeology now plays so dominant a part. These interests date from his days as a student at the University of Uppsala, where History, Nordic Archaeology and Egyptology were among the subjects of his curriculum. They were subsequently nourished by extensive travel, and by contact maintained with scholars in many parts of the world. His patronage of numerous learned societies, his participation in exhibitions, and his collaboration in important research expeditions are further evidence of an involvement in these fields which far transcends generalities. Even today the King preserves an exceedingly active concern for the archaeology of the classical world, and travels to the Mediterranean each autumn, when time permits, in order to assist in excavations there.

His keen enjoyment of these activities is, however, only obliquely reflected in his private collection, which in the main represents tastes of a more purely artistic nature. Its formation has been inspired above all by his deep admiration for the arts of ancient China, and for the peculiar skill and genius displayed by her craftsmen. The late Dr Nils Palmgren, former Curator of the collection and editor of *Catalogue of Selected Chinese Antiquities from the Collection of Crown Prince Gustaf Adolf*, Stockholm, 1948, relates in his Introduction with what enthusiasm the Crown Prince applied himself to the collection and study of Chinese art following his first acquisition, the purchase of a Ch'ien Lung enamelled porcelain dish, in 1907. The time could scarcely have been more fortunate, for these were years of momentous discovery in Chinese art history. So swift has been the process of revelation since, that it is hard to recall how much of its brilliant fabric, as we now know it, was at that time

· ·

Ritual wine vessel,
chia, *in patinated bronze.*
Height 11⅜ ins.
Shang dynasty, 13th–12th century BC

Ritual food vessel,
kuei, *in patinated bronze.*
Diameter 9⅛ ins.
Shang dynasty, 12th–11th century BC

Right: *Ritual wine goblet,*
ku, *from An-yang, Honan province,*
in bronze with a greenish patina.
Height 11⅜ ins.
Shang dynasty, 12th–11th century BC

still buried beneath the soil. Its recovery has been piecemeal, resulting from the activity of dealers rather than of trained archaeologists, and the art historian's task has in consequence been very largely an empirical one. In this work Swedish orientalists have been responsible for outstanding contributions which must, one feels, have derived a considerable part of their impetus from the King's example and support. Wide interest was aroused in Stockholm by an important loan exhibition held there in 1914 under his patronage; and this was further sustained by his lengthy journey to the Far East in 1926. Meanwhile the growth of the collection, like that of others in Sweden, was accelerated by the willing aid of certain Swedish collectors resident in China itself. Today it numbers more than two thousand examples of Chinese artistry and workmanship in a variety of media, and forms a corpus for study whose value is in certain fields matched only by the collections of the greatest museums.

Despite increasing burdens of state in latter years the King's interest in the collection has appeared undiminished and his personal expertise as keen as ever. The creation of a new, comprehensive Museum of Far Eastern Art in Stockholm in the Spring of 1963 is the fulfilment of yet another of his cherished projects; and it should ensure the continuance in Sweden of the fine tradition of research which he has so extensively fostered.

The King's early interest in Chinese porcelains of the more recent periods was soon displaced by the excitement of the rich finds of excavated material arriving yearly in Europe, which opened progressively new fields of enjoyment and discovery. Many fine specimens of ceramics of the T'ang, Sung and Ming periods were thus added to the collection. In subsequent years, however, his attention turned increasingly to the art of the archaic era, notably to bronze and jade objects of the period from the Shang dynasty to that of the Han. These objects would seem to mirror more faithfully than most his attachment to the finest craftsmanship, as well as his concern for the special problems of Chinese archaeology, and it is accordingly from among them that

the greater number of the illustrations have been selected.

The archaic bronzes constitute by far the most significant body of works of art that have survived from the ancient Chinese world. Throughout the Shang and Chou dynasties (fifteenth to third centuries BC) imposing ceremonial vessels were cast and treasured for their distinctive role in the solemnization of religious and civil rites. Western connoisseurs were not slow to recognize their marked aesthetic qualities, not least among which is the handsome patina they have acquired during their long burial; and closer study has revealed in them an unexpected sophistication of design which is complemented by technical skill of the highest order. In China itself they have long been venerated as the classic, archetypal forms of their culture, and they have thus provided there a source of inspiration even greater, perhaps, than that which European art has derived from ancient Greece. Controlled excavation has shed light on other aspects of the gifted Shang civilization under which the manufacture of these bronzes began. Their rulers built extensive walled cities, and were equipped with chariots and bronze weapons which ensured their superiority over the less advanced peoples who surrounded them. Remains have been found also of pillared buildings of impressive size, as well as those of workshops for metal-casting, pottery, and jade and ivory-carving. Their ideographic script provides a recognizable basis for the written Chinese language of today, while their religious observances, which were apparently centred upon the propitiation of spirits and the cosmic forces controlling Nature, would seem to bear a like relation to those practised by their descendants.

In conformity with their sacrificial purpose both the shapes and decorative motives of the bronze vessels adhere closely to a prescribed repertoire, although the more stultifying effects of convention were happily avoided. Of the variety of forms represented in the collection none, perhaps, is more graceful and satisfying than the wine goblet known as *ku*: the slender, flaring profile, the central 'knop' section and slight, serrated vertical flanges could hardly be more exquisitely balanced, or the reliefs which ornament the sides disposed with greater harmony. The curiously shaped, tripod wine vessel *chia*, and the food receptacle *kuei*, are forms, the origin of which has been traced back to pottery wares of the Neolithic period. The *chia* is an especially impressive specimen, notable for its fine tapering legs and for the strange, capped pillars set on the upper rim, of which no definitive explanation has yet been forthcoming.

Their unified style of ornament adds massively to the symbolic power and impact of these ritual vessels. The motives are predominantly linear in character and cast with the piece itself, forming a crisp pattern of low relief or intaglio

23

Below: *Bronze fittings, possibly from a coffin. The upper
fitting is in the form of a t'ao-t'ieh monster mask.
Breadth of top fitting 3 ins. Height of bottom fittings 2⅜ ins.
Warring States period, 5th–3rd century* BC

Right: *The reverse sides of two bronze mirrors. The first
is ornamented with an arabesque dragon design on a scroll-
work ground. Diameter 7½ ins. Han dynasty, 3rd–2nd century* BC.
*The second is decorated with animals and T-shaped motives.
Diameter 7 ins. Warring States or Han period, 4th–3rd century* BC

over its surface. At first sight they might appear as pure abstractions; closer examination, however, reveals everywhere among them the conventionalized forms of animals, mythical or otherwise, especially the dragon and tiger, and those of birds and cicadas. Not infrequently, these are combined with marked ingenuity to form larger designs, such as the monster mask known as *t'ao-t'ieh* plainly visible on the wine vessel *chia*. The human figure is conspicuously absent, and the entire repertoire would seem to be related to animistic beliefs, each motive having its place in a complex iconographical scheme.

In addition to vessels the collection is uncommonly rich in bronze objects of a less esoteric use, including a variety of weapons, chariot fittings and other adornments. The jingle, probably from a horse's accoutrements, is a fine piece of this kind, ornamented with a central gem setting flanked by four birds. Two finials of uncertain purpose show the gradual naturalization of animal motives which began under the Chou rulers, who supplanted the Shang during the eleventh

century BC. The latter, in the form of a demonic head perched on the shoulders of a monster, is a particularly fantastic example of early Chou style.

This inclination towards fantasy and virtuosity was carried even further towards the end of the dynasty. On the bronze fittings which may have provided handles to a coffin, for example, the meaningful symbols of earlier art appear almost dissolved in the web of teeming, near-abstract forms whose animation is nevertheless reinforced by a rich textural quality. The fitting in *t'ao-t'ieh* mask form shows an especially inventive use of this florid manner.

As well as influences from beyond China's borders, new techniques enriched and refreshed the metalworker's craft at this time. Sumptuous inlays of gold, silver and semi-precious stones adorn objects made for personal use, such as belt hooks, of which there is an especially handsome series in the collection. Contact with the less disciplined, but undeniably vital 'animal style' art of Central Asia inspired a steady movement towards naturalism which finds its reflection in

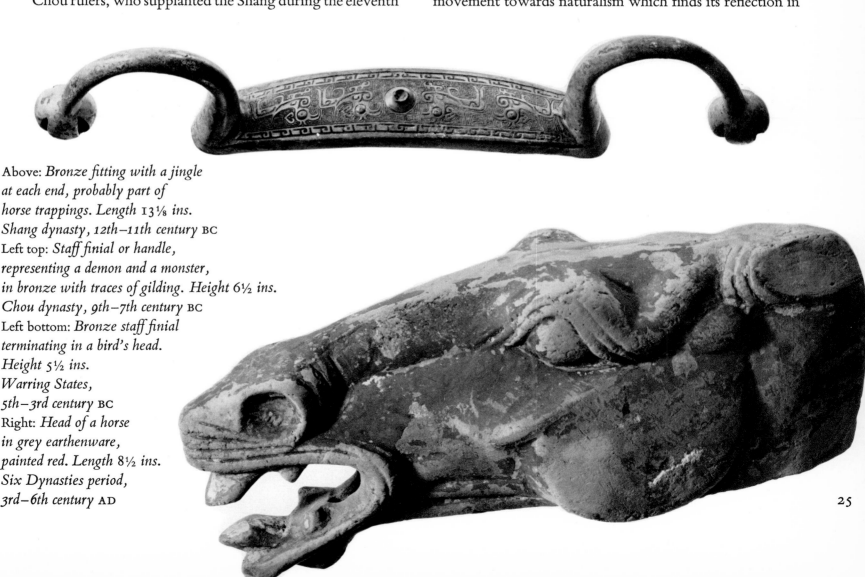

Above: Bronze fitting with a jingle at each end, probably part of horse trappings. Length 13⅛ ins. Shang dynasty, 12th–11th century BC
Left top: Staff finial or handle, representing a demon and a monster, in bronze with traces of gilding. Height 6½ ins. Chou dynasty, 9th–7th century BC
Left bottom: Bronze staff finial terminating in a bird's head. Height 5½ ins. Warring States, 5th–3rd century BC
Right: Head of a horse in grey earthenware, painted red. Length 8½ ins. Six Dynasties period, 3rd–6th century AD

25

Above: *Astronomical disc, hsüan chi,*
in veined greyish-white jade.
Diameter 5½ ins.
Shang or early Chou dynasty, 1100–1000 BC
Right: *Ceremonial axe in veined greyish-white jade*
with serrated edge and perforations for the attachment
of a handle. Length 5¾ ins.
Shang or early Chou dynasty, 1100–1000 BC

the angular dragon arabesques encircling the bronze mirror-back. The ornamentation of these mirrors, too, is pregnant with a magical symbolism. The strange 'т'-shaped motives of the second mirror take their form from the written character *shan* ('mountain'), and represent the four peaks which were believed to stand at the four corners of the universe. The surprisingly naturalistic animals, a dog and three (?) deer which prance over its surface belong therefore to a celestial rather than an earthly habitat.

The fine array of jade carvings in the collection represents every aspect of this peculiarly Chinese art, although specimens of the archaic periods are once again the most numerous. The nephrite stone, which was transported from far-off Turkestan, was in those times accorded an almost religious reverence; and, indeed, the Chinese have regarded it as the

most precious of materials ever since, equating its qualities with the highest human virtues. The earlier jades, therefore, are often linked with ritual, however obscure time may since have rendered their functions. The strange, tapering cylinder known as *ts'ung* is certainly among the more mysterious of such objects, although we know that in Chou times it served as a token of high authority. On slender evidence, it has been described as a 'symbol of Earth'; and rather more plausibly, the Swedish scholar Karlgren has attributed its origin to the cylinder containers of ancestral scrolls. The ring disc *hsüan chi* has also aroused much speculation: ancient records, however, lend substance to an ingenious theory of its use in astronomical calculations of the calendar; and by experiment the rim notches have in fact been shown to correspond to the positions of major

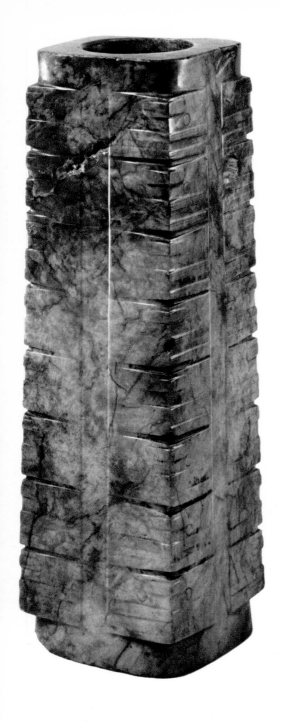

Two-handled cup, in the form of the archaic bronze kuei, *in pale green jade.
Breadth 7 ins. Late Sung to Ming dynasty, 13th–15th century* AD
Left: *Ritual cylinder,* ts'ung, *in mottled brown jade with green and yellow tints
and russet markings. It is enclosed within a block of square tapering section,
with incised striations. Height 8¾ ins. Chou dynasty, 11th–7th century* BC

constellations. The axe-head is another carving whose distinction points to a ceremonial, rather than practical, use.

The aesthetic appeal of such objects results equally from the careful choice of the stone as regards colour, texture and pattern, and the restrained shaping of planes which creates varied nuances of light over their surfaces. The jade-carver's imagination takes wider flight in the design of lesser pieces intended for more personal use, which are found in increasing numbers towards the end of the Chou period. The collection is rich in pendants and other ornaments on which the forms of dragons, tigers and other animals are realized with the utmost vividness of profile and surface detail, their low relief style following closely that of the contemporary bronzes. From this time onwards jade served a widening multiplicity of uses. A writer's waterpot in the collection

dating from the third to sixth centuries AD may remind us that in this period lived several of China's most celebrated calligraphers, as well as her first great painters. Of pale green nephrite carved in the form of a crested bird with finely delineated plumage, it embodies a charming fancy to lighten the austerity of the scholar's study. Scholarly antiquarianism must have inspired the making of the two-handled cup, which dates from about the thirteenth to fifteenth centuries. In form and ornament, this magnificently executed carving is a close replica of a bronze *kuei* from the beginning of the Chou dynasty.

Jade has established a special primacy over the Chinese heart; but to the West, the art of China has long seemed to be epitomized in the skill of her potters, which their consummate technical achievement, the invention of porcelain, 27

HM The King of Sweden

Wine ewer in stoneware with brownish-black glaze, showing 'oil spot' markings. The vessel was filled through a hole in the base. Height 4⅞ ins. Sung dynasty, 960–1279 AD

Opposite left: Ewer in white porcelain with incised decoration under the glaze. Height 7½ ins. Ming dynasty, early 15th century AD

Opposite right: Two women holding hands, grey earthenware painted in red, white and black pigments. Height 6⅛ ins. Northern Wei period, 398–534 AD

has made universally familiar. It is the pottery of the older dynasties, however, which nowadays attracts the deepest admiration. The King possesses many fine earthenware vessels and tomb figures from the Han, Six Dynasties and T'ang periods, from among which three examples of the latter are selected for reproduction here. The group of two young women holding hands is a particularly charming burial piece of about the fifth century. This smiling pair, who are perhaps dancers, are dressed in the long-sleeved robes and wear the piled hair ornaments fashionable at this period. The fine, nervous head of a horse shows a more penetrating sculptural treatment, and its straining posture and dilated nostrils suggest the extreme exertions of the cavalry horse. The squatting figure with bowed head must, one supposes, represent a mourner: it is a unique model, above all remarkable for its expressive power of emotional characterization.

The most admired of all Chinese ceramics are those made under the Sung dynasty, when glazes of unmatched perfection were developed for both stoneware and porcelain bodies. The stoneware wine ewer, with thick, lustrous black glaze minutely sprinkled with silvery 'oil-spots', is of singular refinement and rarity; it is the most prized of many Sung pieces in the collection, and has been frequently exhibited. Of quite a different character is the ewer, displaying the flawless white porcelain introduced in the early part of the Ming dynasty. In the form of the so-called 'monk's cap jug', it has a brilliant, almost colourless glaze which covers incised decoration of lotus scrolls, above which appear the Eight Buddhist Emblems of Happy Augury. It was probably made for use at the court of the Emperor Yung Lo (1403–24).

The collection is not limited merely to objects of the kind here described: amongst other things, for example, it contains some outstanding carvings in rhinoceros horn, ivory, and lacquer. The extent to which it represents every facet of Chinese craftsmanship is indeed a principal factor contributing to the collection's unique character as an instrument of study. Pre-eminently, however, it is an outstanding assemblage of works of art: one which bears witness to His Majesty's keen connoisseurship and unusually perceptive taste.

JOHN AYERS

Above: *Writer's waterpot in the form of a bird,*
in light green jade.
Length 2⅝ ins. Six Dynasties period, 3rd–6th century AD

Right: *Weeping figure in earthenware.*
Height 3¾ ins. Six Dynasties period, 5th–6th century AD

Drawings and antiquities

OVER A PERIOD OF SOMETHING more than thirty years Walter C. Baker has formed a collection which is an exceptionally personal record of the growth of his aesthetic interests. Every private collection formed by an individual in a lifetime is in a way a collection of souvenirs, a record of travel and discovery; but the objects in a great private collection must be of such a quality that they can stand alone, disassociated from their setting and their owner. The selection of sculpture and drawings belonging to Walter Baker reproduced in this volume amply testifies to the importance of his collection, one of the richest and certainly one of the most personal to be formed in America in the last few decades. The range in time, the span of art history covered by the collection, is vast: it spreads from Cycladic marble figures and an Akkadian basalt head to drawings by Picasso and Despiau. But the collection is in no wise encyclopaedic or didactic; nor has Walter Baker ever wanted to make it so. It is essentially a collection of small sculpture and of drawings. The sculpture is limited to works of preclassical and classical antiquity; the drawings range from the fifteenth century to the present day and, with a few exceptions, are works of Italian and French artists. This collection of sculpture and drawings has an exceptional unity due to Walter Baker's concern for plastic values, for form seen in the round. The firm contours, the easily intelligible forms of the classical tradition, have always attracted him. This partiality is evident in the magnificent Greek and Hellenistic bronze and marble figures in the collection, and it is also apparent in his choice of drawings. His own preference has always been for draughtsmen who were concerned with firm contour or sculptural draughtsmanship in light and shade, rather than with calligraphic meanders or merely surface ornament.

The history of this collection is essentially the story of the growth of the collector's knowledge and of the intensification of his personal preferences. But it is also the story of his travels and of his hard-sought opportunities to buy objects of the very first quality over a period of years when great works of art were becoming increasingly rare on the international market. Indeed, the fact that this collection was formed in the last thirty years makes its exceptional quality even more noteworthy.

A great collector's first enthusiasms and purchases are always worth recording. In the mid 1920's Walter Baker bought a number of small pieces of ancient glass, many of which had that fascinating iridescence which chemical transformation gives to buried glass. His interest in the form and colour of these small vases and alabastra led him to the study of ancient art. He has long since parted with these early purchases, and they have been replaced by a fine small group of ancient Egyptian and Greek glass vessels. But they served their purpose as the precipitating cause of his collection.

An active business man until his retirement a few years ago, Walter Baker had relatively little time for travel. His vacation trips to Europe could never be long, but each year they increased his knowledge and enthusiasm. In 1929 and 1930 he travelled to Etruscan sites and visited the principal Italian museums of Etruscan art. By 1930 he had acquired several pieces of Etruscan bronze work: a helmet, a girdle, two shield bosses. Then in 1931 he made his first important purchase, a splendid Etruscan bronze statuette of a warrior. This figure, datable in the first half of the fifth century BC, is still an important piece in the collection, and it established

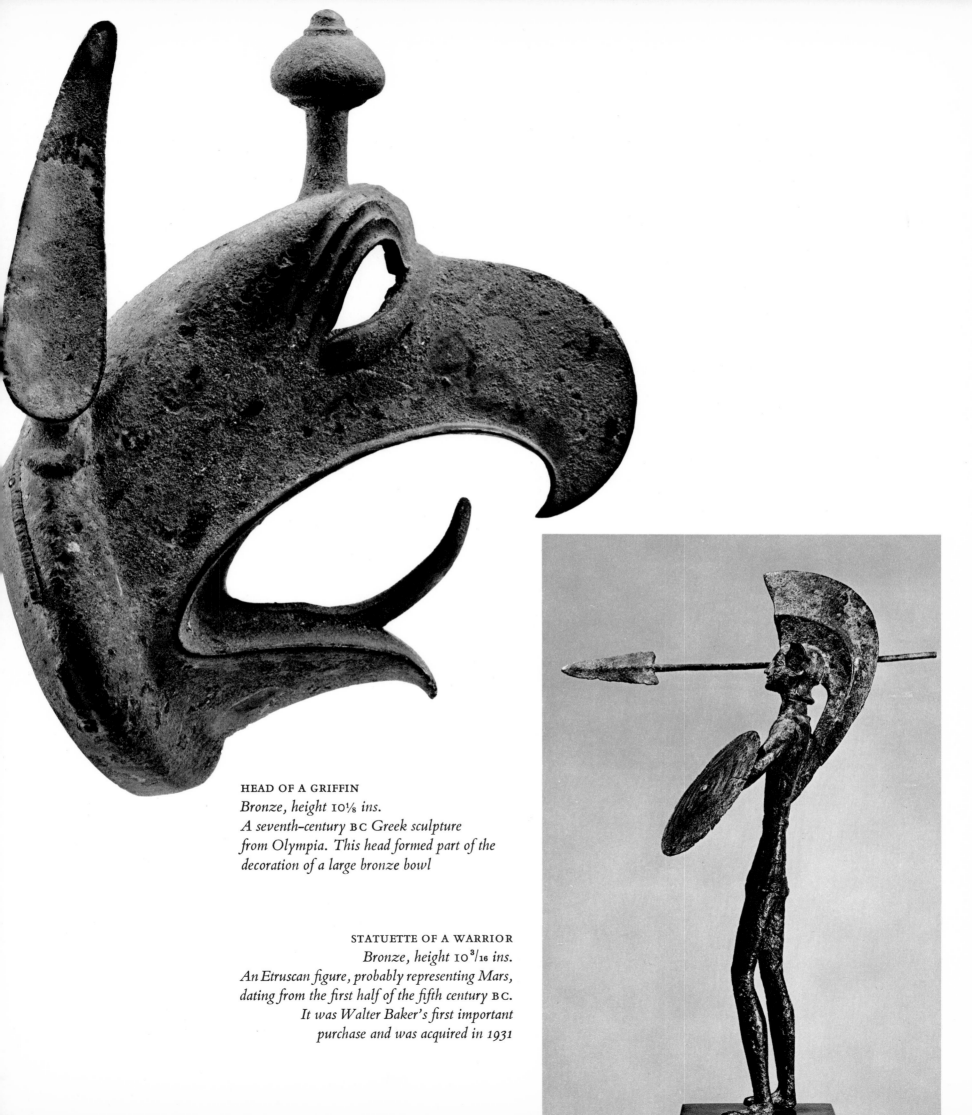

HEAD OF A GRIFFIN
Bronze, height 10⅛ ins.
A seventh-century BC Greek sculpture
from Olympia. This head formed part of the
decoration of a large bronze bowl

STATUETTE OF A WARRIOR
Bronze, height 10³/₁₆ ins.
An Etruscan figure, probably representing Mars,
dating from the first half of the fifth century BC.
It was Walter Baker's first important
purchase and was acquired in 1931

Walter C. Baker

RELIEF OF A HORSEMAN *Marble, height* 16½ *ins.*
A late fifth–century BC *Greek relief acquired by Walter Baker*
shortly after his return from his first visit to Greece in 1935.
At the broken right edge a young warrior can be
distinguished hiding behind a tree

HEAD OF A HORSE *Marble, height* 13⅜ *ins.*
An Attic sculpture dating from
the first half of the sixth century BC

Above: VEILED DANCER *Bronze, height 8⅛ ins.*
c 225–175 B C.
A Greek statuette, probably from Alexandria

Left: HEAD OF A YOUNG WOMAN *Marble, height 15³/₁₆ ins.*
A late fourth-century B C Greek work.
The head was intended to be set into a full-length grave statue

that note of high quality and authenticity which characterizes all his ensuing purchases.

It was shortly after his acquisition of the Etruscan bronze that Walter Baker came into contact with Joseph Brummer, a New York dealer in ancient and medieval art who played an extraordinarily important and creative role in the formation of many of the most significant American collections, public and private. Brummer, born in Yugoslavia, had been a pupil of Auguste Rodin in Paris, but from 1914 he maintained a gallery in New York. From that time until his death in 1947 an astonishing number of objects of the first importance passed through his hands. Walter Baker insists upon the importance of his acquaintance with Brummer in the formation first of his own taste and then of his own collection. Weekly visits to Brummer's gallery over a long

period of years enabled him to learn the feel, the colour, the weight of ancient objects, all qualities which are well nigh impossible to discern through the inevitable glass barriers in public collections. In the first years of this 'apprenticeship' he made a few purchases, all significant acquisitions. A green schist head of Osiris from the xxvith Dynasty and a Greek fourth century BC marble head of Zeus should be mentioned. But it was in 1935, upon his return from a first trip to Greece, that he was able to acquire one of the finest Greek marble sculptures in his collection: the late fifth-century BC Athenian relief of a horseman. The possession of this magnificent piece could hardly fail to be a positive stimulus for an already discriminating collector. Further trips to Greece and to western European collections of classical antiquities marked all the following years. In New York Walter Baker

33

Walter C. Baker

THE ADORATION OF THE MAGI
Fra Bartolomeo (1472–1517)
pen and brown ink 11 × 9½ *ins.*

made the acquaintance of Miss Gisela Richter, then curator of Greek and Roman art at the Metropolitan Museum; and her knowledge and enthusiasm brought him encouragement. He was further sustained by his active membership in the Archaeological Institute. In six years, from 1935 to 1941, he enriched his small but important collection of Greek vases, of Greek terracotta figures, of antique silver, and acquired examples of ancient glass which gradually replaced his first purchases. In 1941 Walter Baker was able to acquire the splendid fifth-century bronze mirror here reproduced. Then over a brief period of seven years he purchased a dazzling succession of objects of the greatest importance: the late fourth-century marble bust of a young woman; the early sixth-century Attic horse's head in marble; the bronze head of a griffin from Olympia which is

to be dated in the middle of the seventh century BC. Then in 1948 came the bronze statuette of a veiled dancer, datable about 225–175 BC, which is one of the most exceptional and certainly one of the most fascinating pieces in the collection. The reproduction here of all these objects speaks for their importance and their beauty. They are works of art which transcend archaeological and historical interest; their rich and noble simplicity gives them an independent existence intelligible to any observer sensitive to the plastic forms of the Mediterranean and Latin tradition.

Walter Baker purchased the first drawing for his collection in 1935. It was a study of a nude male figure by the sculptor Despiau, whose work had interested him in a New York exhibition the previous year. This drawing, a fine example of Despiau's draughtsmanship, is still in the collection, and

34

STUDY OF A NUDE MAN
HOLDING TWO BOTTLES
Jean Antoine Watteau (1648–1721)
black, red and white chalk 11 × 8⅝ ins.
Study for the figure of a satyr
filling Bacchus's cup in Autumn'
one of four pictures painted by Watteau
to decorate Pierre Crozat's dining room in Paris

Above: THE ENTOMBMENT *Rembrandt van Rijn (1606–1669) pen, brown ink,*
brown wash, heightened with white, over preliminary design in red chalk 11 × 15 ins.
A free copy after an engraving by Andrea Mantegna

Below: THE GIANT CACUS *Annibale Carracci (1560–1609) black chalk*
heightened with white chalk 14¾ × 19⅛ ins.
Study for the figure of Cacus in a fresco representing
Hercules and Cacus in the Palazzo Sampieri–Talon, Bologna

Walter C. Baker

has set the tone of all that was to come by its sculptural force and simplicity. Nearly thirteen years elapsed before he purchased another major drawing. Then in 1948 he was shown the superb chalk study of a female nude by Prud'hon illustrated in these pages. The acquisition of this sheet and of two Ingres drawings, portraits of the Comte and the Comtesse de Turpin de Crissé, give a new direction to Walter Baker's collecting. Over the last fourteen years he has brought together with exemplary discrimination a group of drawings, relatively small in number, but of an impressive level of quality and importance. Not long after these first acquisitions came the unforgettable Degas black chalk *Self-portrait,* a study for the etching of 1857, and the fine Cézanne *Self-portrait.* Nineteenth-century French draughtsmanship came to be further represented by an exceptional Delacroix Moroccan water colour, given to the Comte de Mornay by the artist; a portrait drawing of the Baronne Duperré and her daughters by Chassériau; fine examples of David, Corot, Daumier, Millet, Renoir and Seurat.

As a collector of sculpture, it is not surprising that Walter Baker should have been impressed by the sculptural force of the Watteau study of a male nude for the Crozat *Seasons.* His Rubens red chalk drawing after a Hellenistic figure of a sleeping hermaphrodite has a similar plastic force. The collector's passion for the lucid forms of the Mediterranean tradition seems evident, too, in the one Rembrandt drawing in his collection, a magnificent free copy after Mantegna's engraving of *The Entombment.*

Walter Baker's Italian drawings have been his most recent acquisitions. They are few in number, but they are remarkable for their quality. The pen study for the *Adoration of the Magi* is certainly the finest drawing by Fra Bartolomeo in America, and a sheet essential to our knowledge of the range and monumentality of this artist's style. Two drawings by Pietro da Cortona, both studies for the frescoes in the Sala della Stufa in the Palazzo Pitti, are capital documents for this brilliant draughtsman. A powerful study for

•••

SEATED FEMALE NUDE
Pierre Paul Prud'hon (1758–1823)
black chalk heightened with white on blue paper 22 × 15 ins.
This was bought in 1948 and was
Walter Baker's second major drawing purchase

36

Left: SELF PORTRAIT *Edgar Degas (1834–1917)*
black crayon heightened with white 11¾ × 9 *ins.*
Preparatory study for the self-portrait etching of 1857

SELF PORTRAIT
Paul Cézanne (1839–1906)
pencil 13 × 10¾ *ins.* c *1880*

the Giant Cacus by Annibale Carracci was purchased as a Rubens, a comprehensible error in attribution, given the exceptional force and freedom of the study. Mr Michael Jaffé has pointed out the very convincing connection with a figure in a fresco by Annibale Carracci in the Palazzo Sampieri-Talon in Bologna. The quality of the drawing was never questioned; what had been thought to be an unusual Rubens revealed itself to be an Annibale Carracci of the first importance, a new testimony to the genius of Annibale.

In the course of his long years of collecting Walter Baker has been a generous ally of a number of American public collections and institutions. Fourteen years ago his passionate interest in classical art brought him close to the American Academy in Rome, of which he is at present the treasurer; and he has for long been an officer of the Archaeological

Walter C. Baker

Above: MIRROR SUPPORTED BY A WOMAN HOLDING A DOVE
Bronze, height 16¼ ins.
Greek, possibly Peloponnesian,
sculpture dating from 460–450 BC

Institute of America and a supporter of its journals. He has been a member of the visiting committee of the Fogg Museum of Art at Harvard, and is a Fellow of the Pierpont Morgan Library in New York. He is president of the Board of Directors of *Master Drawings*, the new quarterly devoted to the study of drawings. And above all, he has been and continues to be associated with the Metropolitan Museum of Art, of which he has been an active trustee since 1948, and a vice-president since 1960.

The sculpture, the drawings, the ancient silver, glass, and pottery which Walter Baker has collected with such model discrimination are housed in his apartment in New York City. The objects are installed with great simplicity throughout the rooms, but some of the finest pieces are close at hand in a small library. In this room the double doors of a sixteenth-century French armoire open to reveal glass shelves where a hundred treasures have been placed with affection in dazzling groups. Those who have had the good fortune to study the contents of this cabinet will realize how impossible it is to make a meaningful enumeration of all the fine things in the collection. Like so many great collectors, Walter Baker has been most generous in lending to exhibitions which can claim to enrich our knowledge of a period or of an artist, and a number of exhibition catalogues describe and discuss objects from the collection. Particular mention should be made of the very considerable number of objects which were lent to an exhibition of Ancient Art from New York Private Collections held at the Metropolitan Museum in 1960. This important manifestation is recorded in a scholarly catalogue by Dietrich von Bothmer. Drawings from the collection have figured in a number of exhibitions in America and abroad, and more recently have been fully catalogued by Claus Virch in a privately printed publication.

Since the appearance of these catalogues, Walter Baker has added both sculpture and drawings to his collection, which is constantly growing in scope and intensity. In recent years the collector has taken an increasingly active interest in the draughtsmanship of a number of young American artists. But the persistence of his passion for the art of the Mediterranean world can be emphasized by mentioning his most recent purchase: a group of drawing by young artists working at the American Academy in Rome.   JACOB BEAN

Right: *A selection of Greek,*
Etruscan and Roman bronzes, silver and pottery
in a vitrine in the drawing room
of Walter Baker's New York residence

George Spencer-Churchill

Antiquities and old master paintings

THE NORTHWICK COLLECTION is now housed at Northwick Park in Gloucestershire. An ancient mansion, remodelled in 1730 by Sir John Rushout from a design by the Earl of Burlington, it proved too small to contain the great collection formed by John 2nd Lord Northwick and, in spite of the addition of a picture gallery in 1832, Lord Northwick was so short of space that he bought Thirlestane House, just outside Cheltenham. An inventory of Northwick Park dated 1705 shows a collection of fifty-three pictures, which were then valued at £24 8s 6d, and were to become the nucleus of one of the greatest collections of pictures in England.

John 2nd Lord Northwick, developed an interest in the visual arts early in life. As a young man he travelled widely and in 1792, at the age of twenty-four, he went to Rome where he stayed for eight years. He was by then laying the basis of a knowledge of works of art that helped him to his position of a highly intelligent, voracious, yet discriminating, collector. To use his own words written many years later, he became 'impressed with a profound veneration for the stupendous monuments of falling greatness... These were the seductive amusements of my youth; they have clung to me through a long life and they are now a solace of my old age.' He succeeded his father in 1800 and returned to

....

PORTRAIT OF QUEEN ELIZABETH OF BOHEMIA
English School, panel 32½ × 43 ins. 1612.
Elizabeth of Bohemia, the daughter of James VI of Scotland, was sixteen when this portrait was painted, and the mourning cord she wears was presumably for her brother Henry Prince of Wales, who died in 1612

England, where he spent the next sixty years indulging his passion for collecting. A study of the important auction catalogues of the period shows that few sales took place without some additions being made to the Northwick Collection. These included not only pictures, but also a large collection of prints, miniatures, coins, Greek vases, gems and porcelain, which was added to Thirlestane House. A generous patron, he wished to share the enjoyment of his treasures and the galleries were open to visitors all the year round.

Lord Northwick never married and when he died in 1859 it was discovered that he had made no will and no arrangements had been made for the future of his great collection. Consequently his property had to be divided among his three nearest of kin. His nephew George, 3rd Lord Northwick, was anxious to keep his uncle's collection intact and made an offer to the other beneficiaries of £80,000. They were unable to agree and there followed the great sale of the Northwick and Thirlestane House collections. Lord Northwick, who does not seem to have had any special interest in pictures, nevertheless showed a very accurate appreciation of the value of the collection which eventually sold for £91,000.

The sales lasted for twenty-two days, over 1500 pictures, works of art and many coins coming under the hammer, and some very surprising prices were paid. Sir Charles Eastlake made several important purchases for the National Gallery and many other collectors of the day made important acquisitions. The new Lord Northwick himself bought in a large number of pictures, a rather haphazard lack of discrimination marking his purchases. However, he did secure the *Stoning of Saint Stephen* by Garofalo for £1,606 10s 0d, and

George Spencer-Churchill

Fra Angelico's *SS Cosmos and Damian* for £77 14s 0d, a picture which had cost John, Lord Northwick, 52s 6d. He also retrieved Lorenzo Monaco's *Presentation in the Temple* for £74 11s 0d but spent £1,370 5s 0d on D. Maclise's *Robin Hood*. However, it must be remembered that at this same sale the National Gallery bought Botticelli's *Portrait of a Young Man* (catalogued as a Masaccio *Self Portrait*) for only £108 0s 0d, whereas T.Webster's *The Dunce Punished* fetched £1,005. Lord Northwick managed to retain quite a large number of pictures, and although much of the collection was dispersed, enough remained to form a continuous, if shadowy, link with the past. He died in 1887 and nothing much of interest happened until the death of his widow in 1912, when the great collection of prints made by the 2nd Lord Northwick was sold at Christie's and fetched prices which would be unheard of today.

In 1912 the Northwick Collection was given a new lease of life, when it passed by descent to Captain Edward George Spencer-Churchill, the present owner, whose scholarship and taste were to restore the collection to the position of importance it holds today.

At the age of thirteen George Spencer-Churchill was sent to Egypt for his health and his stay there marked the beginning of his interest in the world and art of ancient Egypt. He studied the various dynasties and learned to transcribe the hieroglyphs, spending his pocket money on the pottery, bronzes and other objects which could still be obtained at that time. It was not surprising that with such an early start he rapidly became an authority on this subject and his interest spread to include ancient Greece and Rome, and then eastwards through to Asia and China. The ancient world was by no means his only interest, as his extensive knowledge of pictures proves, but it is in his collection of antiquities that Captain Churchill probably takes most delight. It was not long before this new collection became known throughout the world.

Captain Churchill is the least selfish of collectors and although the house is not open to the public, he bears his ownership with the generous spirit of his ancestor the 2nd Lord Northwick. Constant streams of visitors come to Northwick and it is seldom that some of the pictures or objects are not on loan to exhibitions in various parts of the world.

Quite apart from the quality, the quantity of the collection is extraordinary. Captain Churchill has added over two hundred pictures. 'The Northwick Rescues', as he has

Left top: *A Graeco-Alexandrian bust of Gaius Caesar,*
grandson of the Emperor Augustus.
Egyptian green basalt, height 10 *ins. First century* AD
Left centre: *A figure of a stag, attributed to Myron.*
The garland that can be distinguished round the middle
indicates that the stag is about to be sacrificed.
Bronze, height 12¼ *ins.* c 450 BC
Left bottom: *A Cretan figure of a bull with a dancer.*
Bronze, height 4½ *ins.* c 1600 BC

Right: *The picture gallery at Northwick Park,*
built in 1832 by John 2nd Lord Northwick
to house his rapidly growing collection of paintings

described them in a recent catalogue, were chiefly dirty, over-painted and over-varnished pictures in which a hand, an eye, an ear of corn, or petal of a flower excited Captain Churchill's curiosity. Inevitably there have been disappointments, pictures which, when cleaned, did not live up to expectations, but 'The Northwick Rescues' are a formidable list of works by major and minor artists that were literally lost to view, sometimes for about a hundred years, pictures wrongly attributed because of the invisibility of the signature, or pictures so over-painted at a later date that the original work was totally obscured. They hang now mixed in with the older collection in the bedrooms, passages and the gallery, which is so crowded that it is almost impossible to see the walls at all.

'The Northwick Rescues' are particularly strong in the Netherlandish and Early English Schools and this has supplemented the original collection which contained a large group from the Italian Schools, as well as the Netherlandish and later English Schools. So it is the Dutch and Flemish painters whose works are most widely represented at Northwick. Pride of place must go to the *Peasant Wedding* by Pieter Brueghel the Elder, which dates from his later years and is 'signed' with the horse's skull. One of Captain Churchill's most outstanding discoveries must be the beautiful and delicate little panel of the *Madonna and Child* by Dirk Bouts, now well known through exhibitions in London and Bruges. A characteristic work of Bouts, it has the same

mother and child that appear in the National Gallery and Louvre pictures and many others; nevertheless the tenderness of the treatment and the skill of execution make it one of the most desirable of this artist's works. The recurrence of facial types in the works of Flemish painters of the fifteenth and sixteenth centuries, besides being of value in aiding the correct attribution of pictures, makes an interesting study. For example, the young kneeling king in the Northwick *Adoration of the Magi* by Gerard David appears as the Saviour in the *Baptism* at Bruges and the Virgin reappears in the various pictures of the *Adoration of the Magi* in Brussels, the National Gallery and elsewhere.

It was not unusual during this period for artists to paint sitters in the characters of their patron saints. A fine example of such a portrait is found in the *Portrait of a Notary in the Character of Saint Fiacre* by Quentin Matsys. It is one of the artist's most successful portraits and ranks with the rather similar Liechtenstein *Portrait of a Prelate*. Legend associates this seventh-century Irish anchorite saint with the waggons which used to transport pilgrims to the shrine of St Fiacre near Paris during a virulent outbreak of plague.

Moving forward a century or so, one must note the impressive group of flower pictures and still-lifes in which this collection is exceptionally strong. Most of these are 'rescues' and particular mention must be made of the *Vase of Flowers* by Nicholas van Verendael, only the ear of wheat at the bottom of the picture being visible when it was bought. 43

Turning to Italy, there are fewer additions to the collection by the present owner and two of the most notable works are those already mentioned as inspired purchases by the 3rd Lord Northwick – the Fra Angelico panel, *SS Cosmos and Damian* and Lorenzo Monaco's *Presentation in the Temple*. This last painting was catalogued as a Giotto in the Thirlestane House sale, but it must date from about a hundred years later. There is a monumental grandeur and simplicity about this picture and from the photograph one could imagine the figures to be life size. In fact the panel measures only 13 by 15½ inches and to many people is the most outstanding item in the collection. About a hundred years later the Sienese Domenico Beccafumi painted a series of Roman heroines, of which two are in the Victoria and Albert Museum and two, *Tanaquil* and *Marcia*, hang at Northwick on either side of the door to the picture gallery. They date from about 1520, but with their pale tones of green and grey, and their

fluidity of line, they give the appearance of works of many centuries later.

The collection of English portraits hang mainly in the saloon at Northwick and as in the gallery they are hung side by side and one on top of the other to form a solid phalanx of faces from English history. When the *Portrait of Queen Elizabeth of Bohemia* by an unknown artist was added to the collection, its beauty was totally obscured by a layer of dark brown varnish and it was only on cleaning that the Winter Queen's elaborately embroidered dress with its flamboyant red and gold bows and delicate lace collar came to light again. The work is unsigned but dated 1612 and it ranks among the finest examples of English portraiture of this period. About one hundred and fifty years later Sir Joshua Reynolds produced a masterpiece in his *Portrait of Warren Hastings*. Reynolds was paid seventy guineas for this in 1768 when Hastings, 'the ablest of the able men who gave to

George Spencer-Churchill

England her Indian Empire', was thirty-four and presumably on leave from India and the East India Company, for whose sins, real and imaginary, he was later to be the unfortunate scapegoat.

In this same room hang Hogarth's *Portrait of Daniel Lock*, Gainsborough's *Self Portrait*, a Romney of Lady Hamilton, an early *Portrait of Queen Elizabeth* I, and a portrait which can claim to be the best likeness of Shakespeare. On a library table, under the gaze of Warren Hastings to whom the table belonged in his retirement at Dalesford, are over two hundred bronzes all collected by Captain Churchill. There are cats, mice, ibises, goddesses and statuettes from Egypt,

Above: MADONNA AND CHILD *Dirk Bouts (c1414–75)*
panel 11 × 12 ins. c1550
Opposite: TANAQUIL *(left) and* MARCIA
Domenico Beccafumi (1485/6–1551) panel, each 36 × 20½ ins.
Two from a series of portraits of Roman heroines painted by
Beccafumi in about 1520. In the left hand picture Tanaquil,
wife of Tarquinius Priscus and mother-in-law of
Servius Tullius, indicates with a sceptre the inscription
which states her claim to have helped her husband and
son-in-law successively to the throne

Top: *Black figure amphora. Height 16⅜ ins. Attic c 550 BC.*
The figure of Hermes holding a caduceus
can be distinguished in the centre
Bottom: *Red figure stamnos. Height 13 ins. Attic c 470 BC.*
The word μυρτιτος is inscribed on the base,
indicating that the contents were flavoured with myrtle

45

George Spencer-Churchill

PORTRAIT OF WARREN HASTINGS
Joshua Reynolds (1732–92)
oil on canvas 49 × 39½ ins. 1768.
A portrait painted twenty years before his trial,
when Warren Hastings was a young and relatively
unknown administrator in India

javelin-throwing warriors, athletes, and mirrors from Etruria, reclining gods, deities and *aes* coinage from Rome, weights from Babylon, early marble figures from the Aegean, 'geometric' animals from Greece and early stone axe-heads from anywhere from Southampton to Kenya. Also to be seen are javelin heads from bronze-age India, ancient Greek and Etruscan helmets, some with the cheek pieces turned back to show they had been dedicated in the temple after fighting days were over, and nephrite and jade weapons from New Zealand.

In a case over the fireplace with blue faïence Ushabti figures, bronze ritual vessels from China, Cretan gems, Sumerian animals, and Roman and Syrian glass vases, are three outstanding bronzes. First the extremely rare *Chinese Wrestlers* from the Middle Chou period about 600 BC. Their right arms are locked and with their left they grasp each other's

belts preparatory to attempting a throw. From the Crete of about 1600 BC comes the magnificent Minoan bronze figurine of a *Bull with a Dancer*. We know from frescoes at Knossos and the drawings on Greek pots many of the actions in the complicated bull ritual, and this bronze illustrates the moment when the bull digs his forelegs into the sand as he braces against the impetus of his charge and tosses the acrobat who somersaults gracefully between his horns. The sculptor Myron is best known for his *Discus Thrower (Discobolus)*, but a work on a smaller scale that probably also came from the hand of this earliest of the great Greek named sculptors in about 450 BC is the *Stag* that shares the case with the two previously mentioned bronzes. Lifelike and graceful, it is a fine example of the classical period of Attic sculpture.

Arrian, the Greek writer of the second century AD, declared that the greatest quality of the Romans was their

ability to select the best from everywhere and make it their own. The fact that Roman portrait sculpture, a direct artistic descendant from Greece, was no pale imitation nor decadent anti-climax to the art of classical and Hellenistic Greece, can be seen in the Graeco-Alexandrian head of Gaius Caesar. Assuming that it is of Gaius Caesar, the elder brother of Agrippina, and not of his grandfather the Emperor Augustus, as has been suggested, this green basalt head, typical of Imperial portraiture of this time in its refined and academic style, must date from the early part of the first century AD.

Yet another collection within this collection is that of Greek vases and other pottery, and again this has been entirely amassed by Captain Churchill. With more than one hundred examples the whole history of Greek vase painting is covered, from the seventh century BC geometric style through the later orientalizing style, and on to the black-figure and later red-figure styles. The culmination of the black-figure style was reached in the years 550–500 BC, and the vases of Attica of this period, made of good clay and with a highly polished surface, display the most superior workmanship and artistic quality. From the hand of an unknown painter of this period comes the *Amphora* with the drawing of Hermes. Restricted by the technical limits of the convention of the black-figure style, the successors of Exekias and the Amasis painter, the two great exponents in this field, turned to the red-figure style as a medium that would better allow the representation of character and anatomy. They followed the sculptors of the day in cutting away the background and leaving the figure. From Attica comes the *Stamnos* made in about 470 BC shortly before the decline of this form of art.

There can be few private collections in the world today

47

George Spencer-Churchill

which cover such a long period of time and inevitably the question is frequently asked as to what is the oldest object in the collection. In reply Captain Churchill will display a fossilized trilobite, *Calimini Blumen Bachii*, from the Silurian period about 350,000,000 BC or the dinosaur's bones that date from the Jurassic period of about 150,000,000 BC and which he dug from the clay pits near Oxford when he was an undergraduate, or the opalized shells, from the Cretaceous period of 100,000,000 BC that he got from Lightning Ridge in Australia.

The scope and variety of the collection seems endless, with Sumerian cylinder seals from 3000 BC and Luristan bronzes with their strange abstract zoomorphic shapes and bronze weapons from the same part of the world. Then there is the collection of scarabs, the Egyptian emblem of resurrection which was placed in the tombs of their dead. Of extreme rarity is the Cretan scarab of about 2000 BC inlaid with gold; it is inscribed with linear A script and is one of the few examples of this script that is known. There are also two lion scarabs inscribed, 'Amenhotep III, having killed one hundred and two lions fierce in the tenth year of his reign' and 'Amenhotep III, fighting lions as numerous as three swarms of tadpoles'. The collection continues, with coins and gems from Greece, bronzes and glass from Rome, jewellery from the tombs of Egypt, including a

Left: A MIRACLE OF SS COSMOS AND DAMIAN
Fra Angelico (1387–1455) panel 7¾ × 8¾ ins. c 1420. This painting illustrates the legend of the man suffering from cancer of the leg, who prayed in the Church of ss Cosmos and Damian in Rome. He fell asleep and dreamed that he heard the twin Doctor saints resolving to amputate his leg and replace it with that of a Moor who had died recently. On waking he found that he had two healthy legs, but one was black

Above right: THE ADORATION OF THE MAGI
Gerard David (d 1523) panel 27¼ × 28¾ ins. c 1510

· ·

necklace dating from the Eighteenth Dynasty, early Chinese bronzes and jades from the Shang Yin period (traditionally 1766–1122 BC) onwards and Persian miniatures from the hands of the great Moghul painters.

This then is the Northwick Collection, a collection that has had its rise and fall but with a remarkable resurrection to follow. Neither of the two great collectors who built it up allowed themselves to be diverted by the variations of fashion from the essential permanence of quality, and it is in this above all that its greatness lies.   PATRICK LINDSAY

THE PRESENTATION IN THE TEMPLE
Lorenzo Monaco (1370/2–1422/5)
panel 13 × 15½ ins. c 1400.
The Virgin is presenting the Christ child
to Simeon, while Saint Joseph and Saint Anne
can be seen on the left

Below: A PEASANT WEDDING
Pieter Brueghel the Elder (1525/30–69)
panel 27 × 45 ins. c 1560.
The bride in this painting also appears
in Brueghel's Wedding Feast, *now in Vienna,*
which was probably painted in the same year

Brescia Luigi Marzoli

Italian arms and armour

THIS IS THE LARGEST COLLECTION of arms and armour on the continent of Europe to remain in private hands. It has been formed within the last forty years by the burning enthusiasm and devotion of one man, and mostly by purchases made outside of Italy. In doing this, Cavaliere Luigi Marzoli has been reversing the trend of the previous century, when armour flowed out of Italy, where so much of the very finest of it was made, and seemed fated never to return.

Forty years ago Italian armour could be seen in a few public galleries in Italy, in the Armeria Reale in the Royal Palace at Turin, in another royal palace of Capo di Monte at Naples, in the Museo Nazionale in the Bargello, the Museo Stibbert at Florence and the collection of Prince Odescalchi at Rome, now an Italian possession. But these were all static collections that were not in a position to compete with the great modern collections that were being built up in Europe, and especially in America, in the light of modern knowledge and *expertise*. Luigi Marzoli is a leading industrialist of North Italy who has spared no expense or effort to recover the beautiful products of his native land. Two world wars have helped him by effecting the dispersal of ancient armouries and the more recent collections of the nineteenth century, although the Second World War endangered his own.

....

Left: *A late fifteenth or early*
sixteenth-century
barbuta *covered in red velvet*
with gilt copper enrichment
Above: *A 'Norman' conical helmet with nasal, found near*
Salerno and dating from the eleventh or twelfth century

This is more than a collection – it is a great accumulation, for its owner has never allowed an opportunity, however fleeting, to pass him by. The possession of a great family manufacturing business, Fratelli Marzoli, founded by his grandfather over a hundred years ago, has given him the means to bring about this happy result. The tide which had seemed to flow by a natural law from East to West, was halted by the depression of 1929 and the deaths in the ensuing years of the first generation of American collectors. Thus Luigi Marzoli was able to recover some of the finest pieces of the Clarence Mackay, W. R. Hearst and other collections which were thought to have left Europe for good.

Luigi Marzoli's dominating love is for the beautiful firearms of Brescia which were produced in the Val Trompia in the foothills of the Alps, a little to the north of his home. These weapons are famous for their lightness and balance, and for their elegant design. John Evelyn recorded in his diary for the year 1646: 'We came this evening to Brescia, which next morning we traverst according to our custom in search of antiquities and new sights. Here I purchased of old Lazarino Cominazzo my fine carbine, which cost me 9 pistoles, and that workman Jo. Bap. Franco, the best esteemed.' Superb examples of the work of both these two great artist-craftsmen are among those numbered here.

Not far to the west of Brescia is the great industrial centre of Milan. Already in the fourteenth century Milan had acquired an international reputation for the quality of its armour. It lay to the south of the iron-bearing district between the Italian lakes and the Po, and there the craftsmen flourished, each generation passing on his acquired knowledge to the next. Luigi Marzoli's local feeling tends

51

Luigi Marzoli

to make him regard Milan as a mere partner of his native Brescia, which also produced armour, but it is to Milan that the great names of many armourers belong, like the Missaglia and the Negroli. Missaglia is a village a few miles south of Lake Como, and Merate, another armour-producing name, is close by.

Two large rooms on the ground floor of the Palazzolo Sull'oglio contain a veritable regiment of armoured figures. In the larger room they stand shoulder to shoulder in crowded ranks, and have grown in numbers until only a small circular space in the middle of the room is free. Two at least are on armoured horses. They include many familiar figures that until recently graced collections on both sides of the Atlantic. Here one sees the composite Gothic armour originally built up by Sir Farnham Burke, Garter King of Arms, that included two very fine Italian fifteenth-century vambraces. It passed to W. R. Hearst's collection at St Donat's where the latter's armourer, Raymond Bartel, substituted certain other parts, and Luigi Marzoli has done the same, so now little remains of Burke's figure. It now has a very fine pair of Gothic legs, a good breastplate and an Italian armet, not a barbute, on its head. Another composite Gothic suit stands beside it. Much later in date, but perhaps more satisfactory because it is all of one piece, is a finely etched and gilt armour *cap à pie* of the later sixteenth century, and two good Italian sixteenth-century tilt-armours with high grandguards.

Luigi Marzoli's collection is principally of Italian armour, but one finds a few foreigners here and there. There is at least one fluted Maximilian armour, and two harnesses dating from the mid-sixteenth century with embossed borders of scales. But these are strangers here. One is on more familiar ground with the etched halfsuit that once formed part of Sir Samuel Meyrick's collection at Goodrich Court and

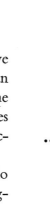

An early armet, probably from Rhodes c 1400

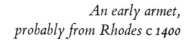

A group of fifteenth-century Italian helmets, the first a sallet with etched decoration, and three fine barbuti

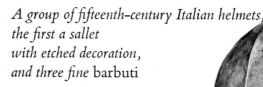

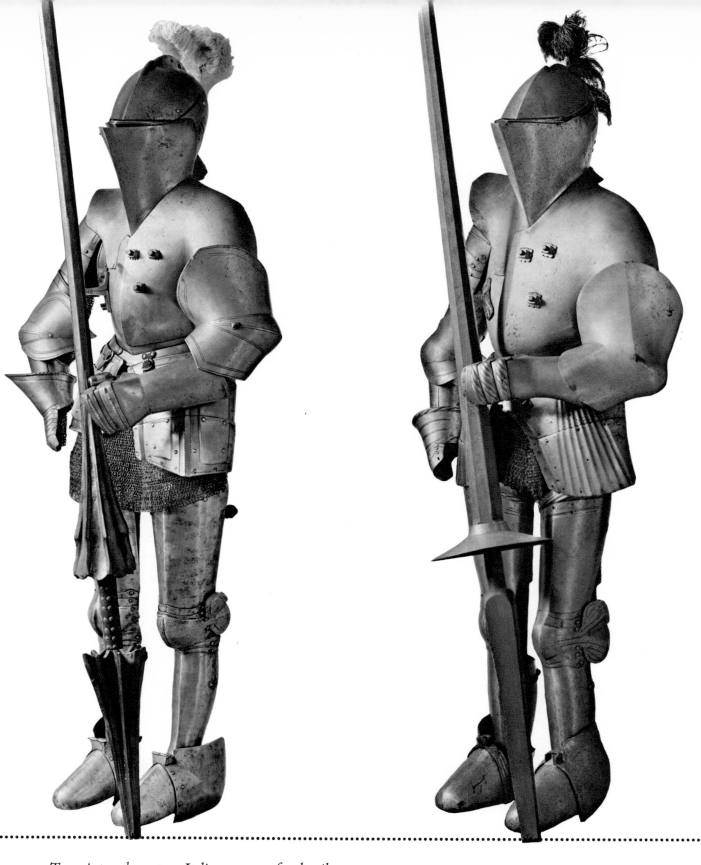

Two sixteenth-century Italian armours for the tilt
with high grandguards. These were found lying in pieces
in a room of a castle near Brescia,
apparently having lain undisturbed for many years

*Two views of a close-helmet
with hollow gadroons at the back,
made for the Duc de Guise in about 1540*

Luigi Marzoli

there are many etched half-armours from later in the century.

The late Field-Marshal Earl Kitchener used to possess a pair of richly gilt and embossed saddle steels which passed to Durlacher of London and are now here. Note too a part of a French saddle, and a chanfron with the ROM ROM mark found on pieces in the Musée de l'Armée and elsewhere.

Upstairs in the painted drawing room Luigi Marzoli has assembled his choicest pieces. There are to be seen here a number of helmets of great interest, many of them bought in the London sale rooms during the twenties and thirties, where his presence always produced spirited bidding. I well remember Marzoli saying to me, 'Whenever I see a piece of armour I become *emotioné*'. The acquisition of fine Italian sallets and barbutes was his great joy. There is a quite lovely sallet very similiar to one worn by one of the playful *putti* in Botticelli's picture in the National Gallery of the sleeping Mars and Venus, which came from the collection formed by Graf Wilzek in the castle of Kreuzenstein, near Vienna. It is said to have been a gift to him from the Emperor Franz Joseph from the Waffensammlung at Vienna. It is delicately etched in the Italian manner and may well be a companion to the Gothic breastplate similarly etched, which is, rightly or wrongly, attributed to the *condottiere* Bartolommeo Colleoni, whose fine equestrian statue by Verrocchio is one of the sights of Venice. At the sale of Clarence Mackay's collection at Christie's in 1939, Luigi Marzoli obtained very reasonably some of the Italian sallets that had figured in the sale of Sir Guy Laking's collection at Sotheby's nineteen years before. One has its original crimson velvet covering and plaques of ornament, and the other the copper enrichments that show it was at one time used as a *stemma* in a Venetian palace. Another, a barbute, is a special favourite of its owner because it carries a maker's mark very similar to a monogram which can still be seen carved on the pillars of an old house in Brescia. Signor Marzoli is a keen partisan of the part played by his native Brescia in the craft of the armourer as against the powerful claims of Milan. He has some fine examples of plain barbutes with T-shaped face openings, one with the PR mark found on similar helmets at Churburg. Of later helmets he possesses a very fine and unusual close-helmet with deeply sunk gadroons at the back which is by tradition said to have belonged to the Duc de Guise. Several good fifteenth-century armets of typical North Italian type, including a tall early one which probably came from the island of Rhodes with other fragments

A sixteenth-century target
by Lucio Piccinino of Milan,
damascened in gold, and embossed
with a scene depicting
Apollo on Mount Parnassus

Saddle steels by Negroli,
dating from the mid-sixteenth century,
with an embossed and etched
chanfron on the right

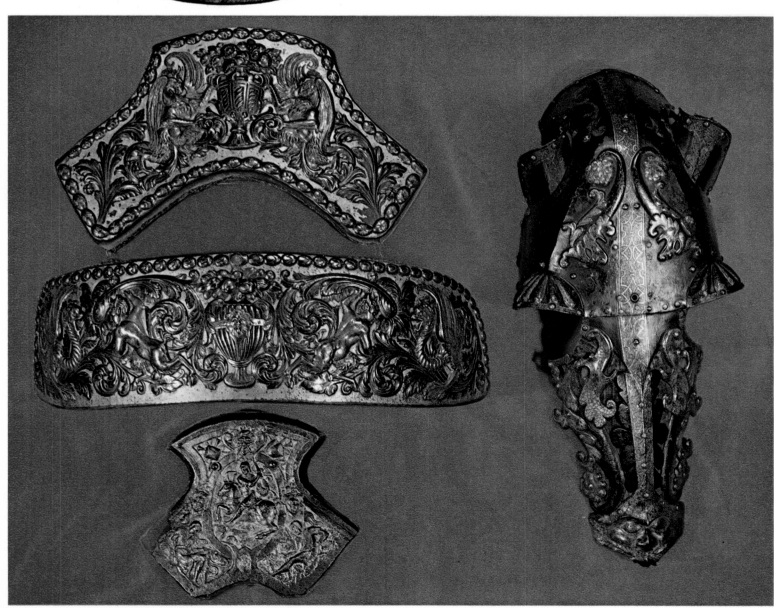

55

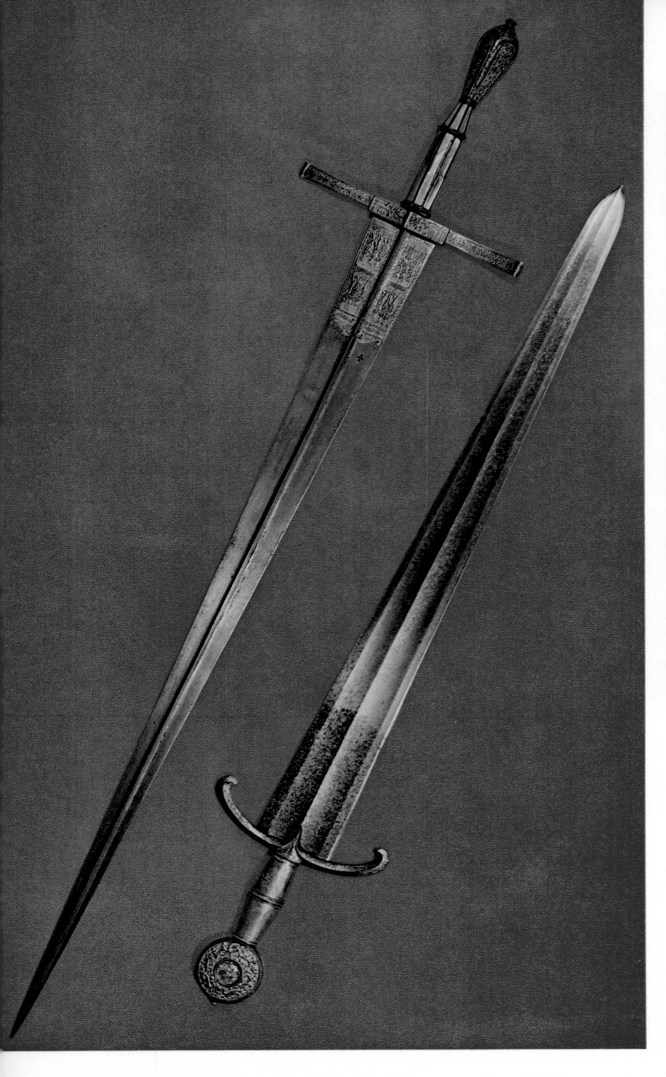

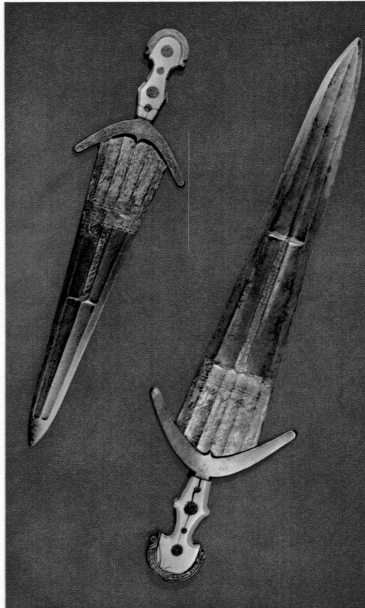

Above: *Two fine Italian cinquedeas,
the broad blades etched and gilt, dating
from the late fifteenth
or early sixteenth century*

Left: *A hand–and–a–half sword
with a mother of pearl grip and an etched
and gilt blade, and beside it
a broad-bladed Renaissance sword,
etched and gilt*

Luigi Marzoli

*A sixteenth-century
curved falchion
with a bird-shaped pommel*

*Two early sixteenth-century
ear daggers
in the Spanish style*

of the armour of the knights of St John. There were apparently several separate *reprises* of these. Major Lefroy had the first pick on his return from the Crimea. These were presented by him to the Rotunda Museum at Woolwich and are now in the Armouries of the Tower of London. A second and larger consignment was obtained by Bachereau, the Paris dealer in armour, some forty or fifty years later. He sold some of these individually to collectors, but the greater number were bought *en bloc* by the late Dr Bashford Dean for the Metropolitan Museum of Art at New York. The remaining pieces were acquired by Marzoli, because, however fragmentary, they were all truly and incontestably Italian. He has been able to put together two *cap à pie* armours, but I think his tall armet has come from the second (New York) group.

A rare early piece is the conical 'Norman' helmet with nasal, found near Salerno, which dates from the eleventh or twelfth century. The best known example of this type is that in the Waffensammlung at Vienna, which came from Central Europe. He has several examples of embossed helmets of the sixteenth century, both morions and casques, and many examples of the etched and gilt morions of the later part of the century.

Apart from armours and half-armours already mentioned, the collection at Palazzolo contains some very fine detached pieces of body armour. First of all, one must mention two very fine pairs of Gothic legs, cuisses, knee-pieces (or poleyns) and greaves of the best North Italian style. One notes with interest the spikes projecting from the side-pieces of the knees. This is a feature that one finds on other examples, as at Churburg, and even on sculptured figures in wood. He has a very fine fluted breastplate of the early sixteenth century, the flutes being boxed and deep. It is enhanced by Italian etching including the usual frieze of saints across the upper part of the breast. It came from the Zouche and Mackay collections.

There are two fine, embossed circular shields, or targets, richly etched and gilt, and probably the work of Lucio Piccinino of Milan, one showing the Triumph of Bacchus and the other Apollo on Parnassus.

The collection is rich in swords. One that first springs to the eye is an early Renaissance hand-and-a-half sword, very similar to Lautrec's sword which the famous French commander himself presented to the church of Treviglio in an episode in the Italian Wars. It came from the S. J. Whawell

57

sale at Sotheby's in 1927. There are several rich Renaissance swords, one with a plaquette pommel, three cinquedeas at least with their flat blades etched and gilt in characteristic manner, and a fine Renaissance falchion. Good rapiers too are here, one with richly chiselled hilt, and a group of a dozen cup-hilt rapiers in the Spanish style. One is inscribed at the forte IL . RIVOLTA . IN . MILANA [sic] . ALLA . CORONA, while the blade bears the name SESESTANO [sic]. FERNANDEZ, apparently a corruption of the name of the well-known Madrid swordsmith Sebastian Fernandez. Mention should also be made of two rare ear daggers in the Spanish manner decorated with minute gold damascening. It is just such an ear dagger as is seen in Holbein's portrait of King Edward VI at Windsor Castle.

The collection of firearms requires a separate article to itself. Luigi Marzoli has made a point of acquiring every good Brescian gun or pistol that has come his way. Many are of the very finest quality and in beautiful condition. It is not possible to deal adequately with them here, but one can pick out a few, such as a pair of long double-barrelled side-by-side snaphaunce pistols, a case of fine pistols presented by the Duke of Calabria to an English nobleman, and a very large Brescian single pistol – the largest I have ever seen. The illustration of the confused view of a single show-case perhaps gives the best idea of the profusion of fine Brescian firearms to be seen here.

Cavaliere Marzoli lent much of his collection to the exhibition of *Armi Antiche* held in the Castle of Brescia in 1954. It is a pity that the catalogue was so sketchy, for Luigi Marzoli has been so busy collecting that he has never been able to compile a catalogue of his own. Here is a rewarding task waiting for the right man to do it.   JAMES MANN

A pair of fine pistols with Miquelet locks

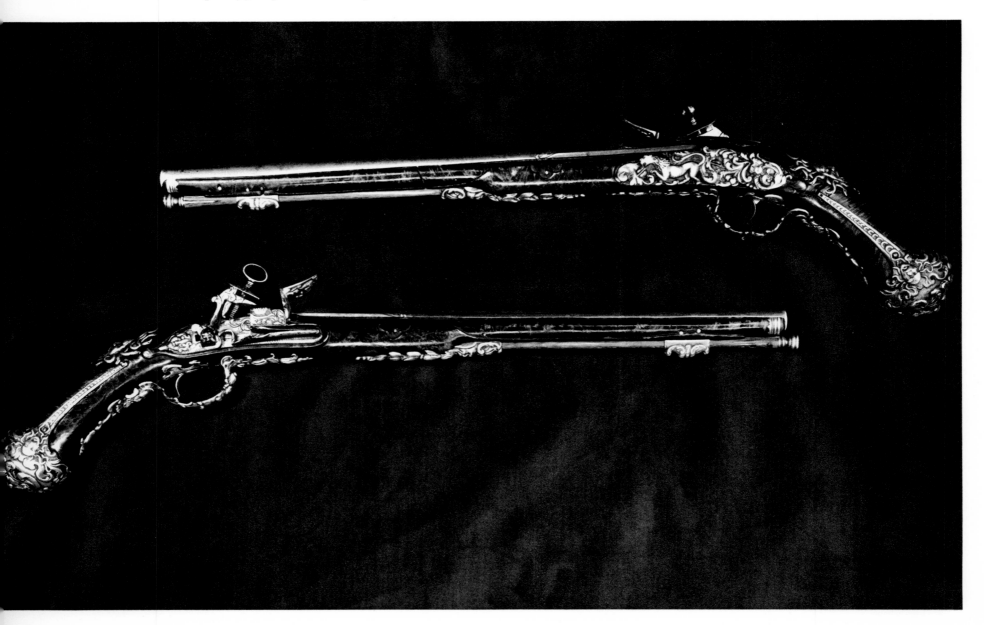

Luigi Marzoli

The finely chiselled snaphaunce lock of a seventeenth-century sporting gun

A group of Brescian wheel-lock pistols

Bernard Berenson

Early Italian and Oriental art

TO FRIENDS AND ACQUAINTANCES ALIKE, Bernard Berenson always denied that he was a collector. He denied it even in print, in the last pages of his *Sketch for a Self-Portrait*. This book was written while Italy was at war with the western powers, and he was not sure that he would end his life among the treasures he had gathered in his villa, 'I Tatti', near Florence. Even then, when the destruction of his possessions could have occurred at any moment, he did not consider his 'collection'; he only hoped for the survival of his 'home'.

This may come as a surprise to many who know about him, but not to those who knew him. True, no other art historian has been more deeply involved in the dispersal and creation of collections than Bernard Berenson, not only when he was Duveen's adviser on Italian art (1907–36), but both before and since. He gained his livelihood from being the greatest authority on Italian Renaissance painting, but he did not enjoy being an expert, however much he loved the pictures he recommended to the American buyer. In 1895, aged thirty, while still possessing no riches other than his exceptional sensibility, his fabulous memory and his intense capacity for work, he wrote to Mrs Gardner: 'If you permit me to advise you in art matters as you have done for a year past, it will not be many years before you possess a collection almost unrivalled – of masterpieces and masterpieces only.' He kept his word and obtained for her not only Italian masterpieces like the unforgettable *Europa* by Titian, but also works by Rembrandt, Rubens, Holbein, Dürer, Velazquez, Manet and Degas. This opportunity to collect on a grand scale before he had the money to buy a house of his own, may have allayed his urge to collect, if indeed he was ever so inclined. But Berenson did not have an acquisitive nature, he was an enjoyer of life. Eventually, the vanity or greed (or both) of most collectors wearied him. The redeeming feature of his activity as an adviser was that he longed for Americans to discover new worlds through the visual arts. In 1887, as a Harvard undergraduate, he had complained: 'One can study literature after a fashion here, *but art not at all!*' Forty years later, he decided to leave his hard-won possessions to Harvard University in order to help his younger countrymen experience the civilizing influence of art and beauty. In fact at the time of his death in 1959, the seed of his enthusiasm had born fruit and a tour of the United States galleries had become the ambition of the European student of art.

America had helped Berenson by using his services in Europe. Europe very soon meant for him Florence. The international character of the town may have prevented Berenson – an uprooted Lithuanian educated in Boston – from realizing at first that he was hankering for a home, after years of wandering. The financial reward of his discriminating work for Mrs Gardner had meant for him, first of all, photographs and books; but when, by Christmas 1897, he could rent a house of his own, his joy was touching. He described every room in detail to Mrs Gardner, and it is

....

MADONNA
Gentile da Fabriano (c 1360–1427)
fragment of a panel 9⅞ × 7½ ins. c 1425

Three treasures from
the Berenson Collection:
ST CHRISTOPHER
Bernardo Daddi
(c 1290–1355)
panel 16⅛ × 6¼ ins.
A wing
of a portable altarpiece

JOHN THE BAPTIST
Michele di Matteo
(mid 15th century).
Panel 10⅜ × 3⅛ ins.

and SAINTS DOMINIC,
FRANCIS, AND
BONAVENTURA OFFER
ST CATHERINE OF
SIENA THE ROBE
OF THE
DOMINICAN ORDER
Neroccio de' Landi
(1447–1500) panel
15¾ × 19¼ ins.
Fragment of
a predella

Bernard Berenson

fascinating to note that many features of the villino in the Via di Camerata were to be found again in the Villa I Tatti: the same situation on the slopes of the hills north of Florence, the same passages, 'monastically white' (his words to Mrs Gardner), which used to strike the visitors to I Tatti with awe, the same white bedroom with gilt and intarsia furniture, even the same bed. This small divan surmounted by a baldaquin puzzled Berenson's friends when he was eighty and apparently made them laugh when he was thirty, as it seemed fit 'not for a bearded monster but for a delicate creature'. Already he liked velvets and silks and preferred walls to be either white or some shade of green, as the best background for the 'two or three pictures on golden ground' which he hoped to hang on them some day. Possibly, at that time, he possessed only the wing of a portable triptych by Daddi, with *St Christopher* on one side and a *Crucifixion* on the other. Two years later he saw a *St Michael* in London and could afford it. Once the centre of a large polyptych, this masterpiece by Giambono had found its way North from Padua as 'German School'. One day I praised to Berenson the subdued richness of its colours: the reds merging into the brown and gold, the yellowish green of the angels' robes brought into relief by the bottle-green ground. Unlike the average collector, Berenson was critical of his possessions and praise elicited his severity. 'The colour, yes, is good. But don't you see how hopeless the drawing is? It looks like a paper doll with a paper dress on that is too big for it. All the same', he added, 'those arabesques on the dress, and the dragon's tail, are gorgeous.' In the Spring of the following year (1900) he secured the jewel of his collection, the Domenico Veneziano *Madonna* – previously called Baldovinetti – which he bought directly from the Marchesa Panciatichi. It is a brilliant example of early Italian Renaissance painting and a miracle of preservation as well, possible because it was never freshened up to attract buyers.

In December of the same year Berenson married. He was thirty-five years old, had published the *Venetian* (1894), the

··

MADONNA AND CHILD
Domenico Veneziano (c 1400–61)·
panel 33⅞ × 24 *ins. c 1435–40*

A page from the AUTOMATA (Book of Machines)
by al-Jazari. Paper 15 × 10 *ins. Mesopotamia 1354* AD

Florentine (1896) and the *Central Italian* (1897) *Painters of the Renaissance*, the book on *Lotto* (1895) and had nearly finished his vast work on the *Florentine Drawings*, which appeared in 1903. During the Easter weekend of 1890 – ten years earlier – he had met Mary Costelloe, who had disregarded her family ties to become his passionate admirer, pupil and companion. She could now become his vital, energetic wife. They rented the spacious villa I Tatti, and married in the little chapel by the upper gate, where Berenson now lies buried beside his wife.

One day Bernard and Mary went into town to buy a stove at a shop in the Via della Spada. Berenson had no sooner jumped off the *carrozzella*, than a piece of a seven-foot panel glittering from the next-door shop caught his eye. He had some jumble removed and saw a large St Francis ecstatically hovering over a low landscape, his arms open in the shape of

65

ST MICHAEL
Giambono
(active c 1420–62)
panel 44½ × 24¼ ins. c 1430.
The centre panel
of a large polyptych

66

Bernard Berenson

Above: ST JOHN THE EVANGELIST
Perugino (c 1448–1523)
silk with silver and gold thread 12¼ × 5⅞ ins. c 1515.
Embroidery from a cope made to Perugino's design

Left: MADONNA OF THE GOLDFINCH
Bernardo Daddi (active 1312–48)
panel 32⅝ × 21¼ ins. c 1340

67

Bernard Berenson

the cross, his feet crushing three Vices, his eyes raised towards three angelic creatures, Chastity, Poverty and Obedience. It was, as Bernard Berenson wrote in 1903: 'A real theophany – the apotheosis of a human soul that has attained to complete harmony with the soul of the universe by overcoming all that is belittling and confining and opening itself out to all the benign influences of the spirit.' Next day the large triptych was brought to the villa. The shopkeeper-carpenter was pleased with its new home and revealed to Berenson that he had come along just in time. Nobody wanted that stuff, but the old wood was sought after for Angelico forgeries and he was going to chop it up. 'Everyone in Florence laughed at me when they heard that I had paid two thousand lire for that encumbrance', Berenson told me. He later discovered that he had rescued part of the Borgo San Sepolcro polyptych by Sassetta, other parts of which are now treasured by the National Gallery, London, the Louvre, the Musée Condé, and the Hermitage. At the beginning of the century he also found, in Rome, a worm-eaten fragment which showed, where the colour had not fallen off, an exquisitely delicate *Head of a Virgin* by Gentile da Fabriano. He hung it, as it was, in a small Venetian eighteenth-century frame and was not disturbed by the charge of anachronism; in fact, the dainty Gothic embroideries on the Virgin's veil are enhanced by the golden tracery of the frame.

The Berensons had not been at I Tatti for long, when they realized they would hate to leave the house. Their chance to buy it came in 1907, when their landlord lost all his money at Monte Carlo and Berenson acquired a regular income from the firm of Duveen's. Luckily he bought the surrounding farmland as well, and so the access not only to the villa, but also to the strip of rocky forest behind, which first attracted him to the spot, are protected to this day from the advancing suburbs of Florence. Every day until the end of his life, his quick steps would thread the steep paths of that hillside, whose clearings command such lovely views across the Arno valley and whose thickets have been the preserve of generations of lovers. The house itself was a plain oblong building (the existence of which was already recorded in 1563) surrounded by old cypresses and vineyards. Berenson transformed the southern slope into an Italianate garden, and the conservatory at the back into a library. From that first large room the library spread into many more rooms, which were gradually added to the original building. On

CHINESE STONE ALTAR *Height 27½ ins. 570 AD.*
An inscription on the back of the altar reads:
'On the seventh day of the fifth month of the first year of the Wu Ping era of the Great Chi dynasty (May 26th 570 AD) the Buddha disciple Ts'ao Po-lo had this stone image made in order that benefits should be bestowed on him, his family, children and fellow-believers and also that all beings in the boundless universe should share these blessings and reach the others above. Written for the female Buddha believer, wife of Ts'ao Po-lo, and for himself.'

Berenson's death, it contained some 50,000 books, rows of periodicals and a priceless collection of photographs. Not only did Berenson put the traditional name of the villa – a Tuscan family name – above his own; he also made sure that the extensions would blend with the old building and merge into the landscape and even the new roofs were covered with weathered tiles. As for paintings, he gave up having any of a style 'little in harmony with an Italian dwelling'.

Although within a few years his pictures numbered over a hundred, the provenance of more than half remains unknown. The rumour spread in Tuscany that he purchased old pictures, and so pictures came to his doorstep. Once a man brought to him the *Franciscan Monk holding a Book* by Giotto, which is a fragment contemporary with the frescoes in the Bardi Chapel at S. Croce. The inset stones and golden encrustations had been removed from the book, but Berenson saved the painting. The other Giotto (according to Berenson a studio work), the *Deposition*, whose companion pieces are scattered in museums in London, Boston, Munich, New York, was bought in London. Berenson made many purchases in London and Paris between 1909 and 1911 to hang on the walls of his newly decorated house: the *Madonna of the Goldfinch* by Daddi (one of his best), the *Madonna* by Matteo di Giovanni (which looked so well in the chapel on the Feast of Corpus Christi, when the procession climbed the hill from the nearby fifteenth-century church of S. Martino a Mensola), the girlish *Madonna* by Boccatis with the painter's home town of Camerino in the background, the delightful *Nativity* in which Bonfigli surpassed himself, the early Paris Bordone *Rest on the Flight*, the Perugino embroideries, and a few similar things. In rare cases the pictures Berenson bought in Italy, came from known collections (Crespi, Noseda), but usually they turned up from nowhere. It is amazing to think that works by Simone Martini, the Lorenzetti, Nardo di Cione, Lorenzo Monaco, that the enchanting little *Pace* by Perugino and the beautiful *S. Sebastian* by Cima, should have entered his collection previously unrecorded.

The choice of these artists is only partly representative of Berenson's taste. He adored Venetian Renaissance painting, but so did most wealthy Anglo-Saxon collectors, and the prices were unattainable; the same difficulty arose with his beloved Botticelli and the other great Florentine masters of the fifteenth and sixteenth centuries. He had better fortune with the Trecento. He also allowed himself a sprinkle of Mannerism, when he bought the Bachiacca *Leda* and the Granacci *Stories of Female Martyrs* from S. Apollonia (in the last chapter of his *Drawings* had he not confessed that Mannerism was the path to decline but 'its beginnings are so pleasant'). Chiefly, however, Berenson could, and did, take

his pick outside Venice and Florence: the Sienese were still dismissed as ugly and abstruse, the Umbrian, Marquigian, Lombard and minor Ferrarese were forgotten in the limbo of provincial art. The Uffizi Gallery is not rich in Sienese painting, but at I Tatti a Florentine could find a cross-section of that school from Segna di Bonaventura to Brescianino. A few months before his death, Berenson generously gave to the Uffizi his beautiful *Madonna* by Ambrogio Lorenzetti: it was the centre panel of a triptych which the Sienese painted in Florence for S. Procolo in 1332 and thanks to Berenson the triptych has now been reassembled in the major Florentine gallery.

Berenson was a pioneer in the study of drawings but did not collect them, for he never considered them as something with which to decorate his walls. 'I thought of an interior that suited my muscular and respiratory ideations with regard to space and my eyes with regard to shapes and colours… hangings, paintings, art objects were not acquired first and foremost with an eye to making a collection, but almost exclusively to adorn my abode. When that was completed… I stopped buying.' *(Sketch for a Self-Portrait)* Curiously, the inventor of the term 'tactile values' does not mention sculpture among his possessions, although he had several pieces in his home and in his garden. He cherished the painted and partly gilt marble *Madonna* by Gaggini, because it gave an idea of what some antique sculpture may have looked like – almost as warm as wax. Of his cubic *Head* of Vulcanic stone from Borobudur, he once said, 'This is cubism for me.' In fact, about ten years after writing the above lines, he made one addition to his collection: a sculpture in the round by an illiterate woodcutter from near Siena, who carved scenes of his daily life in a style reminiscent of Late Greco-Roman and Early-Christian sarcophagi, of Han funerary edicules, or medieval reliefs. The woodcutter was growing blind and was not moved by his sudden success when Berenson wrote a book about him (*Alberto Sani, an Artist out of his Time*, Florence 1951). Berenson put the sculpture conspicuously in the hall, where until then the impassive Egyptian Bronze Cat of the Saitic Dynasty (*c* 1500 BC) had stood on watch alone.

Because Berenson made his reputation as a scholar of the Italian Renaissance, or because of the widespread ignorance of Eastern art, few visitors noticed the oriental objects scattered about the house, except, possibly, the T'ang terracotta *Horsemen* and *Lady*; but those who understood their value, were thrilled. After the Boxer revolt in 1900, Chinese art – as distinct from Chinoiserie – began to reach Europe. Once, having watched the unpacking of a case just arrived at Vignier's in Paris, Berenson tested his contagious enthusiasm on his cultivated friends of the beau monde. They would

Bernard Berenson

not believe that the Far East could produce anything except porcelain, lacquer and prints. 'De la *peinture* chinoise? Mon chéri, ça n'existe pas!' To Berenson the linear subtleties of the Chinese masters came as a revelation. He mentioned them in his *Drawings*. In his essay on Sassetta he analysed the spiritual and aesthetic parallelisms between Sienese and Chinese art. To Mrs Gardner he wrote that if he could start afresh, 'I would devote myself to China as I have to Italy' (Sprigge, *Berenson*, p 216). He persuaded her to buy some of Vignier's treasures, although in 1915 she had long ceased collecting and the war was in progress. For himself he bought part of a scroll made in AD 1141 after a T'ang painting by Chou-Wen-chü of the Fifth Dynasty, representing *The Hundred Ladies of the Palace*. It describes the daily life of tenth-century China. Other fragments of the scroll were at the Royal Academy Exhibition of 1935–36. This delicate painting was put under glass and could be seen by visitors. Very exceptionally, other scrolls were pulled out of drawers, unrolled, admired, put away. Until recently, no photographs existed of his valuable bronzes. One bronze altar,

Pottery tomb figure of a woman.
Chinese, Six Dynasties, Northern Wei, 386–535 AD.
Height 15 ins.

THE HUNDRED LADIES OF THE PALACE 69 × 14 *ins.*
Part of a scroll painting on paper made in 1141 AD
after Chou-Wen-chü (active c 970 AD)

Bernard Berenson

ST FRANCIS IN GLORY
Sassetta (c 1392–1450) panel 74¾ × 48 ins.
The centre panel from the polyptych in
the Cathedral at Borgo S.Sepolcro commissioned
from Sassetta in 1437 and completed in 1444.
It represents St Francis crushing beneath his feet
Lust, Avarice and Violence and raising his eyes
to Chastity, Poverty and Obedience

Opposite: *I Tatti: The east passage*
to the library showing
St Sebastian *by Cima da Conegliano*
Opposite right: BUILDERS
Alberto Sani. Stone, height 15¼ ins. c1940.
The sculpture in the round
by the illiterate Italian woodcutter
which stands in the hall at I Tatti

Northern Wei, dated by the inscription AD 529, was exhibited in Berlin in 1927 and included by Matsubara in his *Corpus* (Tokyo 1961), but other valuable Oriental bronzes, wooden and stone sculptures are still unpublished. So are the Greek statuettes, the Parthian armrest in the shape of a tiger, the Mexican Snake, the Peruvian Beasts kept in the lemon house, just to mention a few items.

Although Berenson wrote the privately printed catalogues of the Johnson and the Widener Collection (1913 and 1916), he always refused to have a catalogue made of his own possessions as long as he was alive: 'I would not feel in my own house any more.' Now two catalogues have appeared, of his paintings (*La Raccolta Berenson*, Presentazione di Nicky Mariano, Testo e catalogo di F. Russoli, Milano, Ricordi, 1962), and of his Persian miniatures (*Persian Miniatures in the Berenson Collection* by R. E. Ettinghousen, Milano, Ricordi, 1962, and Charles Skilton). Miniatures he liked: fifteenth-century Italian and Mongol, sixteenth-century

Armenian, Tibetan Hells and Heavens, even two leaves from the Mesopotamian *Automata* by al-Jazari, AD 1354.

Unlike the real collector, who is only too pleased when asked to lend one of his possessions to an exhibition, Berenson could not bear to part temporarily with anything. During the ten years that I worked at I Tatti, I recall only one exception to this rule: he was persuaded to allow the portraits of *Camillo* and *Vitellozzo Vitelli* to go to Florence to join the portrait of their father, when that came all the way from Birmingham for the Signorelli exhibition of 1953. Although opposed in principle to lending Old Masters, because travelling affects their delicate physical balance, his main distress was their absence from the familiar place. On the other hand, the gates of his villa were open daily to students and visitors and he never refused them photographs of his treasures, nor permission to publish them under any new attribution.

Whereas historic houses impress one as a whole, in the case of collections one remembers this and that item. All the contents of I Tatti were so impregnated with Berenson's personality, that even for the purely curious or purely learned a visit could, and did, become a human experience. To Berenson his house represented his home, in the narrowest and in the widest sense. A lover of history and art, of nature and literature, he found a corner in the world where they seemed to blend in a serene, if severe, harmonious whole. The hills around the house had been loved before him by Gozzoli, Boccaccio and Leonardo. The landscape was to him always part of his 'collection', and his collection consisted of books as well as works of art. 'Like my body my house has a soul – I hope', he wrote; and could not bear the thought that it might be dismembered. Childless, he handed it over to all his spiritual children. 'I should wish to be the indwelling soul of my house and library. To speak more grossly, I should like to haunt it.' All who knew Berenson can only pray he will.

LUISA VERTOVA 73

New York Robert Lehman

European paintings and works of art

THE LEHMAN COLLECTION HAS BEEN made by a man who does not limit his choice to one kind of object, who does not try to complete a set or to prove or teach anything, but acquires rather only what appeals to his sense of quality, regardless of what the object is. The collection is therefore unique in its quality as well as its size. Nothing like it has been brought together in America during the twentieth century. It contains every imaginable kind of work of art, from paintings, drawings, and sculpture to porcelains, jewellery, and little figures of Nevers glass. Each object was chosen because something peculiar or individual about it appealed to the collector. Robert Lehman's interests in art have no limits. His knowledge is profound and scholarly, as can be seen in the excellent catalogue of his collection, which he wrote many years ago, in 1928.

Begun by the present owner's father, Philip Lehman, the collection is a living, growing thing which has been slowly created during the last fifty years. Hardly a week passes but some new and often totally unexpected addition is made. To its owner, it is a daily preoccupation and a never-ending source of pleasure. He seeks and finds works of art all over the world and the names of the sources from which they come read like an Almanach de Gotha of collecting.

Many of the paintings and other objects are famous, having been frequently lent to exhibitions, written about by scholars, and reproduced in magazines and catalogues. The collection was invited to be shown in Paris at the Orangerie in 1957, the first and only American collection ever to be paid this compliment. It has also been exhibited in the Metropolitan Museum in New York and in the Cincinnati Art Museum.

The paintings in the collection are the most important element; and among them, the gold-ground, Italian group from the early thirteenth, fourteenth, and fifteenth centuries is the most outstanding. This group of early Italian pictures is one of the very few to be formed in our time and is an interesting result of the influence upon Robert Lehman of the paintings he saw as a young student at Yale University. The museum there contains the precious Italian primitives ceded to it by that unfortunate and insufficiently recognized pioneer among American collectors, James Jackson Jarves. Robert Lehman's love of early Italian paintings was further encouraged and developed by his close friendship with Bernard Berenson, the ideal collector's scholar, who combined great erudition with the sharpest 'eye'. He has never lost this taste, and today he is the only major collector of Italian primitives – one of his recent acquisitions is a *Crucifixion* by Lorenzo Monaco.

The painters of the Sienese school are the best represented in the collection. They combine technical mastery and precision with grace and poetry in a way that is especially attractive to Robert Lehman. These qualities also characterize most of the works he has chosen from other schools and periods. The diptych of the *Crucifixion* and the *Madonna*

....

LEGEND OF ST ELIGIUS
Petrus Christus (1444–72/3) panel 39 × 33½ ins. 1449.
Saint Eligius, patron saint of jewellers is presenting
a ring to a young couple. The words Petr Cri me fecit a 1449
can be distinguished at the bottom of the painting

with Angels, attributed by scholars to one of Duccio's closest collaborators, shows a wonderful marriage of delicacy with strength. Its restrained and very unusual harmony of pale colours recalls Byzantine painting and it makes a perfect foundation-stone for the whole collection. The other early masters of the school are also well represented: Segna, Ugolino, Simone Martini, and Lippo Vanni. But the most impressive group is the one made up of paintings by artists who clung to their medieval traditions late in the fifteenth century, when, in nearby Florence, the Renaissance was already in full bloom. The *Temptation of St Anthony in the Desert* is one of the most vivid and moving works of Sassetta and the *Expulsion of Adam and Eve from Paradise* by his follower, Giovanni di Paolo, is a masterpiece of this school, in which the decorative fantasy of the Middle Ages is mixed with a delightful new awareness of nature. There are ten of this master's works and fourteen by Sassetta's charming pupil, Sano di Pietro. To know Sienese painting, one must have seen the Lehman collection.

The fourteenth-century Florentine paintings are less numerous. Two appealing Madonnas by Bernardo Daddi and an impressive Crucifixion by Andrea Orcagna and his assistants bring us close to the style of Giotto. A large panel by Bicci di Lorenzo, works by Agnolo Gaddi, Spinello Aretino, and Lorenzo Monaco, along with others by minor masters, give a complete picture of the development of the school into the fifteenth century.

The small *Annunciation* by Botticelli holds concentrated in jewel-like form all the innocence and freshness of the early Renaissance in Florence. It is difficult to imagine a more exquisite and delectable object for a private collection. Related to it by the purity of its graceful linear contours is the portrait once thought to represent Battista Sforza, attributed to Paolo Uccello, still a lovely and poetic picture in spite of the worn condition of its surface. The very rare pair of profile portraits of Alessandro di Bernardo Gozzadini and his wife, a member of the Canonici family, by Lorenzo Costa evokes a vivid image of life in fifteenth-century Ferrara. These two portraits were among the earliest purchases for the collection. Giovanni Bellini's *Madonna and Child* is recognized as one of the most significant of that artist's early period, when he was still under the influence of his brother-in-law, Mantegna. The richness and variety of painting in Italy at this time is well illustrated by the works of artists from many of the different centres: from Ferrara, Verona, Rimini, Bologna, Umbria and the Marches.

The collection also contains a small number of fine examples of the Renaissance in the North, in Flanders, France, and Germany. The scene from the legend of St Eligius, patron of goldsmiths, signed and dated 1449 by Petrus Christus, is

PORTRAIT OF SUZANNE DE BOURBON
Master of Moulins (active c 1480–99), panel 13½ × 9½ *ins.*
c 1491. It has also been suggested that this may be a portrait
of Margaret of Austria, daughter of the Emperor Maximilian.
The artist, one of the great French fifteenth-century
painters, takes his name from the triptych of the
Madonna and Child with Angels and Donors
in Moulins Cathedral

Right: EXPULSION OF ADAM AND EVE FROM PARADISE
Giovanni di Paolo (c1403–87) panel 17¾ × 20½ *ins. c1445.*
Fragment of a predella showing God the Father pointing out to
Adam and Eve the world into which they will be exiled. The
earth is shown surrounded by the ocean and the celestial spheres
with the signs of the zodiac marked on the outermost circle

Robert Lehman

one of the major masterpieces of this painter and an admirable example of the solid, plastic style that distinguishes him from the other Flemish painters. *The Annunciation* by Memling, with its harmony of cool colours, is one of the master's most original compositions and the *Portrait of a Young Man* is acknowledged to be one of his finest. *The Annunciation* by Gerard David is a wonderful example of this artist's sensitive use of paint. Though a grisaille, it gives the feeling of colour because of its infinitely subtle tonal gradations. Well chosen works by Aelbert Bouts, the Master of the St Ursula Legend, Joos van Cleve, and Isenbrandt illustrate various other aspects of this school.

Few paintings of the period are as appealing as the portrait of a little girl, who is thought to be the diplomat and patron of the arts, Margaret of Austria, as a child. It was painted by the Maître de Moulins and kept in the family of his patrons until 1927, when it was purchased from one of their descendants and became a star of the Lehman collection. French painting of this period is very rare, and it is remarkable that it was possible to surround this picture with the works of other Frenchmen of the time like Simon Marmion, the Master of St Gilles, and the anonymous painter of a lady of the Burgundian court wearing the characteristic hennin.

Two fifteenth-century Madonnas and two small panels by Cranach, a *Nymph*, and *Venus with Cupid Stung by Bees* – symbolizing the brevity of love's pleasures and pains –

THE ANNUNCIATION
Sandro Botticelli (1445–1510) panel 9½ × 14¼ ins. c 1490

Below: MADONNA AND CHILD ENTHRONED WITH ANGELS
Duccio di Buoninsegna (c 1255/60–1318/19)
panel 14½ × 10¾ ins. One wing of a diptych
of which the other shows the Crucifixion

give an insight into the variety of German painting of the period. The *Erasmus* by Holbein is the best example of the second group of portraits of the great humanist, painted from 1530 to 1532, and comes from the Arundel collection, one of the greatest and oldest of English collections.

Complementing the early paintings, there is a selection of pages from illuminated manuscripts that ranges from early medieval German and Italian works to examples of the fully developed style of the fifteenth century in Flanders and in France. The most extraordinary of these is the view of medieval Paris with the cathedral of Notre-Dame, from the Book of Hours of Etienne Chevalier by Fouquet, not only a beautiful painting but also a historical document of great importance. The series closes with a fascinating self-portrait by Simon Benning, the Fleming who carried on the medieval tradition of miniature painting into the middle of the sixteenth century.

Robert Lehman has not collected the works of the seventeenth and eighteenth centuries so extensively, but what he has acquired is of the highest quality. The *St Jerome* by El Greco, by far the most powerful of the versions of this picture, came into the collection long before this artist's works were generally appreciated and sought after. The same is true of the large Goya *Portrait of the Countess of Altamira and her Daughter*. The *Portrait of Gerard de Lairesse*, the paint-

er, is a tragic and unforgettable Rembrandt. The *Interior* by Pieter de Hooch is a beautiful example of that artist's gentle, intimate mood, and the two likenesses of Burgomaster Jan van Duren and his wife by Terborch are unusual in showing so clearly how this artist was influenced by Velazquez after his trip to Spain in 1648.

It was in the late 1920's and the early 1930's that Robert Lehman began to acquire the nineteenth-century French paintings which form a group almost as extensive and complete as that of the early Renaissance. They are dominated by the great *Portrait of the Princesse de Broglie*, Ingres' finest female portrait and one of the most extraordinary pictures of the nineteenth century. The first half of the century is represented by works of Corot and the Barbizon school, but the Impressionists and their successors are the painters whose works have especially appealed to Robert Lehman. His collection of Impressionist pictures illustrates all the revolutionary developments in the art of painting which led up to the twentieth century. The great figures of the movement are well represented: Degas, by the large impressive pastel, *At the Modiste's*, from the Rouart Collection; Renoir, by a charming group including *The Two Girls at the Piano* and two unusual landscapes, one of Versailles; Cézanne, by the freely painted wooded landscape, formerly owned by Gabriel Cognacq. The Monet, a Dutch landscape, is a recent

78

Robert Lehman

acquisition. It is an early work dated 1872, beautiful in its freshness and its clarity. Van Gogh can be seen in an almost classical self-portrait and in one of his most disturbing and expressive pictures of a mother and child. *The Seated Girl in Red* by Toulouse-Lautrec, famous through reproductions, is one of that painter's most finished achievements. There is a subtle atmospheric *Study for the Grande Jatte* by Seurat, and there are also paintings by his followers, Cross and Signac. Vuillard and Bonnard can be seen as Nabis and also at other stages of their careers. The representation of Fauves is particularly strong, including paintings by artists little known and rarely seen outside France.

When a collector has a taste for drawings, it almost always indicates an eye for quality. Ever since he was a young man, Robert Lehman has been acquiring drawings. This was always the most consistently active aspect of his collecting, and it still is. As a result, he now has one of the most extensive collections of drawings in private hands in the world today. They form a remarkable complement to the paintings, widely expanding the range and variety of the different schools that interest him. Among the Italians, there are rare, early drawings by Stefano da Verona, Giambono, Antonello da Messina, and Pisanello. A splendid project for the equestrian monument to Francesco Sforza by Antonio Pollaiuolo and beautiful silver-point drawings by Perugino and Leonardo da Vinci are a few of the many brilliant examples of Renaissance draughtsmanship. The faithfulness and precision

Above: SAINT JEROME AS CARDINAL
El Greco (1541–1614) oil on canvas 42½ × 34¼ ins. c 1600

Opposite left: PORTRAIT OF GERARD DE LAIRESSE
Rembrandt van Rijn (1609–69)
oil on canvas 44 × 35 ins. 1665

Opposite right: SELF PORTRAIT
Vincent van Gogh (1853–90) oil on canvas 18½ × 15¼ ins. 1889

Right: STUDY OF A BEAR WALKING
Leonardo da Vinci (1452–1519) silverpoint 4 × 5¼ ins.
The faintly sketched figure of a woman can just
be distinguished across the figure of the bear

79

Robert Lehman

of the early Flemish masters is also well illustrated. From the German sixteenth century the collection possesses an extraordinarily important group of drawings by Albrecht Dürer. They come from the Lubomirski collection, formerly in Lvow, and beginning with the precocious self-portrait of 1493, show the different stages in Dürer's development. Rembrandt's *Large Cottage on the Edge of a Wood* and his copy after Leonardo's *Last Supper* are both exceptional examples of his work. From the eighteenth century there is a fine Watteau figure, enchanting wash drawings by Fragonard, two powerful miniature portraits by Goya, beautiful views of Venice by Guardi and Canaletto, and numerous works by Domenico Tiepolo showing how varied his talents were.

The nineteenth-century drawings reflect the interest in that period that is evident in the choice of the paintings. There are several fine portrait drawings by Ingres, a large female nude by Prud'hon, and superb portraits by Chassériau. The Barbizon school is represented by very finished landscapes by Daubigny and Harpignies. There are studies by Degas, Renoir, and the other Impressionists, together with a large group of watercolours and drawings by Signac and his contemporaries. The most recent purchase is a small but exquisite pen sketch of a *Harlequin with a Girl* by Picasso.

Along with the paintings and drawings, Robert Lehman has brought together an exceptionally varied and extensive assemblage of works of art of other kinds. The collection is preserved in two places, the town house that belonged to his father and once held the entire collection, and the apartment where Mr and Mrs Robert Lehman now live. In each place the decorative arts are arranged in harmony

....

PORTRAIT OF
PRINCESSE DE BROGLIE
*Jean Auguste Dominique
Ingres (1780–1867)
oil on canvas
47¾ × 35¾ ins. 1853*

82

Robert Lehman

Top left: *A jewelled pendant showing Samson and the Lion. Gold, enamel, precious stones and pearls, 7¼ × 3¼ ins. Late sixteenth-century Italian, probably Florentine, workmanship*
Top right: AT THE MODISTE'S *Edgar Degas (1834–1917) pastel 30 × 32 ins. c 1883. One of many similar genre scenes of women dressing or at their toilet*
Bottom: THE PRODIGAL SON *Giorgio Andreoli Diameter 11³/₁₆ ins. 1525. A majolica based on an engraving by Dürer*

with the paintings and drawings so that the qualities of all are emphasized. In the house the walls are covered with velvets and brocades which make a rich and admirable background. There are three tapestries, a late fifteenth-century Falcon Hunt and two early sixteenth-century religious subjects, one of them *The Last Supper* from a cartoon by Bernard van Orley. Much of the furniture, tables, cassoni, and curule chairs, is of the sixteenth and seventeenth centuries. On the tables and chests are displayed a variety of Gothic and Renaissance metal objects. Among the aquamaniles are a rare thirteenth-century lion with basilisks and the witty German example showing Aristotle ridden by his Campaspe – the triumph of love over wisdom. The Renaissance bronzes include medals by Pisanello and sculptures by Riccio together with numerous works by other less well-known masters. The collection of fifteenth and sixteenth-century majolica is extraordinarily large and fine, numbering more than one hundred pieces. All of the great Italian centres are represented. There are many splendid examples by Giorgio Andreoli of Gubbio and Francesco Xanto of Urbino and numerous *albarelli* from Faenza.

There are painted enamels and a large collection of goldsmiths' work and jewellery, comprising reliquaries, pendants, necklaces, and other jewels from French, German, Flemish, and Italian workshops. To these have been added

83

Robert Lehman

A Louis XV black lacquer commode. Height 33½ ins.
The elaborate decoration of birds and flowers
is in colours with a framework of rococo leafage

in recent years precoius eighteenth-century snuff boxes of gold, decorated with enamels and diamonds, which once belonged to Frederick the Great and later to King Farouk. There is a small group of vessels of precious stones, the magnificent table ornaments of Renaissance princes, ewers and cups or rock crystal, jasper, and jade. Complementing these are more than twenty graceful and delicate pieces of Venetian glass of the same period.

The apartment in which Mr and Mrs Robert Lehman live contains the portrait by Ingres, some of the best Impressionists, and many drawings. The furnishings are for the most part French of the eighteenth century. There are vitrines of Sèvres porcelain, blue and Pompadour-rose, and pairs of Meissen birds of beautiful quality. Among the pieces of furniture are exceptional ones like the upright secrétaire with plaques of green Sèvres and the delicate and elegant porcelain *guéridon*, both signed by Carlin, a splendid black lacquer Louis XV commode, and another secrétaire signed by Weisweiler.

This enumeration, detailed though it seems, gives only a fragmentary idea of the richness of this collection. It certainly follows the tradition formed in the great houses of Europe and carried on in this country by J.P.Morgan, Henry Frick, George Blumenthal, and the H.O.Havemeyers. Only the last, however, so daringly and successfully combined the old with the new. It is extraordinary that a man as active as Robert Lehman in the world of finance should have found the time and the energy to create such an assemblage of works of art. He also manages to be active in the world of art – he is Vice-President and Trustee of the Metropolitan Museum, Trustee of the Associates in Fine Arts of Yale University, and a member of the Governing Board of the Yale Art Gallery. He is also a trustee of New York University and Honorary Chairman of the advisory committee of its Institute of Fine Arts. He can indeed be said to descend in direct line from all the great patrons and benefactors of the arts.   THEODORE ROUSSEAU

....

THE EMPEROR VESPASIAN
CURED BY THE VEIL OF SAINT VERONICA
A tapestry in wool, silk, silver and gold thread.
c 1510. Brussels craftsmanship

84

The drawing room of Mr and Mrs Robert Lehman's
New York residence with El Greco's Saint Jerome *over
the mantelpiece, and two Rembrandt portraits,*
Gérard de Lairesse *on the right and* Portrait of an Elderly
Man *on the left. El Greco's* Christ Carrying the Cross
can be seen on the far left

Left: ARISTOTLE AND CAMPASPE
*Brass, height 13¼ ins. c 1400. An aquamanile
of North German workmanship. The subject is based on one
of the most well-known fables of the Middle Ages,
which celebrates woman's power over man*

85

Venice Count Vittorio Cini

Italian paintings and furnishings

THE CINI COLLECTION IS ONLY of recent origin, and continues to grow. In a necessarily brief description, accompanied by a small group of illustrations, it is possible to make only a rapid survey of the collection.

It had its beginnings between 1910 and 1915, when a few works of local painters, ranging from the old sixteenth-century masters to the Ferrarese celebrity of the day, Giovanni Boldini, were assembled at Ferrara. Since then, during the last decades, the collector has extended his interests to the acquisition of paintings outside the school of Ferrara and of objects from the minor and applied arts. Always, in making his choice, he has been concerned with the quality of the individual pieces and the ease with which they fitted into a house designed to be lived in. The collection has never been influenced by passing fashion, and has retained a distinctly 'domestic' flavour, reflected in the harmony and simplicity with which the works of art (many of them listed as national treasures) are arranged in the Castello di Monselice and the Palazzo Loredan in Venice.

The Castello was restored from 1935 onwards under the supervision of Nino Barbantini, who for many years was also the curator of the collection. This unusually complex building bears traces of all styles from the Romanesque to

··

Opposite: MADONNA AND CHILD WITH TWO ANGELS
Piero di Cosimo (1462–1521) panel 45¾ × 33¾ ins. c1506

Right: MADONNA AND CHILD
Florentine fourteenth-century painted wooden sculpture.
Height 69½ ins.

87

Right: *Silver plate by Giovanni Staderini and Gaspare Mola commemorating the reform of the Gregorian calendar. Diameter 21 ins.*
Below left: *A Venetian sixteenth-century carved walnut cupboard from a design by Jacopo Sansovino. Height 8 ft.*
Below right: *Silver ewer by Antonio de Castro bearing the arms of Megollo Lercaro. Height 16½ ins. 1565*

Count Vittorio Cini

AURORA
Giovanni Antonio Guardi (1699–1760)
oil on canvas 163¾ × 82¾ ins. c 1750

the Rococo, and the contributions of each period have been allowed to remain. Because of their monumental scale and scenic effects, the rooms proved most successful as settings for sculptures and bas-reliefs of Tuscan, Umbrian, Ferrarese, Lombard and Venetian origin from the fourteenth to the sixteenth centuries. There are also Flemish tapestries, furniture (particularly Renaissance Tuscan and Venetian) and a collection of arms and armour.

The pieces of special historical or artistic interest, combined with the more simple objects which illustrate the daily life and costume of the times, give character to the interior, whether it be the intimacy of the lower or upper studies, or the austere magnificence of the Sala del Camino or the Salone d'Onore. In this way the domestic life of the Middle Ages and the Renaissance is re-created in an authentic and evocative manner. The visitor is left with the impression not of a period museum, but of an ancestral home which is still lived in.

The Palazzo Loredan in the San Vio quarter of Venice, which was built at the end of the sixteenth century, radiates the same feeling of an inhabited and welcoming private house. There, to an even greater extent, the many different types of works of art are used as furnishings or fittings with a fine sense of their original purpose. This is true of the painted Tuscan and Veronese chests of the fifteenth century, decorated with gilt stucco, the noble Tuscan and Venetian furniture of the sixteenth century, the delicate eighteenth-century Venetian lacquer, the pieces of sculpture, the Chinese carved jade, the enamel, the porcelain, the bronzes, the ivory, and the silver objects which may be as valuable for their artistic merit as for their historical associations, like Lercaro's ewer and basin or Gaspare Mola's plate. It is no less true of the medals, plaques and engraved stones, the Greek, Roman and medieval jewels, and the work of the European goldsmiths from the fifteenth to the nineteenth centuries.

A quiet secluded room houses the series of drawings by Gianantonio Guardi, the illustrated books and the miniatures. The nucleus of this last collection previously belonged to Hoepli, but during the last few years it has been enriched by several codexes and illuminated pages of great interest.

Left: MAESTÀ (MADONNA AND
CHILD ENTHRONED, WITH ANGELS)
Master of Badia Isola
(active late 13th–early 14th century)
panel 67¾ × 41¼ ins.

Above: MADONNA AND CHILD WITH ANGELS
School of Rimini, panel 32¾ × 25½ ins.
c 1340–45

Opposite: MADONNA AND CHILD WITH
ST JOHN THE BAPTIST AND ST FRANCIS
Bartolommeo Montagna (c 1450–1523)
panel 58¼ × 71 ins. c 1490

Particularly noteworthy are the *Martyrology* of the Brotherhood of the *Battuti Neri* of Ferrara, which dates from the beginning of the fifteenth century and is the work of Venetian and Emilian artists; and the little breviary illuminated by Lombard artists and given by Ludovico il Moro to Charles VIII of France.

But the part of the collection which is best known and most prized is the collection of paintings. It is clear from his choice that the collector had a preference for pictures dating from the thirteenth to the middle of the sixteenth centuries, and for Venetian painting of the eighteenth century. Most remarkable among the pictures painted before Giotto are the *Madonna Mediatrix* of the Roman School, with its wide chromatic range recalling the colours of Imperial Rome, and the little painted crucifix by Giunta Pisano, formerly in the Gualino collection, painted on both sides. From the fourteenth century come pictures of the Umbrian School, the School of Rimini, and the Master of Santa Cecilia, a polyptych usually attributed to Orcagna, but possibly from the Pisan School, and finally, the *Maestà* of the Master of Badia a Isola, the quality of which, revealed by the removal of over-painting, leads one to suppose that the artist was not merely a follower, but the active collaborator, of Duccio di Buoninsegna.

Passing to the fifteenth and sixteenth centuries, a few gem-like panels by Cosmè Tura and Ercole de' Roberti represent the School of Ferrara together with works by Ludovico Mazzolini, Lorenzo Costa, l'Ortolano, Dosso and Battista Dossi, Garofalo and Panetti. Southern Italian painting is represented by five little panels which were once part of a *retablo* by Colantonio as well as the large triptych by Cristoforo Scacco; Umbria and the Marche contribute outstanding examples of the work of Giovanni Boccati, of Girolamo di Giovanni da Camerino, and of the Master of the Barberini panels.

Tuscan and Venetian painters claim, however, the place of honour in this collection. Among the former must be mentioned Lorenzo Monaco, Sassetta, Fra Angelico, Pietro di Giovanni Ambrosi and Botticelli, while of particular importance is Filippo Lippi's *Madonna and Child with Saints, Angels and Donor*, painted in the artist's youth under the direct influence of Masaccio; the *Madonna Villamarina*, which is attributed to the later years of Piero della Francesca; and the *Madonna with Child and two Angels*, which should be counted among the finest achievements of the eccentric Piero di Cosimo.

Of greatest interest in the Venetian paintings of the fifteenth and early sixteenth centuries are two *Saints* by Nicolò di Pietro; a small *Saint Francis* by Giambono; the earliest known work of Carlo Crivelli; works by Cima da

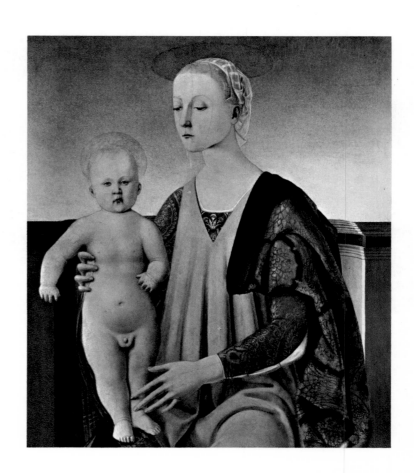

Count Vittorio Cini

Opposite top: MADONNA AND CHILD
WITH ANGELS, SAINTS AND DONOR
Filippo Lippi (c 1406–69)
panel 19⅜ × 15½ ins. c 1430–35
Opposite bottom: MADONNA AND CHILD
Piero della Francesca (1415/20–92)
panel 25¼ × 21¾ ins.
A late work
Below: TWO FRIENDS
Jacopo Pontormo (1494–1557)
panel 34½ × 26¼ ins.

Above: ST GEORGE *Titian (c 1488–1576)*
panel 50⅜ × 26⅜ ins.
c 1517–20

Count Vittorio Cini

Conegliano and Benedetto Diana; and the *Caregiani* altarpiece by Bartolomeo Montagna, in which the austere and geometrical design is softened and made more human by the after-glow of a beautiful sky, reminiscent of Giovanni Bellini's sunsets.

As we advance into the sixteenth century there are the portraits attributed to Sebastiano del Piombo, Bartolomeo Veneto, Giovanni Cariani, Bernardino Licinio and Lorenzo Lotto, and the paintings by Jacopo Tintoretto. Of particular importance is the *Saint George* attributed to Giorgione or Titian, but which perhaps formed part of the painting commissioned from Vecellio by the Republic of Venice in about 1517 as a tribute to Odet de Foix, Vicomte de Lautrec, Maréchal de France and Governor of Milan.

Although Mannerism is scarcely represented in the collection, there is an outstanding painting from this period: Pontormo's *Two Friends*, painted in a subtle combination of greys.

Eighteenth-century Venetian painting is shown in some of its most characteristic aspects. The splendour of Giambattista Tiepolo's decorations (illustrated by a ceiling fresco of *Aurora*) and the poetic vein of his sketches blend with the disenchanted elegance of Alessandro Longhi's portraits and the Arcadian prettiness of the landscapes by Zuccarelli and Zais. The international Rococo taste of Sebastiano Ricci is seen beside the provincial, but no less valued, art of Pittoni and Fontebasso. Canaletto and Francesco Guardi are naturally included in the collection: two youthful and romantic works by the former show him under the spell of the Roman countryside; and the latter is represented by some excellent *capricci* and other landscapes.

From the last flowering of Venetian painting come the great canvases representing *Neptune, Vulcan, Venice* and *Aurora*. Whether these paintings should be attributed to Francesco Guardi or to his brother Gianantonio, whose preparatory drawing for the *Aurora* is known, is one of today's controversial questions among Venetian art-critics. Whatever the truth may be, these mythological figures are among the most important expressions of Rococo painting in Europe.

Finally, it should be emphasized again with what care all the works of art in this collection have been restored to their original condition. This loving care reveals to the sensitive visitor the extent to which this cultural heritage forms an important part of our lives today. FRANCESCO VALCANOVER

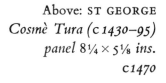

Above: ST GEORGE
Cosmè Tura (c 1430–95)
panel 8¼ × 5⅛ ins.
c1470

Right: ST JEROME,
ST CATHERINE OF ALEXANDRIA,
ST GEORGE
Ercole de' Roberti (c 1450–96)
panels each 10⅜ × 15½ ins.
c1475–77

Above: *The Salone d'Onore in the Castello di Monselice.*
The red and white chequered decoration of the walls is
derived from the arms of the Carrara family, Padua.
The walls are hung with sixteenth-century tapestries
made in Brussels depicting episodes in Roman history,
and the furniture includes some fine sixteenth-century
Tuscan pieces. In the left foreground is a bronze Chinese
wash basin of the late Ming dynasty

Left: *A room in the Palazzo Loredan, Venice. On the left-hand*
wall is Botticelli's Judgement of Paris *and* Nativity *by*
Parmigianino. On the left of the door is Piero della Francesca's
Villamarina Madonna *and over the door* Portrait of a Man *by*
Bernardino Licinio. Through the door, in the adjoining room,
can be seen Tintoretto's Portrait of a Young Woman

Baron H. H. Thyssen-Bornemisza

European paintings and sculpture

HEINRICH BARON THYSSEN-BORNEMISZA (1875–1947) started to build up his art collection towards the middle of the 1920's. The plan he set out to fulfil was in the tradition of the great museums, and will always be an ideal for a picture gallery to aim at: to illustrate by representative examples the whole course of development in European painting. However, the Baron's personal tastes proved too strong for this plan to be followed rigidly – its fulfilment would have required the detachment of a professional art historian. Certain periods and artists are given special emphasis – evidence of the collector's personal preferences. His ultimate concern was with the artistic unity of all culture, and in selecting the sculptures and the pieces exemplifying the useful arts his collector's taste and sensibility was allowed free play, unhindered by academic preoccupations. To appreciate what he achieved, this marvellous collection has to be looked at as a whole, including the carpets, tapestries, goldsmiths' work and furniture.

The collection was first brought together from the great cities of Europe and exhibited to the public in 1930, at the New Pinakothek in Munich, under the title Schloss Rohoncz Collection. In 1937 a three-volume catalogue was published to coincide with the opening of the exhibition at Lugano-Castagnola, where Baron Thyssen had been living since 1932. Here he built a special gallery for the pictures, which was completed and opened in 1939. The whole building retains the arrangement, proportions and above all the style of a noble house, so that the exhibits are seen to their best advantage. On arriving at the Villa Favorita, one of the most beautiful on Lake Lugano, the visitor approaches through a long avenue of cypresses leading to the tall,

austerely built house, in the Tuscan style. The vestibule, staircase and spacious rooms, rich yet restrained in style, contain a number of sculptures, tapestries, pieces of furniture and pictures – the most beautiful being Tiepolo's *Death of Hyacinth*. In the last and highest room, as cool as a Renaissance studio, hangs El Greco's Venetian painting, *The Last Supper*. From here a narrow white marble stairway leads up to the clearly-lit gallery, where the rhythmical alternation of one large room with two pairs of smaller ones, all lit from above, has made it possible to arrange the pictures in their national and historical groupings. Baron Heinrich's son and successor has shown sympathetic understanding of his precious inheritance and increased its value. Like his father, Baron Hans has not been afraid to emphasize the collection's special features and augment its qualities, even where this has meant further abandonment of the original plan and an occasional exchange. All nineteenth-century pieces, except the five Rodin marble sculptures commissioned from the artist by August Thyssen, have been excluded from the exhibited collection. Baron Hans Thyssen's personal interest in the development of art has led him to purchase some more modern pictures, for example Monet's *La Barque Bleue*, even including some with abstract tendencies. This group, however,

....

THE DEATH OF HYACINTH
Giovanni Battista Tiepolo (1696–1770)
oil on canvas 113 × 92½ *ins.* C 1757

HENRY VIII
Hans Holbein the Younger
(1498–1543)
oil on canvas 10¾ × 7¾ *ins.*
A pendant to a portrait of
Jane Seymour (now in The
Mauritshuis, The Hague).
Both were painted by
Holbein in 1536–37,
apparently with the
intention of gaining the
98   *patronage of the king*

Baron Thyssen

is kept separate from the historic collection, and reserved for the day-to-day intimacy of the private apartments.

In its general arrangement the gallery follows a chronological sequence, beginning with Italian Romanesque and Gothic painting, which includes the Sienese school, here represented by Giovanni di Paolo with a painting of great merit. The starting point is a thirteenth-century panel of the Madonna, solemn and hieratic, as yet untouched by Cimabue's innovations. There are numerous pointers towards Byzantine art in the small *Crucifixion,* which is unmistakably Tuscan and close to the classicism of Cavallini in its clarity of construction, nobility of line and beauty of texture. The juxtaposition of these two pictures, the monumental composition and the small cabinet-piece which has to be seen from close to, creates an effect of tension which is several times repeated at Castagnola – here, significantly, one finds it at the very beginning of the collection. If one compares these two marvellous pictures with the more than life-size sculpture of the Virgin and Child which stands nearby, one is forced to recognize the boldness with which painters of this period approached their work. This sculpture, the *Madonna of Sionviller,* was made in Lorraine towards the middle of the thirteenth century and is a rare and impressive example of French cathedral sculpture; from the harmonious movement of the soft-flowing drapery it seems to have affiliations with the art of Champagne. It was also in the thirteenth century that panel painting had its earliest tentative beginnings north of the Alps – there is an example on a small altar from Cologne of the kind intended for private devotions, a characteristic expression of the mystical elements in religion at this time. The collection's first peak is reached with the works representing the period around 1400. It has only recently been recognized that this school, whose style is common to all European countries, is better represented at the Villa Favorita than in any public collection: the *Face of Christ* by Meister Bertram – a reiteration of the Byzantine Acheropoiiten, the Cologne diptych,

Above: PORTRAIT OF A WOMAN *Albrecht Altdorfer (1480–1538) panel 23¼ × 17¾ ins. c 1520. The only known portrait by Altdorfer who was primarily a landscape painter*
Left: CHRIST DISPUTING WITH THE DOCTORS
Albrecht Dürer (1471–1528) panel 26⅜ × 31½ ins. 1506.
A painting showing the influence of Leonardo's character studies

99

with its rich vocabulary of symbols; the majestic *Portrait of a Prince in Blue* – an incunabula of portraiture; and finally the great panel of the two St Johns, with the minute figure of the donor clad in full court regalia kneeling between them. This last is a truly astonishing picture, in which the cultural achievement of the age which produced it is explicit in every detail – in the human types, their physiognomy and bearing, in the fall of the draperies and in the delicate colouring; its recent attribution to an English master and the identification of the donor with Henry v must be correct, and relates the picture in iconography, though not in style, back to the Wilton diptych in the National Gallery. One of the most beautiful sculptures, the figure of Guillaume d'Auniers holding his shield, is a further choice example of the courtly nature of art at this period, as is shown by the portraiture and the surviving traces of colour.

Much space and emphasis is given to early German painting. Until very recent times there was such a large number of extant works in this field that purchases were relatively easy to make. This made it all the more difficult for a collector not to squander his resources and to content himself

THE ANNUNCIATION *Jan van Eyck (c 1400–1441) diptych, each panel measuring* 15⅛ × 9¼ *ins. c 1440. Grisaille imitations of stone figures often decorate the outside of altar wings. Here they are made by the artist to form a diptych complete in themselves*

with a representative selection. For this reason it is rare to find a really sound collection; despite much careful research into details we still have no clear picture of the main stages of German development to set beside that of contemporary Italian painting. There is a multiplicity of masters and schools, the area covered is wide – from the Tyrol to the North Sea, from the Danube to the Upper and Lower Rhineland – and split up by internal barriers; moreover, the local schools followed their own lines of development which touched or ran criss-cross at several points. Michael Pacher and Rueland Frueauf were active in the south of this region, Hermann Koerbecke in the north. Koerbecke's panel with the *Assumption of the Virgin* was once part of a now completely dismembered altar from Marienfeld in Westphalia (1457); with its mass of blue on a gold ground this picture is at once retrospective and forward-looking – an anticipation of the later classicism of Cologne.

The restraint and sobriety of four fragments from a large altar panel by Dirk Baegert are typical of the second half of the century; the general effect is one of harshness and economy of line and colour, with the painter's efforts concentrated on the exposition of his subject, the Crucifixion. The forcing ground for German painting, the region where it most fully matured, was the area comprising the Danube valley, Swabia and the upper Rhineland. Cranach is the central figure in this section of the collection, represented by a variety of works, including altar panels, mythological subjects and portraits. Baron Thyssen was obviously attracted by this artist's idiosyncratic style and his preoccupation with the aesthetic effects of his craftsmanship, which is of the highest quality. The wide range of the period – and of the collector's sympathies – is again evident in the juxtaposition of Hans Baldung's magnificent nude *Adam and Eve* with Bernhard Strigel's *Annunciation* altar. Both have a Renaissance-like classicism in their melodious line and feeling of suppressed emotion, but what a difference there is between the subtle grey tones of the Strasbourg master and the rich darkness of Strigel, which recalls the Venetians!

The Netherlands dominated the art of this period, as this collection convincingly makes clear. The small group of Dutch and Flemish works acquired by Baron Thyssen is not only the most valuable but also the most edifying and instructive of the entire collection. Jan van Eyck's *Annunciation* is a work of genius pure and simple. The ivory-coloured stone figures, their draperies reflected in the black marble of the recess, create an imaginative effect which has concentrated in it the essence of the European soul and goes beyond and above mere artistic invention. The sense of reality which Jan van Eyck imparts to his work becomes with

Baron Thyssen

YOUNG KNIGHT IN A LANDSCAPE
Vittore Carpaccio (1460/65–1523/26)
oil on canvas 86×60 ins. 1510. The white animal is a
symbol of the Order of the Ermine, founded in 1483,
of which the knight must be a member

Roger van der Weyden a refinement of aesthetic imagination and accomplishment, as displayed for example in the collection's second great masterpiece, the *Madonna of the Cave*. The Netherlander who after Roger did most to influence German development was the Master of Flémalle. He is represented here by a male portrait, worthy to be set beside the portrait at Berlin, and more impressively still by the studies which Gerard David used in his youthful *Crucifixion*. In this there is more of the true Flémalle – indeed more of Robert Campin – than in the *Nativity* of Jacques Daret, which all too obviously betrays its Dijon prototype. One sees Northern Holland asserting its individuality as against the southern provinces as early as the fifteenth century, with the Master of the *Virgo inter Virgines*, whose original style can be seen here in his magnificent *Crucifixion*. Three portraits from successive generations show clearly the artist's changing conception of style, his outlook on social class and his awareness of character: Roger van der Weyden's *Unknown Noble of the Burgundian Court*; the burgess for whom Memling painted on the back of his portrait one of the earliest still-lifes, as a warning that youth is transitory; and the *Portrait of Joan the Mad* by Juan de Flandes.

In Italy the paths so clearly mapped out in the fifteenth century in Florence, Milan and Venice led directly to the High Renaissance. This second peak of European painting is represented only patchily at Castagnola, so that it never emerges in its full range. Mannerism, however, is epitomized by the four splendid El Grecos. If the huge and powerful Caravaggio is excepted, the baroque style has only the Flemings and the Dutch and to a lesser extent the Spaniards to uphold it. The eighteenth century comes into its own with Fragonard's delightful picture *The Seesaw* and with Hubert Robert in France, and with Guardi and Canaletto in Venice.

The Villa Favorita is strikingly rich in portraits. This part of the collection seems to reflect most faithfully the personality of its founder; here one seems to make direct contact with him. Indeed, one might imagine that Baron Thyssen first started to collect pictures under the compelling attraction of these strong-featured faces of the Reformation period, so expressive of their inner character. Even if this is fanciful, interest in portraiture was certainly a decisive factor when it came to building up the collection. A special gallery was built for the portraits, a corridor containing twenty-two pictures hung on wood panelling, with a row of busts of six Roman Emperors above. This arrangement and the sense of space give the impression of one of the earliest Italian galleries of the Renaissance period. German painting only came into its own when the emphasis shifted to portraiture. The series begins about 1480 with peasant

101

FERDINAND VII *Francisco de Goya y Lucientes*
(1746–1828) oil on canvas 33½ × 24¾ ins. 1814.
One of a number of portraits
of the Spanish royal family by Goya

PORTRAIT OF GIOVANNA TORNABUONI
Domenico Ghirlandajo (1449–94) panel 30⅜ × 19¼ ins. 1488.
A portrait painted after Giovanna Tornabuoni's death
in childbirth

faces, like woodcarvings – the young bridegroom from the lower Rhine, the Bavarian monk depicted against a yellow background, the bride from Styria – and ends with figures recognizable as simply European, the married couples depicted by Barthel Beham and Bruyn, by Christopher Amberger and, with somewhat less success, by Hans Wertigen. Between these two extremes stands the work of the elder Holbein, Baldung Grien, Cranach and Wolf Huber, in which firm cranial outlines, expressive features, clothing and ornaments all combine to produce portraits of unique and unmistakable individuals. The only known portrait by Albrecht Altdorfer found its way to Castagnola and not to one of the Berlin museums. The crowning piece among the portraits – and the third great masterpiece of the collection –

is Holbein's *Henry* VIII, at once a miniature and a monument of political portraiture. Indeed, the best-known pictures in the entire collection are portraits – Ghirlandaio's *Giovanna Tornabuoni* and Carpaccio's *Knight*. The whole atmosphere of the early Renaissance seems concentrated in the unresolved mystery of this last portrait, as though in a burning-glass. Sebastiano del Piombo's *Portrait of Cardinal Carondolet* is an expression both of human dignity and the High Renaissance; the *Portrait of a Young Woman* by Palma Vecchio provides a feminine companion piece. The Thyssen collection also contains an unusually complete series of fine group portraits. Lorenzo Costa's *Bentivoglio Family* (incorporating a self-portrait of the artist) is one of the earliest examples, followed by Dürer's portrait studies for what is perhaps his

Baron Thyssen

FAMILY GROUP
Frans Hals (1580–1666) oil on canvas 79½ × 112¼ ins.
c 1645. Apart from the picture in the National Gallery,
this is the largest
of Hals' family groups

Baron Thyssen

greatest painting, *The Boy Jesus Disputing with the Doctors*; the series ends with another important work, the *Family Group* by Frans Hals. No attempt has been made to emulate the example of the Uffizi Collection: the only self-portraits are Jan Steen's cheerful version of himself and a possible Joos van Cleve.

Still-lifes and large-scale compositions – which usually come under the heading of narrative pictures – are almost completely absent. However, Baron Hans is now on the point of acquiring one of Willem Kalf's finest still-lifes. Dutch landscape painters are well represented in the academic sense, and it is worth noticing in particular the pictures by Hobbema and by Jacob Ruisdael illustrating various stages of his career, including two important early works.

Stripped to essentials-painting depends on brushwork and colour; in a collection of this quality both are naturally seen at their best. There can scarcely be any other place where the potentialities of paint can be better appreciated; the whole of European painting is spanned by the arch which

Above: VENUS WITH CUPID AND A LOOKING GLASS
Peter Paul Rubens (1577–1640)
oil on canvas 53⅜ × 43¼ *ins.*
An imitation of Titian's famous painting
made during a visit to Madrid in 1628–29

Left: PORTRAIT OF AN UNKNOWN BEAUTY 'LA BELLA'
Palma Vecchio (c 1480–1528)
oil on canvas 37⅜ × 31½ *ins.* c 1512.
One of the outstanding half-length portraits
which are characteristic
of Venetian painting of the Renaissance

Opposite: THE SEESAW *Jean Honoré Fragonard*
(1732–1806) oil on canvas 47 × 37 *ins.*
One of a pair of compositions painted in the style of
François Boucher in about 1750. The pendant,
Blind Man's Buff, is now in the Toledo Art Museum, Ohio

Baron Thyssen

GUILLAUME D'AUNIERS
*Unknown Burgundian. White stone, height 34 ins. c 1410.
Traces of colour can be distinguished
on this sculpture*

Right top: *The portrait gallery
built by
Baron Heinrich Thyssen in 1939*
Right bottom: *Swiss tapestry
dating from about 1450*

runs from Van Eyck's little grisaille altar to the marvels of colour achieved by Tiepolo; within it are contained all manner of formats, and diametrically opposing ideas about the social and aesthetic purposes of art.

A particular feature of the Thyssen Collection is that it combines systematic exposition with the exhibition of individual masterpieces. As the giant mountains of the Alps raise themselves above a sea of peaks, so here a few of the greatest masterpieces of European painting stand both among and above the surroundings from which they came. Some private collectors make a point of covering one field as completely as possible, others elect to concentrate on masterpieces, and are necessarily very restricted in their choice. Baron Thyssen was able to combine the two: for him a work of art was a unique creation and at the same time as indispensable as a link in a chain. Some of his most important purchases were made at the dictates of his personal taste and in the face of academic convention. In this he displayed that same unorthodoxy and daring which so often marks the work of a great artist in the early stages of his development. Examples of such boldness include Gerard David's *Crucifixion,* in which the artist echoes both Van Eyck and the Master of Flémalle; the small panel, as delicate as a miniature, which bears witness to the subtle art of Roger van der Weyden; and one of the most touching works of Rembrandt's early genius, *Tobias and his Wife.* This thoroughly baroque Allegory of Love painted by the artist at the age of twenty-eight, in the year of his marriage with Saskia, has both irony and wisdom. And it most certainly needed courage to acquire Tiepolo's huge canvas. The last of the great Venetians transformed this piece of mythology, taken from the *Metamorphoses* of Ovid and seldom depicted in the figurative arts, into a hymn to the beauty of life.

On leaving any private collection, one is entitled to the pleasure of deciding for oneself which painting deserves the prize. Like the collector himself, one may also take a certain delight in thinking about the provenance of many of the paintings. At Schloss Rohoncz the works on view can boast of provenances which include the greatest names in the history of European collecting.   MAX HUGGLER

Jean Furstenberg

Rare books and bindings

BIBLIOPHILES HAVE THE REPUTATION of being among the most secretive of collectors. Jean Furstenberg proved that this belief is not entirely well-founded when he invited the visitors to the International Congress of Bibliophilic Societies, which was held in Paris 1961, to view an exhibition of Renaissance bindings, which he had arranged specially in his apartment. That one evening did not, however, suffice for his guests to discover every facet of their host's taste. Besides his library in the Avenue Foch and the collection he keeps at Beaumesnil in his Louis XIII château in Normandy, Jean Furstenberg also has an apartment in Geneva where he houses his collection of English authors as well as his most precious *incunabula*. Every specialist is familiar with the incomparable collection of original editions of the German classics which he has presented to the French nation (*Catalogue de la Collection Furstenberg*; foreword by Julien Cain, Paris, 1940) and which is now accommodated in the Bibliothèque Nationale. The importance of these various collections is known to bibliophiles through an article by Martin Breslauer in *The Book Collector* (November 1960), and through Rudolf Adolph's book *Hans Fürstenberg* (Aschaffenburg, Paul Pattloch Verlag, 1960), while those who can read between the lines will quickly discover the physiognomy of this great collector in Madame D. Levy's catalogue for the exhibition of his Renaissance bindings, which also contains a preface by Jean Furstenberg himself (Paris, 1961, mimeographed).

Pictures, drawings and objets d'art all have personalities of their own. Books deserve our attention for many reasons: for the beauty of their text, the quality of their typography and illustrations, and for their rarity. Ever since printing was invented and a uniformity imposed on each copy of the same edition, books have owed their individuality to the first owner who annotated them or chose their binding, and to the bibliophile who collects and groups them. Above all, what makes a library interesting is the underlying conception which determined its growth and the often unconscious portrait it reveals of the collector. Jean Furstenberg has not confined his choice to Renaissance bindings, French illustrated texts of the eighteenth century, or original editions of German authors, but has endeavoured above all to acquire important works in editions which are remarkable either for their typography or their illustrations, and to find copies with contemporary bindings, many of them coming from famous libraries. This is an attractive idea which other people have tried to carry out, though never perhaps on so large a scale. As one glances along the shelves of the Furstenberg library, one is struck by the fact that it contains masterpieces of literature in all languages. He has that intellectual curiosity for all things international which business men often possess, and which he shares with those great sixteenth-century bibliophiles, Grolier and Fugger, who were also financiers. A true Parisian when in Paris, but travelling constantly on business, Jean Furstenberg is also a country

....

Eustratius Commentaria in Ethicam Nicomacheam Aristotelis. *Venetiis, in aedibus haeredum Aldi, 1536. Themistius* Opera. *Venetiis, in aedibus haeredum Aldi, 1534. An outstanding binding executed for Marcus Fugger, who often patronized the Paris workshops. The cut-out morocco strapwork backed by blue silk, betrays Venetian influence.* 13¾ × 8½ *ins.*

Heures de Nostre Dame a l'Usaige de Romme. *Paris, F. Regnault, 1550*

Platon Opera a Marsilio Ficino translata *Lugdunium, J. de Tournes, 1540*

Homer Ilias, Ulyssea. *Firenze, heredes di F. Giunta, 1519*

Optati Galli de Cavendo Schismate *1640*

Almanach Royal, Année bissextile MDCCLVI. *Paris, Le Breton. Undated*

Francesco Patrizi Il Sacro... Regno... *Venezia, T. de Monferrato, 1547*

Top: *The bow and crescent accompanying the royal fleur-de-lis indicate that this binding was probably made for Diane de Poitiers.* 7⅝ × 4¾ ins.
Bottom: *A magnificent French inlaid binding by Padeloup decorated with medallion portraits of the duc and duchesse de la Vallière.* 6⅜ × 4 ins.

Top: *A volume bound for Marcus Fugger and decorated with morocco inlays, a technique rare in the sixteenth century.* 5⅛ × 3 ins.
Bottom: *The arms of Louis Phelypeaux, comte de Saint-Florentin, duc de La Vrillière are painted on the inlaid oval.* 8¼ × 5¼ ins.

Top: *An Italian Renaissance binding of dark brown morocco with gold and silver decorations and small leaves enamelled in green.* 6¾ × 3⅞ ins.
Bottom: *An Italian Renaissance binding with enamelled strapwork, known as 'Lyonnaise' binding.* 8⅞ × 5⅞ ins.

Jean Furstenberg

The library of the Château de Beaumesnil,
Jean Furstenberg's Normandy home

squire in Normandy and a resident of Geneva during his brief holidays. He is a former president of the *Freunde der Preussischen Staatsbibliothek* and one of the few European members of the Grolier Club in New York.

Jean Furstenberg made his first acquisitions when he left school. His father, one of the great German bankers of his day, rewarded his success in examinations by sending him on a visit to Paris. It was there on the banks of the Seine that the young man made his first discoveries among the stalls of the secondhand dealers. Later, as a student at the universities of Berlin and Munich, he began to look for editions of the German classics. Later still, during his business apprenticeship in London, he bought the volumes which were to form the nucleus of his collection of English authors. At this time he also began to write his first book, and thus the two passions which have come to dominate his life more and more, appeared early on in his career. As he readily admits, his love of collecting has often been at the back of his intellectual pursuits, even encouraging his philosophical speculations.

Yet this library, reflecting as it does very personal tastes, would perhaps have had a different character in other circumstances. Jean Furstenberg had already assembled very important collections, when political developments in his native land forced him to leave Germany and settle in France. From then onwards – and this detail will not be overlooked by future generations of bibliophiles – the engraved red and gold book-plate representing a woman in classical drapery over the inscription *Ex Museo Hans Fürstenberg* which had hitherto been pasted inside his volumes, was replaced by a plain label with the printed text *Ex libris Jean Furstenberg*.

Nevertheless this collector was not proof against fate. Through his connoisseurship and the breadth of his knowledge he had become friendly with many officials in the national libraries and archives, and as war approached these men thought of Jean Furstenberg and his library in a secluded château in Normandy. Thus it happened that in addition to the owner's private collections, Beaumesnil was used for storing quantities of books and documents from the private archives of the King of the Belgians, from the Archives Nationales and the Bibliothèque Nationale in Paris, as well as the public records of Rouen. But as the German advance brought enemy troops nearer, it became necessary to move these irreplaceable possessions from Beaumesnil to the south

The Book of Common Prayer.
London, R.Barker – J.Hill, 1633.
This dark blue morocco binding
is a fine example of English
eighteenth-century workmanship,
executed over a hundred years
after publication of the book.
$10\frac{7}{8} \times 7\frac{1}{4}$ *ins.*

of France. Jean Furstenberg succeeded in chartering a special train and himself supervised the loading of the precious crates. Although he managed to move the rarest pieces from his own collection, he was forced to leave part of his library on the shelves at Beaumesnil. He was able to recover only a small proportion of these books at the end of the war. The rest were and still are missing.

Jean Furstenberg therefore decided to build up another library. He has done this without going to the book sales, preferring to buy from dealers, since his many journeys have enabled him to acquire a good knowledge of the workings of the international book trade. Thus he has been able, for example, to buy French illustrated books in England rather than in Paris. Nor has he lost his delight in acquiring information, and he does not attempt to conceal the pleasure he derives from poring over antiquarian booksellers' catalogues as soon as they come in. There are, moreover, no limits to this personal interest, for just as he writes out his

own index cards, so he insisted that no one but himself should choose the volumes to illustrate this article.

His connoisseurship was proved long ago. He organized for the Prussian State Library an exhibition of books belonging to Napoleon and Marie-Louise; he has written a scholarly article on that curious figure Nicolas von Ebeleben, a sixteenth-century bibliophile who travelled round Europe with Damian Pflug; and his volume on eighteenth-century French illustrated books is still considered an authoritative study.

Jean Furstenberg's reconstituted libraries comprise some ten thousand volumes. Before the war he possessed a very large collection of incunabula, and today there are still some two hundred and fifty examples, an impressive quantity when one considers the rarity of fifteenth-century books. Among the early editions it is the great centuries, the sixteenth and eighteenth, which are most impressively represented. In particular, among sixteenth-century volumes

Luigi Alamanni. Gyrone il cortese...
Parigi, R. et C. Chaudière, 1548.
This binding in brown calf, with white enamelled strapwork
outlined with silver fillets, bears the emblems
of Diane de Poitiers. 9¼ × 6⅜ *ins.*

The Government of the Tongue. Oxford, At the Theater,
1674. A black morocco binding attributed
to the Queens' Binder A, *the unknown artist*
who worked for Catherine of Braganza, wife of Charles II
and Mary of Modena, wife of James II. 7⅛ × 4⅜ *ins.*

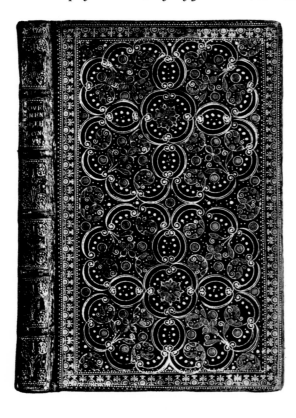

Jean Furstenberg

the library contains copies of the *Editio princeps* of Plato (1513), of the first translation of the *Novum Testamentum* (1522) made by Luther with illustrations by Hans Cranach, and of the *Theuerdank* (1517) printed on vellum. He possesses one of the finest collections in the world of the beautiful illustrated books which were published in France in the eighteenth century. On the other hand, it is curious to note that this great connoisseur, who sets such store by master-pieces of book production irrespective of their time or place of origin, has apparently never been attracted by con-temporary illustrated books or bindings. The only modern works in his library are the publications of various societies of German bibliophiles, and this lacuna appears all the more striking after reading his recent publication *Les Sources de la création artistique*, Editions du Rocher (Monaco, 1962), from which it is clear that he is far from indifferent to the problems of contemporary art. Like all true art-lovers, he must have known that he had to keep within certain limits.

This library, which embraces masterpieces of so many kinds, contains a preponderance of French and Italian literature. This is not the expression of a literary judgement only, but is in part the result of the collector's preference for books in their contemporary bindings, and for sump-tuous specimens originating with some famous previous owner. Inevitably this preference has led him to pick out French and Italian books because it was in France and Italy that the early examples of the art of binding were the most magnificent. This also accounts for the fact that on occasion he has acquired some book – generally a devotional work or an almanac – purely for the beauty of its external appearance.

Apart from a few notable manuscripts, Jean Furstenberg has included only printed books in his library. There are no Romanesque or early medieval bindings of the thirteenth century, when books intended for study were bound in wooden boards covered with blind-tooled leather, while illu-minated manuscripts were given a more elaborate binding. The bindings for liturgical books were sometimes examples of the goldsmith's art as elaborate as church vessels, whereas those executed for some princely bibliophile were generally covered in silk or cloth of gold. This ornate style of binding ceased with the invention of printing and the Renaissance. In the Orthodox Church as well as in Jewish communities in Germany and the Low Countries, however, it persisted for several centuries more. The old tradition is perpetuated in a seventeenth-century English binding in the collection, made

of velvet with gold and silver thread; and in the series of tortoiseshell and chased silver bindings on some Hebraic books which are displayed in glass cases together with hanaps and gold and silver objects evoking the splendour of the taste of the merchants of Augsburg or Amsterdam.

In the early days of printing, books were still costly and were generally kept on chains in libraries, a custom retained from the method of storing manuscripts in earlier times. Several bindings in Jean Furstenberg's collection, bearing iron rings, are reminders of this practice. The ancient technique of blind-tool decoration was also long-lived and there are several interesting examples of this on fifteenth-century books in the library. Later, after the invention of printing had made it possible to produce books in greater numbers, the binders were obliged to work faster and simplified their methods of ornamentation. For small tools they substituted rollers which could be pushed across the cover, or else a carved panel which covered the whole surface at a single stamping. Jean Furstenberg has acquired several fine examples from various countries which illustrate different forms of the techniques. He possesses one particular example known as 'the acorn binding', which is characteristic of the panel type, many of whose motifs were inspired by illustrations from books of hours; some of these, which may be attributed to Jehan Norvins, bear witness to the persistent success of this model. These panels had a special vogue in Germany, where one of the great protagonists of the Reformation, such as Luther or Melanchthon, or some powerful

sovereign and famous bibliophile, was usually the subject represented. Examples of this type, some of which exist in Jean Furstenberg's collection, reveal the importance attaching to an image in those days of political and religious strife.

In the early sixteenth century a decisive step was taken, however, in a completely different direction, first in Italy, then in France. Reversing what had happened in the past, it was now to be the countries of Germanic culture, which had been won over to the Reformation, in which the medieval tradition was to linger on, whereas in the Roman Catholic countries there was an infiltration of Islamic influence. The technique of gold-tooling, the use of morocco leather – its name betrays its origin – and the choice of tracery and abstract motifs whose patterns often suggest the designs of Persian rugs, all came from the Near East. However, the technique of gold-tooling met with some opposition in Italy, and we need only look at the Furstenberg copy of the *Songe de Poliphile*, one of the most splendid books of all time, to see that the cover of its original vellum binding was decorated simply with its owner's arms drawn with a brush.

The new style, which was to make the Renaissance the golden age of binding, came into use in Europe gradually, but certain books in the Furstenberg collection enable us to follow its progress. It began in Italy, where certain bindings have a rare charm and distinction; these Italian prototypes soon became known in France, as a result of the campaigns of Charles VIII, Louis XII and François I, and were copied in Parisian workshops. Some of the most famous and beautiful

Jean Furstenberg

Far left: *Nicolas Guillebert*. Psaumes de David
Paris, P.Rocolet, 1647.
Red morocco binding bearing the arms
of Nicolas-Louis de Bailleul,
to whom the work is dedicated. 7½ × 4⅞ ins.
Left: *Thouvenin*. Parergorum specimena *Paris 1822.*
A unique pattern book bound in violet morocco,
containing designs for bindings and impressions of the tools
and plaques employed by him. 9⅞ × 6½ ins.

Right: Schatz auserlesener Gebete Christlicher Seelen.
No place or date.
A silver binding executed in Augsburg, with pictorial
decorations consisting of the Baptism of Christ (shown here)
and the Resurrection on the lower cover. 7¾ × 4⅞ ins.

books in the Furstenberg collection reveal the influence exercised in this field not only by sovereigns but also by bibliophiles such as Jean Grolier. And what was done by this humanist and financier was imitated, in varying degrees, by other men of taste, many of them Royal functionaries or great bankers, for example, the Englishman, Thomas Wotton, or the German Marcus Fugger, while others were scholars like Nicolas Ebeleben and Damian Pflug, who made a point of stamping their name and the date of their acquisitions on the books which they had bound. The story of how, in the course of their wanderings, these two young men took French bindings into Italy, and Italian bindings into Germany, is familiar. Their influence on the development of this art was therefore considerable, as Jean Furstenberg has shown as far as German binding is concerned in his *Ebeleben in Deutschland* in the *Jahrbuch der Einbandkunst* (volumes III and IV, 1931, 90–96).

At the end of the sixteenth century a new and particularly brilliant type of binding emerged, a style known to historians as *à la fanfare*, which was preponderant until the eighteenth century. France was to maintain its lead and, although the seventeenth century was less inventive, nevertheless it was a century which saw the creation of many masterpieces. The new technique of pointillé-tooling, which replaced gold-tooling, brought added delicacy and lightness to designs which were noteworthy for their magnificence. As in the preceding century, the English at first imitated Parisian models, particularly on religious books. But the originality of English design was to assert itself in bindings with natural flower patterns, which evoke the Englishman's love of gardens and, like the Dutch, his passion for tulips. While poetic bindings of this kind were being executed in England, French binders preferred the delicacy of dentelle ornamentation and the colourful richness of mosaic designs, which made their craftsmen famous. Monsieur Furstenberg possesses an example of this type of binding which is of capital importance, if for no other reason than its unusual size.

The world of the European bibliophile was shattered by the French Revolution and its aftermath. Then began a search for new materials, straight-grained morocco for instance, and for new colours for dyeing leather, at the same time as earlier techniques, such as blind goffering, were revived. This led occasionally to a certain stiffness, but on the whole bindings of this period are notable for their delicate design and inventiveness. The Furstenberg collection is rich in pieces to illustrate this phase. One particular volume, executed by Thouvenin, one of the greatest craftsmen of his day, gives examples of all the different gilding tools he had, and is a magnificent specimen of the bookbinder's art.

The above is a summary outline of the history of bindings as illustrated by some outstanding books in a famous collection. It must, however, be understood that this is purely an appreciation of their external appearance, and that if we looked inside to admire their typography, their illustrations or the valuable autographs which many of them contain, a great deal more could be said. JACQUES GUIGNARD

Denis Mahon

Seventeenth-century painting in Italy

THIS COLLECTION IS HOUSED in a Victorian mansion in Cadogan Square. The collection already consists of about seventy-five paintings, some of them nine or ten feet high in their heavy frames, one – the Guercino *Hagar* – over eight feet wide, a few, little bigger than the palm of a man's hand. As in a great ancestral home, the pictures are hung everywhere – on the ground floor literally down to floor and up to ceiling, over bookshelves and doors, in dining-room, book-rooms and drawing-rooms, up the staircase, all along landings and passages. You can't always get close enough or far enough away or high enough up to see them properly. But there is nothing to be done about this. Of all styles of architecture since the seventeenth century, the Victorian mansion is the least unsuitable for a collection on this scale, and Mahon has made the best of a not ideal job. In any case you forget about the hanging and the occasionally poor lighting – only interior decorators fret about such things – as you become absorbed in peering into landscapes, flashing torches, climbing ladders, backing up a staircase to gaze on an enthroned Pope from the correct distance.

You cannot make sense of the collection without realizing that Mahon is an art historian, and that his interests, and if you like his prejudices, are directly reflected in the works of art he surrounds himself with. Being an Irishman, he is exceptionally determined and single-minded. He made up his mind as a young man in the early 1930's to learn all there was to be learnt about seventeenth-century Bolognese painting, and while his Oxford friends were enjoying themselves in frivolous ways, he embarked on a minute investigation of the life and work of Guercino, pressing as far as Leningrad in search of his pictures, poring for months over illegible manuscripts in Bolognese and Modenese archives. He had no difficulty in turning himself into a leading authority on these subjects (about Guercino in particular he knows more than anyone since Guercino), for he had the money to travel and to buy the necessary books and photographs, and he possessed two qualities essential for this type of activity: sensibility and a passion for hard work. Moreover, he did not need to take a regular job and could devote his whole time to research. The result was a series of books and articles which have become prescribed texts for American graduate students. Outside his chosen field he has preferred to remain silent, unlike the rest of us who are only too eager to come forward with views on any artist between Giotto and Picasso. Mahon is a cautious, self-effacing man who never raises his voice unless he knows exactly what he is talking about.

Since these early days he has extended his horizon. The painters he first elected to study were for ever moving up and down Italy and he had to pursue them to Rome, Naples and elsewhere. This enforced pursuit has encouraged him to investigate what was going on in these other artistic centres, so that he has now built up a reputation as an authority not only on the Bolognese School (on the Carracci and Guercino, on Guido Reni and Domenichino), but on the Rome

ELIJAH FED BY THE RAVENS
Guercino (1591–1666) canvas 76¾ × 61⅝ ins.
Painted in Ferrara in 1620 for Cardinal Serra,
the governor of the province,
this picture passed into the Barberini collection in Rome
and was acquired by Mahon in 1936

REG.III
CAP.XV

117

of Caravaggio, Pietro da Cortona and Poussin, and on the Naples of Salvator Rosa and Luca Giordano. But he has never strayed beyond the frontiers of Italy unless his painters had the effrontery to do so themselves, nor has he pursued his researches further back in time than the late sixteenth century or further forward than the early eighteenth, except in order to discover what light these earlier or later centuries might shed on the period in between. It has been a life dedicated to a small slice of history. And all this time he has been festooning the walls of his house with the fruits of his learning and experience.

The collection has followed the pattern of his intellectual development. Just as in his researches he began by concentrating on the painters of Bologna and extended his scope

Denis Mahon

LANDSCAPE WITH A FORTIFIED BUILDING
*Domenichino (1581–1641) canvas 44 × 76 ins.
Probably painted during Domenichino's visit
to Rome in 1634–35, this free variation of
a lunette by Annibale Carracci was formerly in
the Orléans and Bridgewater House collections*

to take in other parts of Italy as well only as his knowledge grew, so he began by acquiring only Bolognese paintings and then went on to acquire works by artists of other schools. Between 1934 (the year of the acquisition of his first picture, needless to say a Guercino) and 1949, he bought little that did not originate in or around Bologna, except a wind-swept Gaspard Dughet, a Genoese *Madonna*, and one of the masterpieces of the collection which we shall describe later, the *Fall of Phaëthon* by a German from Holstein, Johann Liss – who would never have been granted a visa to Cadogan Square had he not settled in Venice.

These were the heroic years of the formation of the collection. For before, during, and immediately after the war, nobody in England paid the slightest attention to the Seicento except a few poor scholars who were happy so long as they could pick up the odd Carracci drawing in a junk shop, and a few rich patrons of Rex Whistler, who would rather have hung the clumsiest Monsù Desiderio or the flashiest Magnasco on their smart new Victorian wall-paper than a once famous Guido which they would have condemned as pious. The coast was clear for Mahon, and he bought all the best Guercinos, Carraccis, Guidos and Domenichinos which came on the market. His first are naturally his most sensational purchases. Any Bolognese pictures of comparable importance for sale since then have grown too expensive as the taste for them has spread to the United States. Even so he has added to the collection since 1949 exquisite early Guercinos, including the *Mystic Marriage of St Catherine*, which preserves all the lusciousness of a Correggio, and one important late work by this artist, a *Cumaean Sibyl*. I dare say the reason why he was able to purchase the latter as late as 1954 is that the taste for this rather forbidding period in Guercino's career lagged behind the rediscovery of his relatively charming early works.

The difference between the early and late Guercino can best be illustrated by two superb examples, both acquired as one would expect before 1949: the *Elijah fed by Ravens* and the *Angel appearing to Hagar and Ishmael*. The first, of 1620, is an impression of a man, not a clear statement about him. So much is left to the spectator's imagination, as often in real life when we have to make what sense we can of any ambiguities. Clothes, trees, beard, landscape all seethe together in a cauldron of paint, and little lights flicker here and there on the surface, so that we can never be sure where one shape begins and another ends, where a wisp of hair becomes a twig

Denis Mahon

touched by the sun. In the second, over thirty years later, the three figures are kept rigidly apart; the landscape shows no inclination to disturb them, and the light makes no attempt to break up their forms; the gestures, the slope of a body, the tilt of a head are as sharp and as stylised as in a classical ballet. Whereas one would learn nothing from a written description of the appearance of the *Elijah*, an account in words would convey roughly to someone who had never seen it what the *Hagar* looked like.

Mahon has been buying Annibale Carraccis all his life but his first acquisition was the best: the *Coronation of the Virgin* of about 1596. It has all the solemnity that the occasion demands but manages to combine this with a typical Bolognese love of the intimate: those young musicians sprawling about on clouds with that splendid indifference to the appropriate that only children have, remain unabashed by the stiff ritual in progress above them. Mahon had to wait until 1960 before finding the Ludovico Carracci which satisfied him. This is the moving *Agony in the Garden* where the mysterious forms of sleeping Apostles, floating on the canvas like ghosts in the fading light, one still clutching his sword-hilt in an impotent fist, are perfectly wedded to the mysterious vision portrayed.

His best Domenichino and Guido were also acquired before the prices began to soar. The Domenichino occupies a key position in the rise of classicism, since it applies to landscape (more systematically than ever before) those classical principles of design which tended until then to be reserved for figure compositions. We are reminded of Poussin's mature, heroic landscapes, but it was painted earlier, in the mid-1630's, before Poussin had attempted anything of the kind; and it is tempting to believe that Poussin, who could well have known this very picture, was influenced by it. How strange the late Guido *Europa* looked in 1945 when Mahon bought it! I remember on my first visits to Cadogan Square after the war, that I could find nothing even coldly polite to say about it. With the passage of time and the shift in my own taste, I have come to see poetry in the refined pastel colours, and in that generous sweep of sea and sky.

In 1948 Mahon began to branch out in other directions. That year saw the purchase of the extraordinary picture by Liss which seems to make a mockery of art criticism. Critics like to believe that art obeys rules, undergoes a series of steady and more or less predictable changes. But when a German of genius swoops down on Venice, takes over what he finds

there and bends it to his will, turns draperies into rivulets of blood coursing down stones, leaps over two centuries into the Romantic movement, into the world of Etty and the young Landseer – then one can understand the critic doubting the validity of his generalizations.

Between 1950 and 1953 – his most active period as a collector – Mahon acquired, besides Emilian works, two Genoese ones, five from the Roman School, one by Stomer from remote Amersfoort, who, like Liss, would never have been admitted to the collection had he not worked in the South, and no less than fifteen paintings by two Neapolitans, Rosa and Giordano. One of the three Rosa landscapes, illustrated here, conjures up all that is most lyrical in English landscape painting in its heyday from Gainsborough to Turner – but it was painted in the 1640's. All but one of Mahon's Giordanos are oil studies for the frescoes in Palazzo Riccardi-Medici in Florence (1682–83). We illustrate from the series a mythological scene representing *Agriculture* which like the Rosa foreshadows the eighteenth century, but another aspect of it, the pastoral. In its lightness of touch, its brio, the sensation it gives that the art of painting is as effortless and as natural as breathing, it leads on to Boucher; but whereas Boucher flooded the market with an easy formula for charm, Giordano retained in his airy fantasies a firm hold on real life.

The group of Roman pictures grew steadily alongside the Neapolitan and Genoese as Mahon's understanding of this school deepened. He acquired a very early Pietro da Cortona before the craze for Cortona got under way; and two little scenes of everyday life by the Dutchman Pieter van Laer, who chases the inhabitants of Brouwer's taverns out into the hot Roman sun; but the painter, the first realist of consequence in the South working on a tiny scale, was too honest to pretend that life out-of-doors on this economic level was any less sordid than indoors in the cold North. Quite recently Mahon has bought a Sacchi which, with his Gaspard Poussin landscapes, is as close as he is now ever likely to get to possessing a painting by the great Nicolas Poussin himself. It must be a source of distress to him that the two artists outside Bologna on whom he has lavished most love and energy, Caravaggio and Poussin, have never found their way to Cadogan Square, and presumably never can, now that the taste for them, which Mahon himself has contributed towards fostering, has pushed up their prices to levels where only the richest can reach them. In this sense, Mahon the scholar is at war with Mahon the collector: for by praising in print those artists whom he admires most, he is putting them out of his own reach.

Mahon buys nothing that he does not know intimately. He takes no risks – and this is why he has never made any serious mistake, as other collectors have who rely too much

THE CORONATION
OF THE VIRGIN
Annibale Carracci (1560–1609)
canvas 46½ × 56 ins. c 1596

THE AGONY IN
THE GARDEN
Ludovico Carracci (1555–1619)
canvas 39⅞ × 45 ins.
c 1587–89

Denis Mahon

THE ANGEL APPEARING TO HAGAR AND ISHMAEL
Guercino (1591–1666) canvas 76×90 ins.
Guercino's manuscript account book records
the payment for this painting in 1653 by a Sienese client

MYTHOLOGICAL SCENE
ILLUSTRATIVE OF
AGRICULTURE
Luca Giordano (1634–1705)
canvas 47⅝ × 75¾ ins.
A study for a section of one of the
enormous ceiling frescoes in
the Palazzo Riccardi-Medici,
Florence, executed in 1682–83

LANDSCAPE WITH
TRAVELLERS ASKING
THE WAY
Salvator Rosa (1615–73)
canvas 42¾ × 68¾ ins.
A picture painted during
Rosa's stay in Florence in
the 1640's, and still there
in the following century
at the villa of
the 3rd Earl Cowper

Left: THE RAPE OF EUROPA
Guido Reni (1575–1642)
canvas 68½ × 50¾ ins. c 1634–37

Below left: NOLI ME TANGERE
Giuseppe Maria Crespi (1665–1747)
canvas 21 × 16½ ins.
*This was painted in about
1688, possibly for Giovanni Ricci,
Crespi's chief patron in his early days*
Below centre: A ROMAN STREET SCENE
WITH CARD PLAYERS
Pieter van Laer (1592–1642)
canvas 17 × 13½ ins. c 1630–35
Below right: THE MADONNA AND CHILD
IN GLORY APPEARING
TO ST STEPHEN AND THREE
OTHER SAINTS
Corrado Giaquinto (1699–1765)
canvas 18¾ × 8 ins.
*A sketch for a ceiling composition
probably executed between
1750 and 1760*

Denis Mahon

THE FALL OF PHAETHON
Johann Liss (c 1597–1629/30) canvas 50⅜ × 43¼ ins.
One of the few paintings in the collection
by a non-Italian artist.
Painted at Venice c1625–26

on that treacherous criterion of judgement, taste. It is inconceivable that in his youth he could have bought a Sacchi, let us say, before he had had a chance of studying all the ramifications of the intellectual circle to which Sacchi belonged; or that he could have owned at any time a mythological scene from the school of Raphael, or a sketch by Degas about whom he would claim – not quite truthfully – that he knew nothing. Mahon would never feel happy with a picture outside his period, however much he liked it. So he has stuck to the 140-odd years of Italian art that he knows best, buying as he learnt, learning as he bought, never exploring further back than the 1580's, the date of his earliest Annibale Carracci, nor (until quite recently) later than the threshold of the Rococo with Pellegrini, Locatelli, Solimena and the last of the great Bolognese, Crespi. And if he has now acquired a ravishing little sketch by the Neapolitan Corrado Giaquinto of the mid-eighteenth century, and a Pompeo Batoni of about the same time, this can only imply, not that he has ventured outside his period, but that at last he has decided to annex part of the eighteenth century as well.

I am not suggesting that he allows knowledge, divorced from personal taste, to determine his purchases. A collection formed on knowledge alone would be sterile. But he will allow other considerations in addition to purely subjective ones – such as the glamorous history of a picture, its past fame,

its importance for later artists, its significance as representative of a new stylistic departure – to influence his choice. He may even have bought a picture, as only a scholar could, partly for reasons which would appear irrelevant to anyone who uses contemporary art as a yardstick for judging the art of the past, but which to me seem quite legitimate: for the fact that it was once enormously admired; and he may only have come fully to enjoy it himself in the process of living with it. This could explain the wide range of taste reflected in the collection, and the fact that he has bought pictures as difficult to swallow as the Reni *Europa* and the Sacchi, as well as such obviously attractive ones as the Guercino *Mystic Marriage*, the Luca Giordano and the Giaquinto. Only the scholar knows that when we speak of works of art as being difficult or attractive, all we are describing are our own states of mind at a given moment. Thirty years ago the early Guercino, now so much to our taste, was dismissed as melodrama by all but a few admirers. Thirty years hence new habits of mind may condition us to find the late Guercino more desirable. By refusing to pay too much attention to ephemeral taste, by acquiring whatever, within the limits of his purse and powers of assimilation, has at one time or another haunted the imagination of men, Mahon has collected around him a group of pictures which any museum in the world with a sense of history would covet. BENEDICT NICOLSON 125

Paris Arturo Lopez-Willshaw

Seventeenth and eighteenth-century French silver

IS THERE SUCH A THING as a Lopez-Willshaw Collection? Many people will say that there is. The collector seems to have answered the question himself a few weeks before his death, by producing for his friends a magnificent volume which is almost a catalogue; indeed had he proudly included the word 'collection' in the title, no-one could have disputed his claim. Instead the title he chose – *14 rue du Centre* – reveals modesty and satisfaction, and speaks of the purpose he set out to achieve, namely the establishment of a home, and pride in his success in creating so harmonious a whole.

Arturo Lopez-Willshaw would like to have lived in the reign of Louis XIV surrounded by objets d'art of that period. He was passionately attached to Versailles and he would have loved to recreate the vanished splendours of the *roi soleil*. However, his house at Neuilly, built by Paul Rodocanachi with his help, is eighteenth-century in style. Given patience and flair, the connoisseur can still find fine pieces of eighteenth-century furniture and precious objets d'art, whereas nowadays very little is available from the Louis XIV period. And so, wanting objects which he could use and which would at the same time be in keeping with the style of his house, Arturo Lopez-Willshaw turned to the furniture and tableware produced by the countless artists and craftsmen of the reign of Louis XV.

The silver which forms part of this ensemble was made for the table and like almost everything else in the house dates from the eighteenth century. There are, however, just two or three Louis XIV pieces to remind one of the collector's regret that he had not been able to find more seventeenth-century pieces. A large painting by François Desportes, hanging at the head of the stairs, heralds the collection of silver,

for the buffet in the dining room is modelled on this painting, which is dated 1740 but evokes the finest tradition of the *grand siècle*. From amid sumptuous draperies rises an enormous pyramid, on top of which stands a vase of red porphyry similar to those which have survived from the former royal collections; in the centre are two agate urns and two Chinese porcelain bowls, while at the bottom is a lavish display of fruits and meats symmetrically disposed with several large pieces of silver. This forms a perfect introduction to the magnificent buffet which Arturo Lopez-Willshaw lovingly composed, and which dazzles the visitor when he enters the dining room.

The conception of this buffet, with its plaques of pink Languedoc marble, vase of mock porphyry and painted trellis work above, covered with a deliberately opulent array of rare fruits and choice pieces of silver, owes everything to Arturo Lopez-Willshaw's passion for Versailles and its art. This is one of the splendours of the house, and we must pause for a moment to contemplate this superb display, worthy of another age, before considering individual pieces of which it is composed. The arrangement of this mass of silver is perfectly balanced. On the two shelves of this impressive sideboard, grouped around urns and tureens, are

· ·

The magnificent display on the buffet is composed with some of the finest silver from the Lopez-Willshaw collection

Arturo Lopez-Willshaw

Opposite: *The dining room at 14 rue du Centre. Major pieces on view include silver-gilt plates and cutlery from the Orloff Service*

Right: *The painting by François Desportes on which Arturo Lopez-Willshaw based the arrangement of his own* buffet. *The painting, dated 1740, shows silver made by Thomas Germain*

129

Above: *The urn which forms the centre piece of the* buffet *is the earliest piece in the collection. It bears an unidentified English coat of arms. Height 25½ ins. 1661*

Below: *A soup tureen from the Orléans Service stamped Edme-Pierre Balzac and bearing the arms of Louis-Philippe, Duke of Orléans, later King of France. Height 10¼ ins. 1757–58*

dishes of every shape and size: dish-covers, wine coolers, goblets, salt cellars, candelabras and ewers – all of them set out with subtle artistry. One cannot fail to admire the skill with which a piece of the past has been brought to life with none of the deadness of a museum.

It took Monsieur Lopez-Willshaw some fifteen years to assemble not only the objects on the buffet, but all that decorates the table and much that is not always on view – plates, cutlery, sugar bowls, coffee-pots, amounting in all to several hundred pieces of silver and silver-gilt. He liked to acknowledge the debt he owed to his friend Jacques Helft for the help which the latter had gladly given him. Indeed the painting by Desportes, already mentioned, was a gift from Monsieur Helft. We must not leave out of account, however, the remarkable flair of a connoisseur who was always on the look-out and who keenly enjoyed his search.

Perhaps I may insert here a personal anecdote. About seven or eight years ago, I was in an antique shop in the Faubourg Saint-Honoré looking at a piece of furniture, when suddenly Arturo Lopez-Willshaw came in. He could not resist the pleasure of telling me about a discovery he had just made in a shop a few doors up the road. He sent his car to fetch a set of silver-gilt spoons and forks decorated with branches and roses, which looked exactly like those depicted in a drawing in the Musée des Arts Décoratifs. It is strange discoveries like this which sharpen the collector's eye and encourage him to buy more. Each piece generally has a story of some sort attaching to it, though it is often legendary, but they can be worth recalling when looking at these masterpieces.

The oldest piece in the collection is exceptionally rare. It is the silver urn with large chased acanthus leaves which forms the centrepiece of the buffet. It was made in 1661 and has the Paris hallmark. It might easily be mistaken for English work of a slightly later date, so frequently are pieces of similar workmanship found in English museums and country houses. How can we account for this? Is it one of the consequences of Louis XIV's policy which sent many Huguenot silversmiths into exile in England? Parisian silver made in the middle of Louis XIV's reign was almost all melted down as a result of the decrees of 1689 and 1709, so it is now chiefly known to us through foreign imitations rather than through original pieces. This urn might easily have met the same fate, but though, by some chance, the Parisian original has survived, probably because it was taken to England during the reign of Charles II, a replica exists bearing an English hallmark of the end of the seventeenth century.

An octagonal *jardinière* or more probably a chafing dish or centre-piece, chased with medallions and an openwork design, has the Lille hallmark. It belongs to a set of which other

*An octagonal jardinière
or chafing dish,
hallmarked
Lille 1697–98.
Length 16½ ins.*

pieces are in the Château de Vaux, in Philadelphia and chiefly in Monsieur and Madame D. David Weill's collection. The hallmarks are of 1697–1698 and it would be fascinating therefore to know the name of the grandee who, taking advantage of the respite offered by the Treaty of Ryswick, dared to order such a large set of silver in Lille, which Louis XIV had just incorporated into France and was to lose again soon after for a short time. The beauty of some of the silver made in Lille in the reign of Louis XV can only be accounted for by orders such as this.

Objets d'art often have strange adventures and it is curious how pairs can be reunited after a long period. For instance there was a gap of ten years between Arturo Lopez-Willshaw's purchases of two Louis XIV salt cellars, with oddly shaped, jutting out central portions. Yet they are a pair, and bear hallmarks published by Henry Nocq: Paris, 1712–13, Jacques Trouvé. They were first discovered at Foix in curious circumstances which Monsieur Jacques Helft has recounted in his book *Vive la Chine*: the owner wished only to deal with an Englishman, but unwittingly approached a Frenchman. Jean Bloch, the collector, bought one of them. A few years later Arturo Lopez-Willshaw bought the one that remained and then in 1961, through the Bloch sale, he was able to reunite the pair.

One of Arturo Lopez-Willshaw's greatest pleasures was to watch the amazement of his guests on being served from a magnificent seventeenth-century type wrought silver ewer, chased with palmettes. The piece has the Metz hallmark, and as Alsace lagged somewhat behind Paris, it is very probably that it dates from the *Régence*. But apart from historical considerations, the effect of surprise and splendour was complete. A ewer similar to one which might have been used in a royal palace was being used at Neuilly. The table at Neuilly was loaded with objects of royal or princely origin made by all the great silversmiths to the crown in the reign of Louis XV. A pair of sauceboats by Jacques Roettiers, son-in-law of Nicolas Besnier and accommodated by Louis XV in the Louvre, are remarkable for their sober elegance; there

131

Arturo Lopez-Willshaw

is a rippling suggestion of rocaille-work on the rim, but the only ornamentation on these two severe pieces are their graceful handles.

The possession of work by Thomas Germain is the ambition or pride of any collector of silver. Arturo Lopez-Willshaw has one such piece, placed in the centre of the buffet. This large dish, dated 1734, is certainly one of the most vigorous works of this period and the decoration of acanthus leaves instead of *rocaille*, entwining the rim and leading into the delicate moulding of the handles, has a satisfying simplicity and strength. There is a similar dish in the David-Weill collection. Both carry the arms of a Duke of Orléans and formed part of a service which has an interesting history.

The 'Orléans Service', as it is called, consists of about twenty very elaborate pieces of silver plate carrying a later coat of arms, apparently that of Louis-Philippe Duc d'Orléans, which means that it must have been added before 1830. The history of this magnificent set, which came to light in Brussels in the estate of the Duchess of Vendôme, has so far eluded us. It cannot be identified for certain in the somewhat sketchy eighteenth-century inventories of the house of Orléans now preserved in the National Archives. Apart from a magnificent centre-piece or oval dish cover decorated with fish which is now in Lisbon, the Orléans Service, which is now dispersed in France and the United States, seems to have consisted of dishes, tureens, candelabra, wine coolers and salt cellars of two periods. There were pieces made by Thomas Germain during the period 1727 to 1735 or even 1745, and secondly, pieces bearing the hallmarks of Antoine-Sebastien Durand or Edmé-Pierre Balzac and dated 1757 or 1758.

Pieces from this second period of the Orléans Service were also displayed on Arturo Lopez-Willshaw's buffet: two wine coolers and a fine tureen by Balzac. The latter, ornamented with an animal group, is one of a pair, its companion having passed from the Wentworth Collection to the Metropolitan Museum.

There are of course also items from the famous silver collections of the House of Braganza. The table service for special occasions comprising four large candelabra and an unusual centre piece, compares with the finest pieces from the same source now preserved in the Museu de Arte Antiga. The historical background is fully revealed by the complete inscription with the name of F. T. Germain, *sculpteur orfèvre du Roy aux Galleries du Louvre à Paris*, the dates of 1757 or

Above: *An eighteenth-century wrought silver ewer, bearing the coat of arms of the city of Metz, the initials* PP *and three other illegible marks. Height* 10⅞ *ins.*

Left top: *One of a pair of salt cellars made by Jacques Trouvé, Paris 1712–13. Height 3⅞ ins.*
Left bottom: *A pair of sauce boats by Jacques Roettiers. Height 5⅞ ins. 1734*

133

*Two of a set of four candelabra, and the
centre piece with a hunting scene,
all by François–Thomas Germain.
From the Braganza Collection,
they are engraved with the monogram
of Pedro I of Brazil. 1757*

Coffee pot by François–Thomas Germain. Height 11⅝ ins. 1756.
On the right, a detail showing the inscription
F. T. GERMAIN . SCUL . OR . DU . ROY . AUX . GALLERIES .
DU . LOUVRE . A . PARIS
in the furrow of the handle

1758 and the engraved monogram of Pedro I, Emperor of Brazil. But their recent history is not without interest.

Two of the candelabra came on the market in Paris during the Second World War, but luckily found no purchaser. They might have been waiting for Arturo Lopez–Willshaw, because as soon as he returned to France he acquired them. The owner of the other two candelabra, inherited from the Brazilian branch of the Braganza family, then agreed to part with them so that the group of four could be reunited.

The extraordinary mountain of silver chased with hunting scenes, which forms the centre piece, was nearly acquired for the Louvre. It turned up in a sale of predominantly nineteenth-century silver from a large château in the Ile de France at the Hôtel Drouot in November 1950. Experts seeing it among so many later pieces did not at first credit its origin. The brio of the chasing and the P beneath an imperial crown were, however, a better guarantee than any hallmark. With their right of pre-emption, the Louvre might

have been able to acquire this outstanding piece in the dark for a rough equivalent in value of its fifty pounds weight in silver, that is to say, about 250,000 or 300,000 francs. But a leading Parisian antique dealer, who guessed its importance, offered a million francs on the morning of the sale and the piece was then withdrawn. Needless to say, Arturo Lopez–Willshaw paid a very different price, and gave a handsome commission to the intermediary who drew his attention to it. Nevertheless it did come to the Louvre when it was exhibited for a few weeks in 1952, flanked by the four candelabra, and Monsieur Lopez–Willshaw declared his intention of leaving all five pieces to the great national museum.

The Portuguese court is also represented by the coffee pot signed by F. T. Germain and dated 1756 in the furrow of the handle. Similar pieces are in Lisbon and the Metropolitan Museum, all having been commissioned by Joseph I. With its powerful clean-cut outlines and sides decorated only with acanthus leaves and coffee shrub branches, this piece is

135

Arturo Lopez-Willshaw

closely related to those which Thomas Germain had made twenty years earlier.

This account of the treasures collected by Arturo Lopez-Willshaw could go on for a long while. Other pieces, for example, come from former Imperial Russian collections – two dish covers from the Orloff service, and twenty-four silver-gilt plates from the service made for Catherine II by Roettiers. But this brief sketch will have sufficed to show that even in our own time there has been a collector in love with the past who, part Maecenas, part sybarite, has assembled for his own use and pleasure, as well as that of his friends, some of the finest examples of eighteenth-century French silver. **PIERRE VERLET**

Left: *A dish from the Orléans Service by Thomas Germain. Height 26⅜ ins. 1734*

Opposite: *A silver ewer stamped Charles Spire. Height 10⅞ ins. 1758*

Furniture, porcelain and other works of art

THIS COLLECTION IS OF A KIND that has evolved over the last century and belongs rather to an international world before the wars than to contemporary America. Suited to a house or an apartment, it is intimate and personal. Even if rich in examples, it is, in general, defined in scope and considered in approach. It reflects a respect for the achievements of the past rather than the present, a certain delight in group classifications and, as a corollary, completeness within a group. This intimacy inevitably makes quite a different impact from the traditional show place or even country house in which the individual pieces are likely to be part and parcel of some larger decorative whole or of some historical or family sequence. Here nothing demands a vista, there are no pictures or busts that call for distance. Almost every piece is meant to be seen at close quarters. There is no traditional association and the only reason that these objects are together is that their owner chose them personally and bought them because he himself wanted to possess them. Only one bronze belonged to Judge Untermyer's parents before him, and that was bought at their sale.

His family had been established in the United States for some generations. Although not in the intimate circle of the fabulous American collectors, they knew leaders in the field and appreciated fine things. When once asked how all this came about, the Judge's reply was quite simple: 'It was in 1912 when I got married and my parents gave us some nice things for our home and I began to think of adding to them.' This personal approach lies at the root of the collection.

The furniture, porcelain and objects which it comprises were, of course, originally created to add to the pleasantness and elegance of a rich life. They serve today in the New York apartment the purpose for which they were originally intended. The chairs are used to sit on, the commodes and cupboards to keep things in, the bronzes and objects are set about the rooms to be picked up and looked at.

As is only to be expected from a lawyer and a judge, this collection or rather group of collections, reflects an admirably sensible and balanced approach. This is no magpie's nest, for the objects fall into well-defined categories, which represent waves of interest aroused some half a century ago and pursued ever since with knowledge, taste and passion.

With any collector the extent to which the individual will sacrifice everything else to maintain and extend his collection is an important factor. There is nothing of the ascetic abnegation of a Salting about Judge Untermyer and it would probably be wrong to assert that financial considerations have played no part at all in his collection. At the same time the enthusiast no doubt makes to himself a number of excuses when the need arises – as any true collector does. It would be surprising if anything of the recent idea of collecting as an investment had entered his mind.

The categories are implicit in the volumes of the catalogue of Judge Untermyer's collection edited by Yvonne Hackenbroch and published in recent years. The titles of these

....

Cupboard or clothes press in mahogany.
Height 87 ins. English c 1760
Far right: *Bureau cabinet in walnut and burr walnut veneer,*
inlaid with other woods and carved and ornamented
with gilt limewood. Height 82½ ins. English c 1740

Above: *Commode in satinwood
and mahogany, inlaid with other woods.
The yellow marble top has ormolu mounts and the front
is flanked by ormolu draped rams' heads and feet.
The side panels open as doors to reveal drawers inside.
Height 38 ins. English c 1775*

Right: *Spirit case with satinwood veneer,
fitted with bottles and glasses.
The centre section displays the arms and crest
of the Adam family of East Hardwick, Yorkshire.
Height 14½ ins. English 1793*

Judge Irwin Untermyer

volumes include *English Furniture with some Furniture of other Countries*; *Meissen and other Continental Porcelain, Faïence and Enamel*; *Chelsea and other English Porcelain, Pottery and Enamel*; *English and other Needlework, Tapestries and Textiles*; and *Bronzes and other Metalwork and Sculpture*. There is also some notable silver which has not as yet been catalogued.

Within the categories a most reasonable discipline has controlled both quantity and quality, and within these boundaries the formula is quite simple: the best of everything and only the best. Judge Untermyer has been interested only in the very finest pieces that have been produced in his various fields of interest and has made no attempt to amass secondary examples on the grounds of their contribution for comparison or study purposes. When he set himself standards of the finest, the Judge was also fortunate enough to start collecting at a time when the finest was still obtainable and, by comparison with today, still reasonably priced. The initial policy of ruthless selection has been refined by prudent and careful weeding – as essential in good collecting as in good gardening. The results are outstanding, a word which we may use at the outset in the interests of reasonable perspective and even in defiance of the Judge's objection to subjective comment. The ultimate contribution of these possessions to any metropolitan museum would be to make its collections within the main categories, the best, or equal to the best, anywhere in the world.

Let us begin with the primary collection, the furniture, or we may say the English furniture, for this covers all but a handful of pieces. The objects range from Tudor to the late eighteenth century, though inevitably in the search for

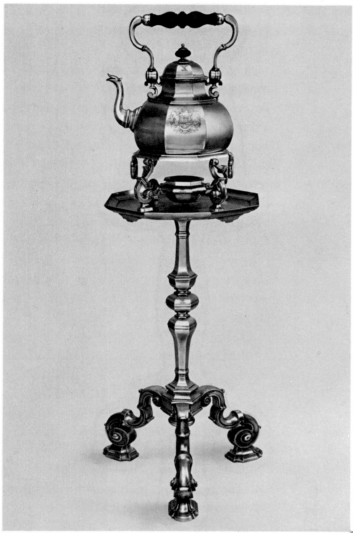

Kettle and Lampstand on tripod stand made by Simon Pantin, London 1724. Silver, height of stand 25¼ ins. height of kettle and lamp 15½ ins.

Right: *Flagon and two cups bearing the arms of William and Mary. The flagon is marked* RF, *London 1660, and the cups* WH, *London 1660. Silver, height of flagon 12½ ins., height of cups 6¾ ins.*

Judge Irwin Untermyer

Two-handled cup and cover
made by Thomas Farrer, London 1732,
and carrying the arms of John Thomas Townshend, later
Viscount Sydney, and his two wives. Silver, height 12½ ins.

every type of rich English furniture – certainly of the eighteenth century – is represented by one or more examples of the finest quality. And though some people might not accord so high a rating to every single piece, it is probably safe to say that out of some four hundred objects only a dozen or so might not rank. The Untermyer collection of furniture probably has only two rivals outside the English Royal collections: the comparatively little-known collection in the Lady Lever Art Gallery and the National Collection at the Victoria and Albert Museum, though the latter is less rich in the most elaborate examples.

Inevitably, in setting a standard of the finest there is always the subjective problem that different individuals, and different periods, may find different interpretations and other assessments. What seems superb to one may not seem desirable to another, just as one period's taste for simplicity may prove boring to another. This is well illustrated by the Untermyer porcelain collections, where the Judge has concentrated on the most luxurious groups and figures, on elaborate garnitures and vases or on examples from special services. Here personal taste has determined the selective choice of only certain English and German factories. As the catalogue titles *Meissen and other Continental Porcelain* and *Chelsea and other English Porcelain* show, the emphasis is on the first in each case. While outstanding examples from other factories are included they have not the representative completeness of the main groups. Indeed the pieces often seem to be an agreeable inclusion that could not be resisted by the humanist and in despite of the judge.

Of the German porcelains some 150 pieces, or well over half the collection, belong to the earlier production of the Meissen factory. Outstanding among these are the great range of pieces by Kaendler which are, of course, the feature of the collection. They include not only most of the well-known groups but also enchanting rococo decorative subjects such as the teapot and castor from the Brühl service. The almost complete series of crinoline figures is without rival. The birds make a notable contribution, while the garnitures and vases, though not numerous, would be no disgrace to any museum. The hundred-odd examples from other German factories make no pretence at offering any particular survey and are the result of more casual collecting. Of these, the du Paquier Vienna and Hoechst demand pride of place. Other factories receive more desultory notice until there is only one group from Berlin and one from Frankenthal. Somehow they failed to find favour. Occasionally, decorative objects of especial charm are included, as in the case of the exquisite Chantilly wall-lights, the Berlin chandelier or the Heroldt snuff box. There are some 'toys', but not as many as from the English factories. The presence of

refined craftsmanship the latter predominates. Chairs, tables, sideboards, chests, commodes, cupboards and desks stand in company with mirrors, clocks, barometers, chandeliers, lights, pedestals, brackets and boxes. There are even notable doorways.

It is perhaps in the furniture, almost more than in any other field, that the collection reflects the owner's personal enthusiasm, and, above all, real feeling for quality and craftsmanship. Although they are all for use, the pieces do not pretend to be other than of the most luxurious kind and generally of an elaborate nature. While some fine simple pieces are included, especially among the walnut, the emphasis is on the carved and decorated examples made for the most exigent patrons of the mid and late eighteenth century.

The source, in almost every case, is either some famous modern collection such as those of Percival Griffiths, Mulliner or Leverhulme, or upon occasion, from the descendants of the families for whom the pieces were originally made. It is invidious to mention individual pieces. But, as an overall comment, it is no exaggeration to say that almost some good Capo di Monte and Buen Retiro is unusual. The few pieces of faïence appear rather as an afterthought. It is perhaps worth recording that the catalogue of this particular section is dedicated to the 'generation of antique dealers from whom we have learned so much that we know of the Arts of Decoration' – an honest and grateful tribute that is not frequently admitted.

With the Chelsea and other English porcelains the standard is just as high – the best – but the net is cast a little wider. The seventy or eighty pieces from Chelsea itself – excluding the 'toys' – offer a broader range as between groups and figures, vases, dishes, candlesticks and objects. The former range from the early figures through a fine group of Raised Anchor to the choicest examples of Red and Gold Anchor. The magnificent group of Chinese Musicians certainly stands out, but for many, figures like the Doctor, or the Pantaloon and Columbine, will have equal appeal. The claret ground vases are of the finest. In this section great pride is deservedly taken in the series of some sixty 'toys' – snuff bottles, boxes and étuis. The addition of some thirty

Nude runner, Adriaen de Vries.
Bronze, height 11 ins. c 1600

fine examples of Bow, including the splendid groups of Fire and Air and a notable pair of chinoiserie busts, rounds off this remarkable collection of London wares, and above all reflects Untermyer's personal taste and feeling for the best in eighteenth century English art. As with the German porcelains, other factories receive more casual attention, although all the pieces, including the agreeable and selective series from Derby and the Worcester garnitures and vases, would be welcomed anywhere. With the emphasis on the finest craftsmanship, it is not surprising that the pottery section is desultory, though some thirty pieces of enamel make their presence felt. The Judge's interest in birds is again manifest in a fine assembly not only of the Chelsea, but also Bow and Derby models.

The collection of bronzes and metalwork has elements of surprise by comparison with the other groups and series. The general traditions of collecting before 1914 no doubt account for its presence and indeed for its composition. Yet the German Renaissance and rather Germanic Italian examples which predominate in the bronzes, appear as an antithesis to the refined, elaborate eighteenth-century predilections of the furniture and porcelain. The Italian bronzes include examples ranging from Bellano and Riccio to the eighteenth century, and include a notable group of mortars.

The metalwork from countries north of the Alps includes a rare sequence of dinanderie plates and objects, boxes, knives, plaquettes and some miscellaneous objects.

In this particular context one is led to recall the rather similar situation at Waddesdon Manor, where alongside the finest Sèvres and French furniture comes a miscellany of early bric-à-brac ranging from powder flasks to daggers and from statuettes to beads, trinkets and boxes. Occasionally objects of the finest quality stand out, but some of the others do not. In such methods of collection no doubt historical and intellectual rather than aesthetic interests prevail. Here is something akin to the veneration of relics, and many of the objects serve rather as touchstones of history than as works of art. This is not to denigrate a practice which has given great pleasure and interest to many generations, and the approach is of creditable descent. It engendered the baroque *Kunstkammern* and descended through collectors like Horace Walpole to the wealthier contemporaries of Walter Scott and Victor Hugo with their love for astonishing assemblages of armaments and bygones.

In the collection of needlework a combination of discipline and the historic rather than aesthetic sense seems to prevail. Certainly it displays the same controlled and selective approach that is to be associated with the furniture and porcelain. Judge Untermyer has always been interested in needlework, in particular, English examples of the sixteenth and seventeenth centuries. The needlework chairs are notable, as are also the table carpets; these with the remarkable group of Elizabethan and Stuart panels of landscapes with figures, birds and beasts make up some two-thirds of the two hundred and thirty odd items of the catalogue. These last are justifiably the great pride of the collection. The rest are mainly French pieces, with some few examples from other European countries and America, including – *mirabile dictu* – two fairly modern American pieces. Again, almost all date from sixteenth and seventeenth centuries and are concerned with narrative scenes or flower and insect themes, often acting as borders for New Testament scenes. The use of the word 'tapestries' here refers to smaller work, such as the Sheldon cushions, akin to needlework, rather than to a group of wall coverings. It is noteworthy in view of the marked rococo bias of the porcelain and furniture, that examples of the embroideries of this period find no place.

As in other categories, only pieces of high quality are allowed, and for the specialist and admirers of this work the whole series make a fascinating and colourful display. At the same time although they represent the best of their kind, not even the most ardent enthusiast would claim for them the highest aesthetic interest. Their appeal lies much more in their evocative qualities. Indeed, the extent to which this has influenced the Judge is emphasized in his own introduction to the catalogue in which he dwells on the human and domestic aspect of these pieces and their association alike with the activities of 'ladies of quality' or of more humble sempstresses. It is the witness they bear to the period's love of nature, their general charm and even their naïveté which have won them a place in the collector's affection.

Judge Irwin Untermyer

Above: *Magpies*
Meissen porcelain, height 21½ and 21 ins. c 1733

Left: *Chinoiserie busts*
Bow porcelain, height 10¾ ins. c 1750

Right: *Chinese musicians*
Chelsea porcelain, height 14½ ins. c 1755

The living room of
Judge Untermyer's New York apartment
showing some fine pieces of furniture
and the amazing wealth
of his collection of
bronzes and needlework

Cheval fire screen
with a woven Fulham 'Savonnerie' panel
showing a parrot and a squirrel.
Height 35½ ins. English c 1755

Judge Irwin Untermyer

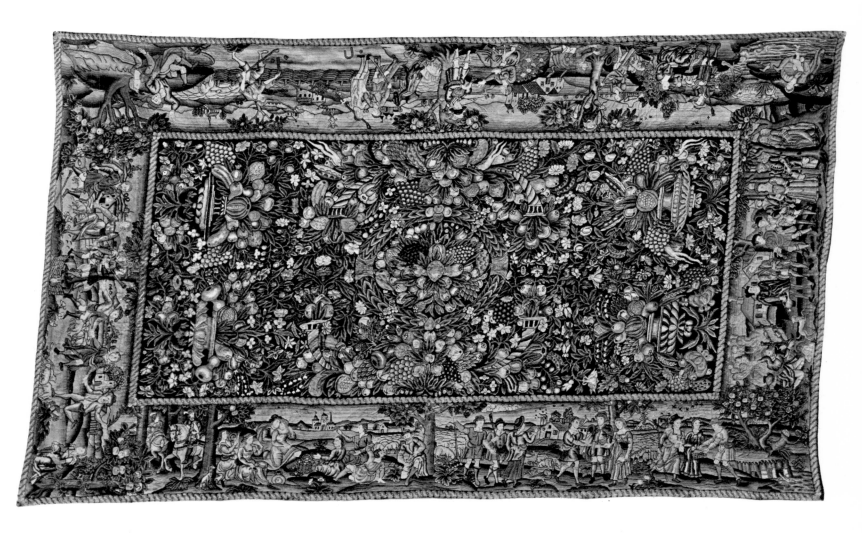

Table cover showing a scene from the story of Gombaut and Macée.
Wool and silk embroidered on canvas. 9ft × 5ft 4½ ins. Flemish 16th–17th century

The English silver comprises examples from the early Tudor period to that of George II. There are tigerware jugs, salts and standing cups, revealing the influence of ornamental engravings by German and Flemish masters. Outstanding is a pair of gilt flagons made for Sir Edward Coke whose arms impaling those of his wife, née Paston, appear beside the dates of 1597 and 1598 respectively. The all-over shell pattern forms a pun on the name of Coke, derived from the French *coquille*. Steeple salts and steeple cups recall Elizabethan emblem books, where the steeple or pyramid symbolizes a long and glorious reign. A large ewer and basin with the badge of Henry Frederick, Prince of Wales, dated 1610, is indebted to engravings by Hans Collaert. There are goblets and grace cups of Charles I's reign, endowed with the refinement of a society whose portraits were painted by Van Dyck. Among the Charles II silver is a pair of large gilt dishes with the Brownlow arms, and a gilt flagon and cups of 1660 from the Royal Jewel House. There are tankards of generous proportions and capacity and domestic silver of the Queen Anne period, revealing the quiet taste and sense of proportion of that period. A kettle and lamp on tripod table with the Bowes arms bears the marks of Simon Pantin, a pair of *jardinières* with the arms of Sir Robert Walpole is by William Lukin and a pair of salvers with the arms of Sir George Treby by Paul de Lamerie. The contribution of Huguenot masters is evident in these examples of early Georgian plate.

These are a few highlights of a collection brought together with a deep appreciation for balanced design and superb craftsmanship. DELVES MOLESWORTH 147

Forsyth Wickes

Porcelain and the French eighteenth century

FORSYTH WICKES FIRST ATTRACTED the respectful attention of those European collectors and curators who have a special knowledge of and admiration for the art of eighteenth-century France when, in 1935, he contributed a dozen notable loans to the memorable exhibition *L'art français au* XVIII *e siècle* held at the Charlottenberg Palace, Copenhagen. His name had, in fact, appeared before, but as the lender of a single object, a delightful gouache of flawless execution, *La jolie visiteuse* by J. B. Mallet, sent two years before to the carefully chosen exhibition *Three French Reigns* (those of the three Louis, XIV, XV and XVI) organized by Sir Philip Sassoon and installed in his own house in Park Lane, an exhibition mounted as a kind of supplement to the famous French show of the preceding year at Burlington House.

Only after the Second World War did Forsyth Wickes become widely known to American collectors and curators. In 1949, it was announced that he would speak at the Metropolitan Museum on fine porcelains, using as illustrations of his talk, superb examples from his own collection. The lecture hall was filled to overflowing long before the hour announced for the talk. Clearly Forsyth Wickes's audience knew that he would speak of style and quality with knowledge as well as affection.

In 1951 when Gordon Washburn organized his first exhibition at the Carnegie Institute in Pittsburgh, *French Painting 1100–1900*, Forsyth Wickes contributed generously. He sent six drawings, a pastel and a painting to Pittsburgh, each one an outstanding contribution to a notable ensemble.

The impression made at Pittsburgh that the Wickes Collection had been assembled by a man of subtle discernment and a sure personal flair was more than strengthened in

1958–59 when he permitted ten distinguished drawings selected from the many in his possession to travel with the exhibition *French Drawings from American Collections* organized by the International Council at the Museum of Modern Art of New York. That exhibition was shown at the Boymans Museum in Rotterdam, the Orangerie in Paris and the Metropolitan Museum in New York.

The loans to London and Copenhagen had been made from Forsyth Wickes's house in the rue Weber, Paris, a house which he had acquired in the middle twenties when business commitments had begun to require periodic sojourns abroad. His earliest trips to France had brought him a vivid awareness of France's contributions to civilized living. When he acquired a house in Paris it was natural for him to wish to furnish it not only in the French style but in the style of that century which had produced the highest levels of craftsmanship and of refined artistry. His service in the First World War–he was a major in the infantry and a liaison officer with the French Army – had forged strong ties with France. Gradually these brought him the friendship of Frenchmen who shared his tastes. As his experience broadened and his judgment sharpened, his acquisitions began to grow both in variety and distinction.

Three valued friends, the very three who were the members of the committee of organization for the Copenhagen exhibition, Georges Grappe of the Rodin Museum, François Boucher of the Carnavalet and René Huyghe, then of the Louvre, as well as Georges Haumont of the Sèvres Museum, had begun to offer friendly advice and helpful criticism. Georges Grappe died in 1947. The others have remained valued friends.

*Sèvres plate from a cameo service
ordered in 1777 for Catherine II,
Empress of Russia,
and shipped from Rouen in 1779.
Catherine's monogram can be seen
in the centre. 13 × 10½ ins.*

SAPPHO

*Jean Auguste Dominique Ingres
(1780–1867) watercolour 11½ × 8½ ins.
This almost unknown early watercolour,
probably before 1810, is traditionally
known as Sappho, although
there is reason to believe that the
subject makes reference to
Madame de Staël's Corinne in Italy,
first published in 1807*

In 1948 Forsyth Wickes relinquished the house in Paris. He kept, however, a charming property in Normandy, the Chateau de Courtmoulins at Gaillon, which he had acquired before the Second World War. There he passes his summers. The remainder of the year he is generally to be found at Starbord House in Newport, Rhode Island, a house which he acquired in 1945. It is the Newport house that contains the major part and the most important items of his collection with the exception of certain treasures, particularly suitable to their setting, which remain at Courtmoulins, such as a magnificent terra cotta bust by J. J. Caffieri, *Mlle Dorothée Luzi Darinville*, of the Comédie Française, a bust signed and dated 1776; two Lemoyne paintings on pastoral themes; a Desportes *Singerie*; and a variety of ceramics, pottery as well as porcelain.

Starbord House is not large. Its simple, almost severe exterior of grey-brown stone gives little hint of the quality of the treasures in its interior, nor of the happy harmony and elegance of their arrangement. When he bought the house, Forsyth Wickes reduced it to a hollow shell. The inside was then rebuilt to be as perfect a setting as could be planned for a collection that had been assembled with love and understanding, a collection that is cherished and enjoyed even though its owner's failing vision now makes it possible for him to see its fine points only with the eye of memory.

No one who crosses the hospitable threshold of Starbord House is quite prepared for the impact of the ensemble within. No matter how many separate objects have been familiar to visitors, either through knowledge of them in former collections or through loan exhibitions, the effect that they make in their present setting is a perpetual and pleasant surprise. One is immediately aware of an air of graciousness, a brightness of atmosphere, a kind of shining and glowing vibrance that braces one like a magic elixir. The eloquence and smiling harmony of sculpture, painting, pastels, drawings, porcelains and furniture is clear, distinct, assured and restrained. It is as though all the different and distinguished objects which add their individual notes to the subtle orchestration were accustomed to holding court together. The effect deepens with better acquaintance. Nuances of style, of colour, or of juxtaposition are gradually and increasingly revealed.

The main accent is on the work of eighteenth-century French artists, but not exclusively so. Artists of China, Italy, England, and Germany all contribute to the chorus. A T'ang horse greets one in the vestibule. Just inside the hall door, on a Louis XV lacquer commode in black and gold with ormolu mounts, two bright K'ang Hsi cocks stand as pendants to a gay group of two Bacchantes with the young Bacchus, a terra cotta signed by Clodion. Beyond, by the foot of the

Forsyth Wickes

curving stairs, is a charming T'ang *Seated Lady*, a figure of unusual size ($18 \times 7\frac{1}{2}$ inches) glazed in subtle soft greens and oranges. She wears an elaborate bird headdress and watches intently a small bird held in her left hand. Across from her, resting upon an elaborately carved Charles II base is a Chinese lacquer cabinet of extraordinary interest. The incised lacquer in its subtle tones and fine craftsmanship is clearly Chinese in origin, as are the four poems written in black on gold fans on the reverse of the cabinet doors. Yet the wood seems to be English oak, probably prepared in England, shipped to China to be decorated and then returned to England.

In the salon is a bronze Nereid by Giovanni da Bologna, formerly in the Eugen Gutman Collection, Berlin. She rides her sea monster with appropriate nonchalance, a dark foil to the shining brilliance of Duplessis' ormolu mounts to the left and the gleaming whiteness of a nude by Allegrain, a Falconet follower, to her right. Across the room are two seascapes with summer skies by Boudin. They are bright balances to the two paintings by Lancret at the other end of the same wall: a spirited oil, a reduction, painted for La Live de Jully and engraved by P.E. Moitte in 1756, of the painting *Le Déjeuner au Jambon* ordered in 1735 for the dining-room of the Petits-Appartements at Versailles and now at

Above: STUDY OF A YOUNG WOMAN
Jean Antoine Watteau (1684–1721)
black, red and white chalk $8\frac{1}{2} \times 5\frac{1}{2}$ ins. c 1717–18.
One of a number of portraits of the same subject

Left: SEATED LADY HOLDING A BIRD
T'ang pottery glazed in green and orange.
Height 18 ins. T'ang Dynasty 618–907 AD
This is one of the first pieces
seen in the entrance hall of Starbord House

Right: MADEMOISELLE LUZI DARINVILLE
J.J. Caffieri (1725–92)
A life-size terracotta bust, executed in 1776,
of a member of the Comédie Française.
This is one of the pieces from Forsyth Wickes's house,
the Château de Courtmoulins near Paris

Chantilly, and a small picture painted in glowing colours, *Three Figures from the Commedia dell'Arte.* In the smoking room rare Meissen porcelains harmonize with those of Sèvres, Chantilly and Vincennes. In the upstairs study, a vitrine filled with a magnificent display of Worcester of the Dr Wall period, its deep blue background and gold edges and its decoration, some with flowers and some with insects, adds a note of rich dark colour to contrast with the pair of van Blarenberghe pale gouache views of the now destroyed Château de St Simon and the sanguine landscape drawings by Hubert Robert which hang nearby.

The collection contains more than 125 pieces of fine English silver, all of it used on occasion, and many pieces of Jacobite glass ornamented with the engraved rose and two buds, which represent the King, the Prince of Wales and the Duke of York. There is a rare treasure, a Williamite goblet with an engraved portrait of King William on horseback, a glass made probably in 1690 to celebrate the Battle of the Boyne, a piece that was on loan for many years to the British Museum before Forsyth Wickes acquired it.

The English silver, and glass and porcelain have a particular appeal to Forsyth Wickes because of youthful associations. When he was still a small boy his mother called his attention to the special qualities and particular excellences of fine porcelain, beautiful glass and well designed silver. He has never forgotten the instruction she gave him, just as he has always remembered his father's pleasure in beautifully bound books. His eyes, thus early alerted to the accurate observance of colour, the importance of good design and a constant consideration of suitability of substance to use, have continued to have an unusual awareness of a wide variety of objects.

Throughout the house the emphasis is on exquisite craftsmanship and perfection of preservation rather than largeness of scale. In fact and rather curiously two objects of unusual size that yet perfectly suit the décor are drawings: the *Poule de Chevaux* by Carle Vernet and Prud'hon's *Standing Nude seen from the Back.* Hubert Robert's painting *L'Escalier des Lavandières*, signed and dated 1786, is a luminous evocation of his Roman journey, a kind of *recherche du temps perdu*. Yet in spite of the massiveness of its architecture and the majestic effect of its rolling clouds and the shifting play of light and shadow it is not a large painting. It measures only 23 × 15⅛ inches. Watteau's magnificent *Study of a Young Woman*, in black, red and white chalk, measures only 8½ × 5½ inches. The delightful signed Marin, *Girl Satyr*, is hardly more than one hand high. The elegant gilt-bronze clock, whose gold glistens with such a spectacular radiance that it seems to be more than an application, measures only 14½ × 13½ inches. The table by Riesener, with its delicate

yet weighty ormolu decoration, is not more than 30 inches long. The jewel cabinet by BvRB, who has recently been identified as Bernard II van Risenburgh, the *ébéniste* who also signed a commode and two corner cupboards in the Queen's Collection at Buckingham Palace, is truly jewel-like, in size as well as in craftsmanship. This graceful little table can also serve to illustrate another aspect affecting Forsyth Wickes's choice.

Although he has sought first of all objects of striking artistic quality – the artist's name is not the first consideration – whenever possible in flawless condition, he has been particularly pleased whenever such works have had the added distinction of clear lineage or when the circumstances that gave rise to their creation are known. Pertinent facts of history can often be associated with them to add interest to the pleasures of the eye. The jewel cabinet by BvRB once belonged to a princess of the Lubomirsky family. From the late eighteenth century until shortly before the outbreak of the Second World War it remained at Lańcut in Poland. The Chinese lacquer cabinet came from Bretby Hall in Derbyshire, one of the seats of the Earls of Chesterfield, and was sold with the heirlooms of Bretby by the seventh earl. The spirited portrait of the Earl of Huntington by Perronneau was one of the paintings which that artist sent to the Salon of 1753, the very year that he was received into the Academy. A police report of August 29, 1753, describes both the appearance and the social position of the sitter: 'Milord Holtington [*sic*] jeune homme d'environ 24 ans, d'une jolie figure et puissamment riche et d'une des premiers familles d'Angleterre demeurant ici [Paris] ... rue des Petits Augustins.' The Drouais portrait of one of Louis xv's mistresses comes from her descendants. The Meissen *magots* which sit below the Lancrets, on a Hepplewhite side table, come from the collection of Frau Schlotz, the mistress of Franz Joseph, and were acquired from her descendants. The two gaming chairs in blue velvet of the period on either side of the Bretby cabinet in the hall are marked underneath with the original official enumeration of the royal inventory: Garde Meuble de la Couronne Ordre no 3, du 21 Octobre 1787. Voyeuse pour le Salon de jeux du Roi à St-Cloud. The andirons in the Salon come from the Château of Commercy and have the arms of Stanislas, King of Poland. David's pencil protrait of Mme Mère was made when the artist was preparing the huge canvas depicting Napoleon's coronation. The rare blue Vincennes perfume burners once belonged to Horace Walpole and were in the famous Walpole sale of 1842. The brilliant blue Chinese fish in their elaborate chiselled and chased ormolu mounts, attributed to Duplessis probably were made for Mme de Pompadour and make playful if oblique reference to her name: *poisson*. A Sèvres soft paste

Forsyth Wickes

dish with a rose Du Barry ground combined with green in an unusual combination of colours is decorated with the monogram of the marquise, the D in gold, the B a garland of roses. The little nude by Allegrain referred to above was the gift of Sir Richard Wallace to a friend. The famous Sèvres garniture known as *The Coventry Vases* belonged to the sixth Earl of Coventry who, in 1752, married one of the beautiful Miss Gunnings. They were later in the J. P. Morgan Collection, New York. The silver cake basket by Lamerie belonged to the Duke of Montrose. The small and elegant red lacquer desk was made by Pierre Macret (1726–1796) and has been described as the finest piece that gifted *ébéniste* ever made. A drawing by Boucher was given by that French artist to Sir Joshua Reynolds and is so inscribed.

A soup tureen, with cover and *présentoir*, and a plate are of extraordinary interest as well as of the first quality. They belonged to Catherine of Russia. The tureen, of soft paste Vincennes porcelain, its charming cover topped by an orange sheltered by its leaves, is ornamented with playful cupids on white reserves against a brilliant green. Its platter, ornamented with a nosegay and bird decoration, repeats the colour and the flowing rocaille design of the tureen. The pair formed part of a service made for the court of Russia in 1756.

Twenty-one years later, Catherine's ambassador in Paris, Prince Ivan Sergeivitch Bariatenski, ordered another service for the Tsarskoe Selo Palace, a service of 744 pieces, enough for a dinner for sixty people. The names of the gilders and the flower painters are known. It is even recorded that the completed service was shipped to Russia from Rouen in 1779 aboard a Dutch ship. Many pieces were scattered after a fire in the palace. Forsyth Wickes has a platter from the set, a piece that shows how radically style and taste had altered in two decades. Catherine's monogram ornaments the centre. It is surrounded by decorative elements which show the influence of the discoveries of Pompeii, and the new interest in ancient Rome. All the undulant and gay rococo

••

STANDING NUDE SEEN FROM THE BACK
Pierre Paul Prud'hon (1758–1823)
charcoal heightened with white on blue paper
23½ × 13¼ ins. Undated

153

L'ESCALIER DES
LAVANDIERES
Hubert Robert
(1733–1808) oil on
canvas 23 × 15⅞ ins.
A nostalgic evocation
of Rome painted in 1786.
Robert spent eleven
years in Italy before
returning to Paris in 1765

Opposite: PORTRAIT
OF THE EARL
OF HUNTINGTON
Jean Baptiste Perronneau
(1715–83)
oil on canvas
23¾ × 19¾ ins.
A portrait painted
in 1753, the year
Perronneau was received
into the Academy

lines have vanished. In their place are restraint and a show of learning.

In every room, both at Starbord House and at Gaillon, beautiful clocks, all in perfect order, tell the time, bracket clocks, 'pendules' in gilt-bronze and clocks set in porcelain with ormolu. They are of the early, middle and late eighteenth century. One extremely rare one was made at the time of the French Revolution. The clock which Louis XV gave to the Duc de Bourgoyne when that youth finished his education, a very handsome ormolu clock set in a marble base, Forsyth Wickes has presented to Versailles. It is now in the ceramic room of the Petit Appartement of Louis XV.

Diverse as may be their interests, Forsyth Wickes would surely agree with Ruskin's comment that 'The temper by which right taste is formed is characteristically patient. It dwells upon what is submitted to it ... it is good ground, retentive ... And the pleasure which it has in things that it finds true and good, is so great, that it cannot possibly be led aside.' *(Frondes Agrestes)*

Because of failing sight, Forsyth Wickes no longer collects as he used to, but his love for beautiful things has not decreased, nor have his various interests abated. He continues his role as a member of the Administrative Council of the Carnavalet Museum, the chairman of the Board of the French Lycée of New York, a valued friend and patron of the French Institute in New York, and a trustee of the New York Historical Society of which he was once vice-president. He is President of the *Société de reproduction de dessins anciens et modernes* and has done much to make fine French drawings better known in the United States. He remains a charming and marvellously well informed host, a gifted raconteur, and an inspiration to the young, whether his own grandchildren or the coming generation of amateurs who have the good fortune to visit him. AGNES MONGAN

Forsyth Wickes

Above: JEWEL CABINET
Signed BVRB. *Height 39 ins. Pre-1766.*
Formerly the property of Princess Isabelle Lubomirsky, who at the time of the Russian Revolution succeeded in escaping to Poland with a large quantity of furniture and works of art

ANDIRONS *J. J. Caffieri (1725–92)
gilt bronze, height 17½ ins.
A pair of the finest
surviving rocaille andirons*

Above: *The smoking room at Starbord House.*
On the left are drawings by Boucher, Lajoue, Fragonard
and Ingres, and on the shelves Sèvres and Vincennes porcelain.
On the mantlepiece between the Sèvres vases is a fine
Louis XV clock and above it Carle Vernet's Poule de Chevaux

Extreme left: *The entrance hall at Starbord House.*
Portrait of a Lady, *a pastel by Maurice Quentin de la Tour*
hangs above a Chinese lacquer cabinet.
Two Sceaux vases flank François Lemoyne's Portrait of
Fénelon. On the left is a pastel by Claude Hoin and on the right
one by Jean Marc Nattier. Two voyeuses, dated 1787, made for
the game room at St-Cloud, are on either side of the lacquer cabinet
Left: *A display cabinet in the library at Starbord House*
containing Chantilly, Tournai and Sèvres porcelain

157

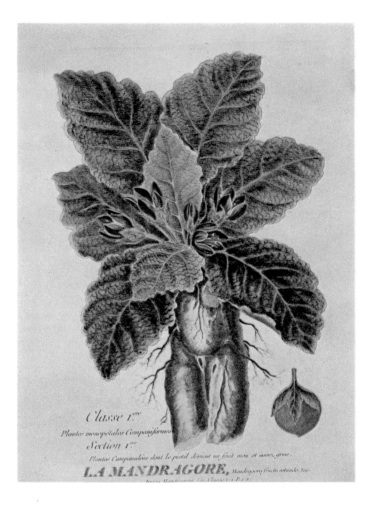

Left: COURS DE BOTANIQUE...
*P.P.Alyon, Paris. For the Author
and M.Aubry, 1787–88.
Colour plate of a mandragora plant
by J.Aubry. 17⅞ × 11½ ins.*

Right: PLANTAE SELECTAE...
*C.J.Trew, Nuremberg, 1750–73.
Colour plate of a lily by
G.D.Ehret, who is considered
to be the greatest botanical
illustrator after Redouté.
20¾ × 14¼ ins.*

Left: LE BOUQUET ROYAL
*P.-J.Redouté.
For the Marchands de Nouveautés,
Paris 1843. Colour plate of the
Adelaide Rose by P.-J.Redouté.
18 × 11¾ ins.*

Right: SOUVENIRS
DE VAN SPAENDONCK
*Paris, Castel de Courvel, 1826.
Colour lithograph by
G.van Spaendonck, 11⅛ × 8¼ ins.*

Arpad Plesch

Rare botanical books

'IF I WERE ASKED TO DESCRIBE a happy man, I would reply: a bibliophile, if one can call so rarefied a being a man! From this it follows that the secret of happiness is old books.' In these words the nineteenth-century scholar P.-L. Jacob humorously expressed his love for old books. But is this attitude to the love of old books still valid? Let me answer the question by quoting the views of the eminent bibliophile Dr Arpad Plesch, who has given an informal account of his own aims and experiences as a collector.

'The love of books is like the love of music. It is inborn and cannot be acquired. Our first adventures in reading constitute an initiation which is never forgotten. I do not think I parted with any of the books I possessed, whether they were intended for study or amusement. I kept them all. You can imagine my distress when I learned that the library I had gathered together in the years before the war – literally thousands of books – had been carried off by Nazi troops during the looting of my house at Beaulieu-sur-mer in the south of France. All I was ever able to recover were a few items of furniture, and they had been stamped "Munich". It seemed useless to try and reconstruct my library, which had vanished irrevocably.

'It was then that I decided to collect books that could be cherished purely for their aesthetic appeal, their elegant appearance, the delicacy of their colour illustrations, or their interesting provenance. As there is such a vast number of old books on botany, this field tempted me, especially as it was a subject in which I had always been passionately interested, and I remembered vividly lectures by Lajos Simonkai that I had attended at the Lycée in Budapest. The loss of my Herbarium and Professor Zsimond Simonyi's handbook full

of my student notes had already grieved me. However, at this point chance played its part and I was given a copy of De Candolle's *Histoire Naturelle des Plantes Grasses*, a magnificent set of two folio volumes with superb plates by P.-J. Redouté. Experts are familiar with the bibliographical complications associated with the publication of this book – no copy being identical. The copy I was given, which was to form the cornerstone of my new library, was one of the most complete.

'Apart from my desire to carry on, within the limits of present day resources, the tradition of scholars and noble families, particularly in the seventeenth and eighteenth centuries, in gathering together comprehensive libraries which would assist the progress of science, I also had another aim in view. I wanted to preserve the work of generations of authors and artists complete in its original form, both text and pictures. So many volumes once renowned for their splendour have been torn up and dismembered by vandals from the second hand book trade, and their plates sold to decorate some bedroom or boudoir. Thus not the least satisfaction that my collection affords me is the knowledge that it forms a repository of rare books that can be consulted without fear of disappointment as to the completeness of their contents. Moreover, I am keenly aware of the practical application of botany. As a result of my study of rare species of foreign plants that I grew in my garden at Beaulieu, I have recently published an illustrated work, *Essais d'Acclimatation des Plantes Tropicales en France.*'

The first man to interest himself in the science of botany was without doubt a nature-lover who collected specimens of corn, flowers and leaves, and preserved them by drying.

Dr Plesch owns a curious *Hortus Siccus Pharmaceuticus* dated about 1700. The captions, to be cut out and mounted by the amateur herbalist, foreshadow our modern 'do-it-yourself' craze.

The first painters or engravers to portray the images of plants on parchment or wood had an essentially practical end in view, that of providing the early herbalists and doctors with an inventory of the simples or medicinal plants so that their habitats and properties might be easily recognizable. Once the manuscript era was over monographs made their appearance, for example, the *Herbarius Patauie* (1485) with its unsophisticated woodcuts heightened in green. Then came the *sommes*, compendiums of facts and fiction, blending sorcery with botany, the esoteric with the art of healing. More ambitious in character, the *Hortus Sanitatis*, the *Garten der Gesundheit* and the *Arbolayres* prefigure the birth of a more realistic approach to the subject. The Plesch library

Left: HERBARIUS PATAUIE,
*Passau, J.Petri, 1485. Coloured woodcut
of a mandragora plant.* 7⅝ × 5⅜ *ins.*

Above: HISTOIRE ADMIRABLE DES PLANTES ET HERBES
ESMERVEILLABLES ET MIRACULEUSES EN NATURE...
*C.Duret, Paris, N.Buron, 1605.
Woodcut illustrating a legendary tree whose leaves
were supposed to have a life of their own
and be able to move along the ground at will.* 6⅜ × 4½ *ins.*

Opposite: DELINEATIONS OF EXOTICK PLANTS
CULTIVATED IN THE ROYAL GARDEN AT KEW...
*F.A.Bauer, London, Nicol, (1796–1803).
Colour plate by F.A.Bauer.* 24⅛ × 18⅝ *ins.*

contains the publications of R.Beck of Strasburg which appeared first in German and then in Latin, with vigorous woodcut illustrations.

We do not find a more scientific approach before the first half of the sixteenth century, which saw the publication of Brunfel's *Herbarum vivae icones* (1530), Fuch's *Historia Stirpium commentarii Insignes* (1542) and Bock's *Kreuter Büch* (1546), illustrated for the first time with drawings based on direct observation. Hans Weiditz, who, as Brunet says, 'was the first artist in Germany to produce drawings of plants copied straight from nature', made magnificent woodcuts for Brunfel's work. Fuchs himself extolled the merits of his illustrators, and posterity, through the mouths of Morris and Ruskin, has agreed with him. Examples of all of these volumes have been acquired by Dr Plesch.

Dodoens' *Crüydeboeck*, a rare work, appeared in 1552 printed in Brussels. Other works by the same author issued from the famous Plantin presses, while a conscientious translation of the *Crüydeboeck* was done by Henry Lyte in London in 1578 and dedicated to Queen Elizabeth.

A rather amusing publication in the library is the *Histoire admirable des Plantes et Herbes* by C.Duret, printed in 1605, which abounds in picturesque portrayals of a number of strange and legendary plants, notably at the beginning the description (and even illustration!) of the Tree of Life in the Garden of Paradise (the tree shown is in fact a Musa).

The use of woodcuts gave way to that of metal engravings. F.Colonna illustrated his *Phytobasanos* (1592) and *Ekphrasis* (1606 and 1616) with etchings, while the *Jardin du très Chréstien Henry* IV (1608), the work of P.Vallet, has drypoint illustrations. The *Florilegium* by J.T.de Bry (1641) in the Plesch collection has plates by M.Merian which have been carefully coloured. The enormous folio volume *Hortus Eystettensis* (1613) by B.Besler, is divided into four parts – each devoted to a season of the year. The 367 plates with which it is illustrated were drawn by the author over a period of sixteen years and engraved by six artists, the flowers being represented life-size.

In Paris the sumptuous *Memoires pour servir à l'Histoire des Plantes* by D.Dodart (1675–76) appeared from the Royal Press, illustrated with engravings said to be as fine as anything by Ehret or Redouté.

Journeys and explorations provided the botanists with a rich harvest of new specimens which became the subject of numerous illustrated books. There is in the Plesch Library one on the flora of Mexico by F.Hernández (1651), and another devoted to exotic plants, chiefly American, by J.Breyne (1678). There is also the *Hortus Medicus* of Amsterdam by J.Commelin and his nephew Caspar (1697–1701), as well as J.J.Dillenius' study of the garden at Eltham (1732)

with 325 plates by his own hand, reproducing the rarest specimens, particularly the plants from South Africa and those belonging to the geranium family.

After this local studies began to appear, represented in the Plesch Library by the *Plants of Aix* by G. Garidel (1715) and the *Plants of Paris* by S. Vaillant (1727), as well as B. Langley's *English Fruit Garden* (1729) and P. Miller's book on the plants – both indigenous and imported – of Britain (1730).

A later and richly illustrated monumental work is A. Seba's description (1734–65) of his own natural history cabinet. After hand-coloured engravings came the first attempts at colour printing, a process employed by J. van Huysum in J. Martyn's *Historia Plantarum* (1728–37) and also by J. Weimann for his *Phytanthoza Iconographia* (1737–45).

The fame of G. D. Ehret will always be associated with C. J. Trew's *Plantae Selectae* (1750–73). This superb folio volume contains 100 colour plates and is, in the opinion of C. Nissen, 'the finest botanical work ever printed in Germany. The result of the collaboration of a Nuremburg expert and the greatest illustrator of plants ever known beyond the Rhine, this splendid book can well compete with the masterpieces of Redouté.' The Plesch Library also contains fifteen original *vélins* by this protegé of Sir Hans Sloane, which came from an album compiled by Mary Delany, the friend of George III.

The golden age of botanical illustration came in the eighteenth century when scientific accuracy and elegant presentation went hand in hand. Flowers, fruits and trees no longer appeared rigid like sentries on the page, but acquired pleasing – if at times a little artificial – effects of light and shade and were grouped in bouquets, corbeilles and woodland settings. The compositions of an engraver such as Jacques in his *Nouveau Livre de Fleurs* (about 1750), are a good example of this new trend.

In *A Natural History of Carolina, Florida and the Bahamas* (1754 second edition), Marc Catesby offered a set of 220 coloured plates dealing with new varieties of flora from

Top: HORTUS ROMANUS... *G. Bonelli, Rome, Bouchard & Gravier, 1772–93. A double-page engraving by A. de Rossi showing a garden plan. 26½ × 21⅝ ins.*
Bottom: FLORILEGIUM RENOVATUM ET AUCTUM... *J. T. de Bry, Frankfurt, M. Merian, 1641. Coloured double-page engraving by M. Merian. 14½ × 12⅝ ins.*

DE HISTORIA STIRPIUM
L.Fuchs, Basel, Isingrin, 1542.
Colour portrait of the author.
14¼ × 9⅛ ins.

CRÜYDEBOECK
R.Dodoens, Antwerp (1552–1554).
Colour portrait of the author.
12⅜ × 7¾ ins.

LE BOUQUET ROYAL *P.-J.Redouté, Paris.*
For the Marchands de Nouveautés,
1843. A lithograph of the
author. 18 × 11¾ ins.

foreign parts. With the copy of *Exotic Flora* (1759), we encounter that picturesque figure 'Sir' John Hill, an inveterate jack-of-all-trades – actor one day, journalist the next, 'in a chariot one month, in jail the next'. The twenty-six folio volumes of his *Vegetable System* (1759–75), containing 1,544 picturesque engravings, testify to his fecundity if not always to his scientific accuracy.

A somewhat later publication dealing with exotic plants is F. A. Bauer's *Delineations of Exotick Plants cultivated in the Royal Garden at Kew* (1796–1803), with thirty plates, while the Plesch Library is also fortunate in having Mrs Lydia Byam's two volumes of *A Collection of Exotics, from the island of Antigua* and *A Collection of Fruits from the West Indies*, published anonymously about 1800 and now virtually unobtainable. Unlike the British Museum copy which has five plates out of twelve missing in the first volume, the Plesch copy is complete. A later illustrated volume on the flora of the Indies by Mrs J. Cookson (1830) has delicately coloured lithographs.

In response to the growing interest shown in the Sciences during the century of Enlightenment, the naturalists also took steps to expound their knowledge. An example of this in the Plesch Library is *La Botanique mise à la portée de tout le monde*, published in France in 1774 by N. F. Regnault and his wife. It has 472 plates and deals chiefly with the nutritious properties of plants. In the same category may be placed the *Phytonomatotechnie universelle, c'est-à-dire l'Art de donner aux plantes des noms tirés de leurs caractères*, the work of J.P. Bergeret, published in 1783 in three volumes with 320 plates. However, the most precious of these didactic works is the *Cours de Botanique, Pour servir à l'Education des Enfants de S.A. Sérénissime Monseigneur le Duc d'Orléans* (1787–88) by P.-P. Alyon, of which the Plesch copy with eight engraved and coloured title-pages, plus 104 coloured plates is perhaps the most complete to be found anywhere.

The Plesch Library is also strong in books which show what was being done in countries other than France. In Austria, N.J. Jacquin, whose work was continued by his son, brought renown to the gardens at Schönbrunn with his *Hortus Botanicus Vindobonensis*, published between 1770 and 1776 in an edition of 162 numbered copies (a very rare practice at the time). Other inventories followed, such as the *Selectarum Stirpium Historia* published *c*1780 in a limited edition of twelve copies with original watercolour illustrations, and J.H. Knoop's four volumes on the orchards and forests of Holland published in 1758 with plates whose colouring is rather flat. A work of much finer quality in the Plesch Library is G. C. Oeder's *Flora Danica* of which the first plates appeared in 1766. This publication continued to appear in instalments up to 1883, by which time no less than

Arpad Plesch

3,060 illustrations had been made. The only botanical publication which rivals the *Flora Danica* in length of life is Curtis's *Botanical Magazine*; which was founded in 1787 and is still appearing today. The 110 plates of Mayer's *Pomona Franconica* (1776) offer some delightful specimens of south German flora, while that of Hungary is described in a volume covering Central Europe by M. Piller and L. Mitterpacher (1781) with sixteen plates. We can traverse the Russia of the Tzars in the *Flora Rossica* (1784) of P. S. Pallas, a work illustrated with 101 plates. The Plesch copy has a fine red morocco binding by Bozerian. The flora of Italy is described in *Hortus Romanus* by G. Bonelli (1772–93): a work in eight volumes, bound in contemporary half-vellum and containing 800 plates. Last, but not by any means least, comes J. Sibthorp's celebrated ten-volume *Flora Graeca* (1806–40), which has ten engraved title pages with landscapes and 966 plates by F. Bauer. This work has a strange history. A first edition of some thirty copies (costing about £30,000) was offered for subscription at £254 a copy. Then, between 1845 and 1847 a reimpression of forty copies appeared at £63 a copy. The plates seem to be identical in both editions. With this work we are in the presence of one of the *rara botanica* described by W. Junk.

From England, home of navigators and gardeners, the Library contains J. Edward's *British Herbal* (1770), with 100 illustrations in colour and W. Curtis's *Flora Londinensis* (1775–98), with four times as many. There is also Moses Harris's *Aurelian* (1788), which deals with insects and the plants on which they feed, and a copy of that important contribution to medical botany *An Account of the Foxglove*, by W. Withering. This was the first scientific study of the therapeutic value of digitalis in cases of heart disease and there is a fine drawing of the plant by J. Sowerby as a folding frontispiece.

At the turn of the eighteenth century a new type of non-scientific book began to appear which encouraged the reader – particularly the ladies – to try his hand at rivalling the great flower painters. A typical example is T. Parkinson's quarto volume *Flower Painting made Easy*, published in London around 1750 with seventy-two colour plates. The Plesch Library contains several of these charming botanical copybooks, which are rarities nowadays because the use for which they were intended has lessened their chances of survival. From among the many compilers of such works, one can mention R. Ackermann and B. Hunter, whose *Six Progressive Lessons for Flower Painting* appeared in 1802 with sixteen plates; G. Brookshaw, a master of the genre, who published several treatises on simple methods for copying birds or flowers; and lastly, J. Sillet, whose *Grammar of Flower Painting* (1826), which contains ten plates of models to be

Arpad Plesch

copied, has escaped the notice of bibliographers. Then there is Mrs Peachey, 'Artiste to Her Majesty', who in 1851 launched her *Guide to Wax Flower Modelling*. This vogue was not confined to England. In France, *L'Art de peindre les Fleurs à l'Aquarelle* by a pupil of Redouté, Augustine Dufour, appeared in 1834, with thirty-six plates; while a much rarer example is *L'Aquarelle, ou les Fleurs peintes d'après la méthode de M. Redouté* (1837) compiled by another of the master's pupils, Antoine Pascal.

The Plesch Library is rich in examples of the work of the most famous of all botanical illustrators: P.-J. Redouté. This 'Raphael of flower painting', as he has been called, needs no introduction, though his glory must not cause us to over-look Van Spaendonck, who guided his first efforts and whose own fame is solidly assured by two works: the *Fleurs dessinées d'après Nature* of about 1800, and the *Souvenirs de Van Spaendonck ou Recueil de Fleurs* (1826), containing nine-teen plates, which was published posthumously by his pu-pils. Van Spaendonck succeeded Madeleine Basseporte as instructor in flower painting at the Museum of the Jardin du Roi and it was his support that enabled Redouté and his brother, also a flower painter, to embark on their careers. Another decisive factor in Redouté's artistic education was his meeting with L'Héritier de Brutelle, who instructed him in the science of botany and commissioned him to execute thirty-eight plates for his *Stirpes Novae* (1784). Four years later, another joint work appeared: the *Sertum Anglicum* (1788–92), which is a study of the rare plants at Kew. Be-tween 1799 and 1804, Redouté produced the 169 illustrations for De Candolle's *Histoire Naturelle des Plantes Grasses*, prob-ably Redouté's chef d'œuvre as an example of colour print-ing. He also made eighty-one plates to illustrate Ventenat's *Description des Plantes du Jardin de M. Cels* (1800–3), and others for his *Le Jardin de la Malmaison* (1803–4). Ventenat was botanist to the Empress Josephine, and it fell to him to de-scribe and illustrate the many rare plants in her collection. He produced a magnificent inventory, which appeared in two folio volumes with 120 plates by Redouté. Meanwhile the first of the series of *Liliacées* (1802–16) had begun to leave the presses; there were to be eighty of these bound as eight wonderful volumes with 486 plates. The copy in the Plesch Library, one of twenty on *colombier* paper with plates re-touched by the artist, originally belonged to Chaptal, the chemist and minister of State, to whom the work is dedi-cated and contains an autograph inscription. Another

Ananas lucide virens, folio vix serrato.

splendid example of Redouté's work is the seven-volume re-edition of Duhamel du Monceau's *Traité des Arbres et des Arbustes* (1801–19), which contains 498 plates on large paper and is bound in a rich red morocco stamped with the arms of the Imperial House of Austria. The work which was to make the name of Redouté a household word, the famous *Roses*, appeared between 1817 and 1824, but the Plesch Library can also boast of a copy of *Le Bouquet Royal* (1843), published three years after his death and containing the four last roses which the artist painted.

The first three decades of the nineteenth century also witnessed the publication of works by lesser though still talented artists who made a valuable contribution to botanical iconography. Poiteau, for instance, whose 109 stippled plates, printed in colour and retouched by hand, serve to illustrate J.A.Risso's *Histoire Naturelle des Orangers* (1818–20). About the same time, J.-L.-M.Poiret produced his *Leçons de Flore* (1819–20) for which J.-P.-F.Turpin provides a large and most unusual folding illustration and sixty-four plates, while Jaume-Saint-Hillaire was responsible for the 552 delicately coloured plates in *Flore et Pomone françaises* (1828). Poiteau and Turpin together did the illustrations for one of the greatest undertakings, the *Botanique* of the *Voyage aux Regions équinoxiales du Nouveau Continent*, by Humboldt and Bonpland published in fifteen tall volumes, between 1805 and 1829.

But France was not the only country with a fine group of botanical illustrators at this period. In the Plesch Library we find Dr R.J.Thornton's *Temple of Flora*, which reveals the talents of a Henderson and a Reinagle. Then there are W.Roscoe's *Monandrian Plants of the order Scitamineae* (1824) with 112 plates, and his *Hexandrian Plants* (1831), with fifty striking plates by Mrs E.Bury. Nearby these are the *Flora Javae* (1828–98) and the *Rumphia* (1835–48) of K.L.Blume, N.Wallich's *Plantae Asiaticae Rariores* (1829), the fruit of new journeys, and the great studies of the flora of India by J.F.Royle and J.D.Hooker *Illustrations of the Botany... of the Himalayan Mountains* (1833) and *The Rhododendrons of Sikkim-Himalaya* (1849). And we may conclude this tour of the Plesch Library by paying our respects to Mrs A.Robley's *A Selection of Madeira Flowers ...*

Dr Plesch, on being asked one day which of all these books was his favourite, promptly replied: 'Do you wish me to prefer the reproduction of a lily to that of a sprig of heather? The artists who recorded these images all shared one ideal, no matter how different their talents. They stood in front of actual plants, drew them in outline and then mixed their colours. Then they invite us constantly to confront reality with art, to find the fragile transience of spring permanently on record in a graven image.' Thus in botanical illustrations nature and art mingle and as Wilfred Blunt has written in his classic book *The Art of Botanical Illustration* 'our eyes are opened to the endless variety of nature ... not merely to the obvious charm of bluebell woods in spring, but to the subtler beauties of colour, rhythm, and texture and to the structural miracle of cell and tissue, which are to be found in each individual flower however humble.'

JACQUES PLEY 167

Baron Elie de Rothschild

European paintings, objets d'art and furniture

DURING THE LAST CENTURY and a half, five generations of Rothschilds – settled in Frankfurt, Vienna, Paris, Naples and London – have distinguished themselves by their innate sense of *faste*. They seem to be born with a physical need to surround themselves with the most exquisite, opulent and impressive works of art created by the hand of man. And they are *amateurs* in the true sense, that is, men whose natural taste and flair urges them on to build up their understanding and knowledge. Thus they are not so much active as insatiable collectors, and were it possible to compile a catalogue of the artistic treasures that have been saved from destruction and accumulated by the various members of the Rothschild family, the world would be astonished at its magnitude.

Rothschild collections have embraced – and still do embrace – every conceivable kind of art object: furniture, carpets, tapestries, books, enamels, ivories, paintings, porcelain, bronzes, glass, jewels, gold and silver. Equally, considerations of date, subject or place of origin have never limited the choice of works of art involved. Objects of the pre-Christian and Christian eras, from Egypt and Byzantium, Valencia and Versailles, Pekin and St Porchaire have entered Rothschild houses together, while in their apartments the Gothic has always mingled with the Renaissance, the Romanesque with the Rococo. Admittedly, if one considers the family's collections as a whole, it is perhaps not incorrect to say that they reveal a certain preference for works of art produced in Germany and Italy during the period of the Renaissance, or else in France during the eighteenth century. But this is really the only generalization which seems to be valid except, negatively speaking, that until now each successive generation of Rothschilds has generally shut its eyes to the art of its own time. Thus no member of the Rothschild family was to be numbered among the patrons of the Nazarenes, the Impressionists or their successors in France and elsewhere before 1920, while until recent years no Rothschild had interested himself in twentieth-century art at all. And in the past their artistic outlook was expressed in the conception of two of the great houses which were built for them: Ferrières near Paris, and Waddesdon in Buckinghamshire. The former, built by Paxton in 1857 to the orders of Baron James de Rothschild (1792–1862), founder of the Paris branch of the family, was decorated in a nineteenth-century version of the Italian Renaissance style. The latter, on the other hand, built in 1879 for Baron Ferdinand de Rothschild (1839–98), of the Vienna branch of the family, consists of a composite arrangement of favourite elements from various French châteaux of the Renaissance.

As each generation of the Rothschilds has died, some of the finest pieces in the family's possession have gone to enrich museums, while the rest has been divided up among the children. Many a Rothschild could well have contented himself, therefore, with simply enjoying whatever he had the good fortune to inherit from a father, an uncle or a grandfather and not thinking about buying other things on his own. But Rothschilds are not made like that. Of course, they have not all made sensational purchases, yet most have collected something and are remembered by their personal contributions. Thus Baron Robert de Rothschild (1880–1946), father of Baron Elie (*b* 1917), whose collection is the subject of this article, was the first member of the family to venture into the modern field, and his son has inherited and developed his interest.

Above: *A Louis XIV book cabinet in the style of A.C.Boulle, containing various Almanachs Royaux for the years 1740–90. The cabinet is painted black with brass marquetry and a central medallion depicting Jacob with Laban and his daughters. 12 ft × 2 ft 6 ins. c 1710*

A group of sixteenth-century objets d'art: a pair of tortoise-shell boxes with silver-gilt mounts (Augsburg c1580); two shell and silver-gilt drinking vessels in the form of fantastic animals (Nuremberg c1600); (left) the Elephant Jewel (South German c1585) and (right) an Italian jewel in the form of a siren, both in baroque pearls; in the background three Limoges enamels: portraits of Catherine de Medici (1552) and Henry II (1548) by Léonard Limousin and a stand for a ewer; in front, an Italian rock crystal dish

Many of the pieces in Elie de Rothschild's collection have come down to him from the collection of his great-grandfather Baron James (1792–1868), whose wife was painted by Ingres in 1848. But he is also the heir of two other very active family collectors, his grandfather Baron Gustave (1829–1911), and his father, Baron Robert. He has thus come into possession of a very impressive and substantial selection of works of art of earlier centuries through birthright. But Baron Elie's interest in art is alive, and unlike other members of his family he has not hesitated to extend his patronage to the very latest thing in the art of today, though not to the exclusion of the art of the past. Indeed, his acquisitions in this latter field have been of considerable importance. So Baron Elie's collection has a special interest because it is continually growing and developing, because it brings the past face to face with the present, and because it is in the hands of a young Rothschild with a strong sense of the family's collecting tradition, who nevertheless wants to move forward in time, backing his own taste and speculative instincts.

In 1955, Baron and Baronne Elie bought the house belonging to Comte Etienne de Beaumont in the Rue Masseran in Paris. This severe but elegant *hôtel* was built by Brongniart in 1787–88 for the Prince Masserano, Ambassador of Charles IV of Spain to the Court of St James's in London. Into this Louis XVI interior, refurbished and remodelled, Baron Elie has put new life and splendour with his own collection of furniture and other works of art. Only about half of what he owns has come to him by inheritance. The rest, he and his wife, *née* Liliane Fould-Springer, have acquired during the last fifteen years, and it is important to do justice at the start to their varied collecting activities, which have included the purchase of furniture by Weisweiler and BVRB, of drawings by Ingres, of the *Elephant Jewel* and the silver-gilt *Camel* from Danzig, of the Duc de Noailles' desk from the Château de Maintenon, of an Achemenid silver vase, and of various items such as wall-brackets and candelabra by Gouthière from former royal palaces. But the Baronne Elie has also contributed her share to the ensemble, and two among many pieces which she has inherited deserve special mention. First, the fine *Régence boiseries*, painted white and gold, coming from the former Hôtel de Gargan on the Place

Vendôme, which are now installed in the dining-room of the Hôtel Masserano. And secondly, the seated *Portrait of Madame Du Barry* by Madame Vigée-Lebrun, on which she was working at Louveciennes in September 1789 when the Revolution broke out. 'We could hear shooting in the distance' she writes in her *Memoirs*, 'and I remember the poor woman saying, "If Louis XV were alive I am sure this would not be happening." I had done the head, and outlined the body and arms, when I was obliged to make an expedition to Paris. I hoped to be able to return to Louveciennes to finish my work, but Berthier and Foulon had been murdered…and thenceforth I thought of nothing but leaving France.' Comte Louis de Narbonne acquired the painting during Madame Vigée-Lebrun's years of wandering, but she recovered it some twenty years later, finished it and kept it for herself until she died. Nor is this the only souvenir of Madame Du Barry in the house, for the Elie de Rothschilds also possess a Sèvres porcelain table service which once belonged to her. Today, Louis XV's favourite presides over a Louis XVI *salon*, surrounded by fine furniture and many a portrait, as well as personal souvenirs, of Marie-Antoinette.

A wall of the picture cabinet: Seascape *by Jan van der Capelle above two portraits by Jan Mostaert (c1530) and* Scene in an Inn *by Teniers (1643). Two silver-gilt animals, a unicorn and a stag (Augsburg c1580) and a seventeenth-century bronze cast of a marble sculpture of Mercury by Antoine Coysevox stand on a black lacquer commode signed* BVRB *(c1760)*

Baron de Rothschild

Right: *One of a pair of drop-front secrétaires in the style of Martin Carlin, in mahogany and lemon wood with Sèvres porcelain plaques. c1780*

Below left: THE ROTHSCHILD CAMEO *Dark brown and white sardonyx. Diameter 6½ ins. The portraits are thought to be of Emperor Constantius II and his consort, possibly made in Byzantium c335 AD. The names of St Sergius and St Bacchus were engraved on the stone in Greek script at a later date, indicating that it probably served as a cult object, and the silver-gilt filigree mount is thought to be late twelfth-century Byzantine work*

Below right: *One of a pair of Louis XIV marriage coffers and stands of a well-known type created by A.C.Boulle, executed in ebony with brass marquetry. c1720?*

Baron de Rothschild

A group of prehistoric sculptures.
From left to right: *two female divinities in terra-cotta
from Amlach in Southern Persia,* c 900 BC;
Persian bronze goat, Achemenid, c 500 BC;
two bronze figures of Hittite divinities, c 1500 BC;
two bronze figures of Cappadocian divinities, c 2000 BC;
Sumerian copper bull, c 2400 BC

Chief among these are her japanned foot-bath (1787), the travelling-case *(nécessaire)* with silver table and toilet articles which the Queen took with her on the flight to Varennes, and a pair of mahogany and lemon-wood drop-front *secrétaires*, inlaid with plaques of Sèvres porcelain, in the style of Carlin, made (*c* 1776) for the Tuileries. Other noteworthy pieces of furniture in this salon are a marquetry *commode* (*c* 1775) by Leleu, with many secret drawers and a top made from a marble slab of Roman origin with remains of a painting; a *coiffeuse* (*c* 1780) from the Trianon made by Riesener; and two exceptional Louis XV *consoles*, in a combination of gilt and silvered bronze with steel, which were designed (*c* 1766) by Victor Louis and executed by the metal-worker J.L. Prieur.

The adjoining *grand salon* is dominated by a pair of sumptuous baroque tortoise-shell cabinets with mother-of-pearl, copper and ivory inlay. Nothing is known about these cabinets, neither when, nor where, nor for whom they were made. Traditionally, they are described as French and attributed to A.C. Boulle, but if he designed them they are unique in his work; equally, because of the military scenes with which they are decorated and the three-times repeated monogram 'PV' on their fronts, it has been said that they were ordered by Louis XIV to celebrate the Treaty of Rijswick (1697) and given to his grandson Philip V of Spain. This tradition perhaps makes for confusion. In style, these cabinets suggest a much earlier date, about 1665, while in type they belong to a familiar Flemish (Antwerp?) pattern with

an interior recess and drawers. Some significance not yet discovered must attach to the fact that Cadiz is the only city marked on the map of Spain included in their decoration, while the fact that two pieces of similar type exist in Belgian private collections is perhaps also a meaningful pointer. Elsewhere in the *grand salon* are a pair of very ornate ebony marriage-coffers and stands (*c* 1720?) with brass marquetry, which conform to a well-known Boulle pattern; also a large Boulle-type black book-cabinet (*c* 1700) with restrained but elegant gilt decoration, which contains a selection of *Almanachs Royaux* of the years 1740–90. Two pieces of furniture of later date are also in this room: a writing-table (*c* 1775) by R. Lacroix, and an elaborate stone-encrusted cabinet (1779) from the Château of St Cloud by Weisweiler. Over the book-cabinet hangs one of Baron Elie's most notable recent acquisitions, Gainsborough's large painting of *The Marsham Children* (1787).

Sculpture and tapestries are not prominent in the Elie de Rothschild collection. Nevertheless, mention must be made of one important set inherited from Baron Gustave, which consists of four Beauvais panels and two *portières*, woven with silver thread, designed by Bérain about 1696, bearing the arms of Duke Charles de Lorraine and coming from the Hôtel de Marsan in Paris.

Nor is the Elie de Rothschild collection particularly notable for its Old Master paintings and drawings. There are several fine and interesting works, but as a group they are less important than the objets d'art. Most have been inherited from Barons Gustave and Robert, and the French school predominates. The one masterpiece of the collection is *The Standard-Bearer* by Rembrandt (1636), which was bought in London in the early nineteenth century by Baron James, and once belonged to George IV. There are other Dutch and Flemish paintings by Teniers, van der Capelle and Mostaert. Among the French paintings, the finest are Watteau's *Les Amusements Champêtres* (1716), which is known to have been in the collection of Jullienne in the 1750's, *Dans les Blés* (*c*1750) by Fragonard, a charming pair of Paters, Etienne Jeaurat's *Les Trois Pucelles* (*c*1745) and the marvellously vibrant *Lancier Rouge* (*c*1814) by Géricault, which first belonged to Delacroix and then passed to the Prince Napoléon. This list is by no means exhaustive, for elsewhere in the house are early family portraits, works by Guardi, Greuze and Gustave Moreau, as well as a handsome pair of portrait drawings, *Mr and Mrs Thruston*, by Ingres.

Baron Elie's active picture buying is done in the modern field. He began well by taking over from his father a great Picasso *Still Life* of 1921 which the trustees of the French

National Museums had felt unable to accept in the 1930's. He later bought for himself a fine Rouault *Benito the Clown* (*c*1937), a *Dead Turkey* (*c*1925) by Soutine and a group of works (1909–20) by Suzanne Valadon. This initial contact with the modern artistic sensibility led Baron Elie to his newly-developed interest in the art of primitive and prehistoric civilizations, which are represented in his collection by a large *Cycladic Idol*, two extraordinary terra-cotta tombfigures from the recently discovered sites at Amlach in Persia, and a resplendent silver Achemenid vase with two goats rampant serving as handles. All of this, one might say, represents for Baron Elie the established foundations of modern art. But he enjoys above all his forays into the more speculative art of the immediate present. So he has filled his private apartment with a heterogeneous collection of ultramodern works, many of which are non-figurative. There is a group of Max Ernsts extending from 1925 till 1960, a somewhat larger group of Dubuffets, including the nightmarish *Vagrant* (1954), a less important group of small Klees, a Miró of 1925, and paintings by Matta, Tapiès, Millares,

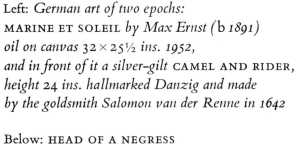

Left: *German art of two epochs:*
MARINE ET SOLEIL *by Max Ernst (*b*1891)*
oil on canvas 32 × 25½ ins. 1952,
and in front of it a silver-gilt CAMEL AND RIDER,
height 24 ins. hallmarked Danzig and made
by the goldsmith Salomon van der Renne in 1642

Below: HEAD OF A NEGRESS
Black marble. Height 17 ins.
Florentine or Venetian? c 1500

Vieira da Silva, Hartung, Bissier and Michaux. But Baron Elie also believes in encouraging the production of contemporary decorative objects, so that he has commissioned an elaborate occasional table (1960) made from an elm root by Stahly, in addition to a metal wall plaque (1956), a pair of andirons (1960) and the stand for a television set (1962) from César.

The Elie de Rothschild collection is rich above all in objects of various kinds. There are French and Italian jewels of the sixteenth and seventeenth centuries, Italian sixteenth-century rock crystal vases and beakers, a quantity of sixteenth and seventeenth-century Limoges enamels by Léonard Limousin, Jean II Pénicaud and others, many sixteenth and seventeenth-century German objets d'art in silver and silver-gilt, and a considerable group of gold and enamel snuff-boxes of the Louis XV and Louis XVI periods, many of which belonged to Madame Adelaïde or Madame Victoire. There is also a selection of china and *porcelaine de Saxe*, as well as the gilt key (1675) to the Royal Chapel at Versailles. Larger

and more impressive is the ceremonial table service in silver and silver-gilt – comprising plates, soup tureens, candlesticks, sugar canisters, salt-cellars, cutlery, etc – which was made for George III of England by Auguste and bears the hallmark of 1765. It is impossible to describe and discuss such a galaxy of fine and fascinating objects in the space at my disposal. I have therefore picked out six objects of exceptional quality, each very different from the others, in order to try to give some idea of the splendour and variety of the collection as a whole. These I shall consider in chronological sequence.

The earliest is the so-called *Rothschild Cameo*, which was acquired by Baron Gustave in Paris in 1889. This majestic object is a finely carved circular piece of sardonyx, the lower layer of which is blackish-brown, the upper layer, in which an imperial double portrait stands out in relief, being white. The Emperor portrayed was for a long time identified (by Reinach, Delbrueck and others) as the western Emperor Honorius (*b* 384 AD) and it was supposed that the cameo and

Baron de Rothschild

its mount had been made contemporaneously in Byzantium on the occasion of his nuptials (400 AD) with his cousin Maria, supposedly portrayed beside him. However, this cameo has recently been re-studied by Etienne Coche de la Ferté, who has shown that while the stone must be much earlier (c335 AD) than was thought, the mount must be much later (twelfth century). His conclusion – based on comparison with portraits on coins – is that the cameo represents the Emperor Constantius II (b317 AD) and his consort and was made at Byzantium to celebrate their nuptials. He further believes that the exquisite quadrilobe mount, decorated with silver-gilt filigree work, was added after the double-portrait had lost the mistaken identification with Saints Sergius and Bacchus (officers of the Imperial Guard martyred in the early fourth century), which it mysteriously acquired during the Dark Ages, and had again come to be treasured as an object of intrinsic beauty.

The next three objects to be discussed are products of the late Renaissance. The first is a black marble bust of a *Negro Girl*, a finely carved, vivacious sculpture whose charm misleads one at first into thinking that it is eighteenth-century. Yet for all that it is most unusual for its period, c1500, one soon sees on looking closely that only a Renaissance craftsman would have handled the subject in this direct unsentimental way. And in fact it has been attributed to the studio of Tullio Lombardo. But is it really Venetian? Its date is clear, but might it not be Florentine? At all events, wherever it comes from, it is an exquisite and unique object. The second object in this group is an imposing blue and white porcelain ewer, decorated with Raphaelesque *groteschi* and the arms of the Medici crossed with those of Austria beneath a Grand Ducal coronet. This ewer is not only handsome but also an object of great rarity, for only some sixty pieces of this special porcelain are known. In 1574 the Grand Duke Francesco de Medici, who had been given a formula for making porcelain in the oriental manner, set up a factory in a village near Florence to work exclusively for his court. The Rothschild ewer was one of its products and must have been made c1576, because the arms of Austria joined to his own refer to his wife Giovanna of Austria, who died in childbirth in 1578. The third object is the so-called *Elephant Jewel*, one of Baron Elie's most striking acquisitions, which comes from the collection of his cousin Baron Maurice. This exquisite piece of South German craftsmanship is full of fun and fantasy and datable about 1585. A large baroque pearl

Above: THE STANDARD BEARER
Rembrandt van Rijn (1606–69)
oil on canvas 50 × 42 ins.
Signed and dated 1636

Opposite left: BENITO THE CLOWN
Georges Rouault (1871–1958)
oil on canvas 21 × 26½ ins. c 1937

Opposite right: LE TRUAND
(THE VAGRANT) *Jean Dubuffet*
oil on canvas 36 × 28½ ins.
Signed and dated 1954

Left: CYCLADIC IDOL
White Parian marble fragment
Height 21 ins. Greek c 2400 BC

THE MARSHAM CHILDREN
Thomas Gainsborough (1727–88)
oil on canvas 94½ × 71 ins. 1787.
Charles, second Lord Romney,
and his three younger sisters
are represented picking fruit

serves as the body of the animal, the rest of whose anatomy is constructed in gold and enamel. A *howdah* containing the figure of a rajah has been delicately placed on its back, while a rider sits on its neck. Pearls and precious stones of different colours have been used to enliven the setting, and the jewel is suspended from three fine gold chains.

The last two objects to be considered belong to the seventeenth and eighteenth centuries respectively. The first, a singularly enchanting silver-gilt *Camel with Rider* (1642), was acquired after the war by Baron Elie. It bears the stamp of the goldsmith Salomon van der Renne, who was commissioned to make it as a gift from the Free City of Danzig to the Tsar. The second, the Choiseul snuff-box, is not merely an object of great charm and beauty, but a unique historical document. This small and simple gold box made for the Duc de Choiseul, Louis xv's Foreign Minister at the time of the Thirty Years' War, serves as a frame for nine tiny gouaches by Nicholas van Blarenberghe (1716–94) showing Choiseul at the height of his power and wealth, inspecting plans of fortresses in the Grande Galerie of the Louvre, receiving visitors, at work or accomplishing his toilet in

Baron de Rothschild

Below left: MADAME DU BARRY
Elisabeth Vigée-Lebrun (1755–1842) oil on canvas 59¼ × 46¾ ins. This portrait, begun at Louveciennes in September 1789, was left unfinished owing to the outbreak of the Revolution. It was not completed until long after Madame Du Barry's death

Below top: LES AMUSEMENTS CHAMPETRES
Antoine Watteau (1684–1721)
oil on canvas 12¼ × 18 ins. 1716

Below bottom: DANS LES BLES (IN THE CORN)
Jean Honoré Fragonard (1732–1806)
oil on canvas 13 × 15¾ ins. c 1750

Baron de Rothschild

CHOISEUL SNUFF-BOX
3¼ × 2¼ *ins. Made for
the Duc de Choiseul, Louis* XV's
*Foreign Minister, by Roucel, orfèvre
du roy à Paris 1770–71. The gold
mounting frames gouaches showing
Choiseul in different rooms of his
house on the rue de Richelieu*

STILL LIFE WITH A JUG
AND A LOAF OF BREAD
*Pablo Picasso (*b *1881)
oil on canvas* 40 × 50½ *ins.
Signed and dated 1921*

different rooms of his glamorous *hôtel particulier* in the Rue de Richelieu. This *hôtel particulier* had been built, in the first half of the eighteenth century, by the fabulously rich Pierre Crozat to house perhaps the greatest private collection of works of art ever made by one man. Choiseul did his best to emulate his predecessor, and it is part of the fascination of this snuff-box that it provides not only an intimate glimpse of the home-life of a *grand seigneur* under Louis XV but that it enables us to see how his house was arranged and to identify many individual pieces among his paintings and furniture. In 1771, Choiseul fell from grace, was banished from Paris and was so heavily in debt that the contents of his house had to be sold. The Elie de Rothschilds also possess a copy of the catalogue of all his paintings, each represented by an engraving on the back of which is marked the price it fetched at the sale in the hand of his sister the Duchesse de Gramont. This snuff-box, the work of the Parisian goldsmith Roucel, bears the hallmark of 1770–71 and must therefore have been made just a few months before disaster overtook him. It shows his walls hung with paintings by Rubens, Claude, Greuze, Teniers and various seventeenth-century Dutch and Flemish artists, some of them now in the Louvre.

It also shows Choiseul working with his secretaries at the famous desk made for him (*c* 1760) by Caffiéri, which was later to be used by Talleyrand and Metternich before passing into the collection of the Baron Edmond de Rothschild.

So, to sum up, the Rothschild tradition of collecting is splendidly represented today in the *hôtel particulier* of the Elie de Rothschilds. The eighteenth century and the Renaissance predominate still, the opulence, fantasy and fine quality which one expects to find in a Rothschild collection are well in evidence, yet the objects around the house are not there merely for show. A great deal has come to Baron Elie through inheritance, but he has also acquired a great deal on his own, and not by any means the least interesting part. For Elie de Rothschild does not buy along set lines of taste, and his collection, which he loves, is neither backward-looking nor stagnant. He may value the historical associations of things he owns or acquires, but he lives in the present and his collection is a vital part of his everyday life. That is why he is the only member of the Rothschild family who can be called an active collector at this present moment, and why he is the first Rothschild who began to buy dangerously in the immediately contemporary field. DOUGLAS COOPER

*A corner of the grand salon in the
Hotel Masserano showing a pair of
tortoise-shell cabinets decorated with
an inlay of mother-of-pearl and ivory.
In the foreground a chaise longue of the
type known as* une gondole, *said to
have been made for Marie Antoinette*

*The private sitting-room
of Baron Elie de Rothschild. Modern
works of art predominate. On the left
a stand for a television set by César;
on the right an elm-wood table by Stahly
and a sculpture by Chadwick.
Paintings on the left wall by Miró
and Vieira da Silva; on the fireplace wall
Max Ernst's* Enseigne pour une Ecole
de Mouettes, *Dubuffet's* Lecture au Sol
*and a metal relief by César.
On the mantelpiece a collection of
prehistoric sculptures from
Persia and Asia Minor*

Antiquities, French furniture and paintings

EVEN TODAY COLLECTORS who possess both wealth and taste are rare, but Mr J. Paul Getty is of an even rarer type in that he accepts self-imposed limits. For many years now the only barriers to possession which he has encountered have been the doors of museums, but it always gives Mr Getty pleasure to visit a museum other than his own, and he has in fact presented works of art to the Louvre and the Los Angeles County Museum. Because he knows exactly what he wants he is spared the pains of temptation; and since his choice is guided solely by his personal inclinations, independent of fashion or financial advantage, his taste is safeguarded.

What then has this exceptional collector chosen? Greek and Roman sculpture, French eighteenth-century furniture and tapestries, sixteenth-century Persian and the earliest Savonnerie carpets, and Renaissance painting. Even when thus described, his tastes could sound eclectic; yet they really amount to a love of sculpture, for what is French furniture but sculpture? The other 'flat' objects play only supporting roles. Mr Getty's friend, the distinguished connoisseur Julius S. Held, has drawn attention to their complementary nature: 'His passionate desire to own a particular work of art has most often been aroused by antique sculpture, eighteenth-century furniture or tapestry.'

....

PORTRAIT OF A JEWELLER
Lorenzo Lotto (c 1480–1556), canvas 31 × 26 ins. c 1519.
The subject has recently been identified as
the Milanese jeweller Gian Pietro Crivelli who sat for Lotto
while the artist was working at the Vatican in 1519

The trend of his tastes was fixed by an experience which he had as a young man. In 1912, as an Oxford undergraduate, on holiday in Rome, he was deeply stirred by the statuary in the Museo delle Terme. The importance of things Mediterranean in English education had already prepared him for the impact of these marble statues, still warm from the sun of antiquity. Several years later he was offered a unique opportunity to acquire several masterpieces of Greek and Roman art from some of the greatest collections, notably the fabulous Elgin Collection.

Monsieur Jean Charbonneaux, Keeper of Antiquities in the Louvre, has singled out three works of exceptional quality in the Getty collection, which has now been assembled in the museum at Malibu, California: the Cottenham relief, the Thasos relief from the collection of Wix de Szolnay, and a fragment of a statue wearing a peplos, from the Elgin Collection – all three from the pre-classical period.

The Cottenham relief which dates from the very end of the sixth or the beginning of the fifth century BC, represents a young horseman curbing his horse, a typically Attic subject. In Monsieur Charbonneaux's opinion it represents one of the highest points achieved by Greek art: 'The horse and rider,' he writes, 'are of equal nobility; the handsome profile of the young patrician rider, the energy and elegance of his gestures, the beauty of the horse's body, erect and straining for action, are wonderfully expressed by the certainty and sharpness of the design.'

The relief from Thasos is Ionian and more archaic: the attitudes of the maidens bringing their offerings to the Goddess still retain the grace characteristic of earlier sixth-century sculpture, while the motionless Goddess, shown

181

J. Paul Getty

Right: THASOS RELIEF
An early 5th century BC *marble relief found on the island of Thasos in 1913. The goddess to whom the maidens are bringing offerings has been identified as Aphrodite, Cybele, or more probably Athena Poliouchos, 'protectress of the city', especially worshipped on Thasos.*
Height 14½ ins. Length 25½ ins.
Below: ELGIN TORSO
An early 5th century BC *Attic marble figure of a woman draped in a* peplos. *Height 30 ins.*

Opposite top: COTTENHAM RELIEF
Fragment of an Attic relief. Height 11 ins.
Length 12 ins. c 485 BC

Opposite bottom: YOUTH HOLDING A RAM'S HEAD
The young man is probably Phrixus, who was saved from the fury of his stepmother Ino by escaping on the back of a ram with a golden fleece given by Hermes
Bronze. Height 6½ ins.

seated full face, is in a hieratic tradition which had fallen into disuse thirty years before this sculpture was executed.

Finally the Elgin torso of a woman draped in a *peplos* hanging in rigid folds represents the vigorous art of the Peloponnese. Severely architectural, it is according to Monsieur Charbonneaux, one of the oldest and most authentic examples of the Dorian reaction at the beginning of the fifth century against the Ionian languor of the sixth.

Mr Getty's taste for the majestic, illustrated by these three masterpieces, does not prevent him from appreciating smaller works or more delicate pieces of later centuries. Thus the two funerary steles from the Elgin Collection, which complete what one might call the noble part of the Malibu Collection, form a happy contrast with two female heads, also funerary pieces in origin, which are much more refined in style. One head which is Attic and of the first half of the fourth century has subtle modelling and a delicate expression, the other which is Hellenistic has a stronger relief and a more emphatic expression. The latter closely resembles another head from Tarsus, now in the Louvre, and both probably originated somewhere on the coast of Asia Minor.

A wonderful bronze statuette of a youth holding a ram's head in his right hand has for long puzzled archaeologists;

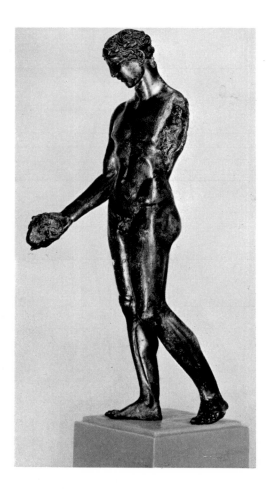

is it a Greek original or an unusually fine replica manufactured in Rome? The best authorities incline to think it a Greek work, in spite of the fact that the left arm was cast separately, a practice in fact favoured by the Greeks, even for small pieces. It is an example of the supple Polycletian style and may well be a reduced copy of the Naucides Phrixus, the hero who was given the ram with the golden fleece by Hermes.

Among other pieces are the Lansdowne Hercules, an excellent and well-known copy of the Hercules by Scopas; the head of a curly-headed young man, which reminds one of the Ludovisi Aries; a head of Venus in the Capitoline style; two Hellenistic female busts; a head of Achilles; and finally three superb Roman portrait busts. Together these amount to one of the most perfectly balanced collections of antiquities, in which no piece is superfluous and everything is of the highest quality.

Mr Getty's collection of pictures reveals a quite different purpose. He has bought paintings for the pleasure they give him, and he has not, therefore, shown the same jealous passion as in his purchase of antiquities. He saw no need to confine himself to any special period such as Venetian, eighteenth-century French or the Impressionists. His choice of canvases was broadly based, and his only criterion was that they should be both simple and noble. The advice of Dr Held has assured that they are of fine quality. Thus in the Getty collection one finds Florentine fifteenth-century painted *cassoni* side by side with a Monet, Flemish paintings next to those of the Venetian school. At no moment does one feel that the collection has abandoned its general character for the eclecticism forced upon national museums.

The outstanding pieces are not necessarily by painters with great names like Rubens, Rembrandt or Tintoretto. It is true that the famous *Diana* by Rubens, which aroused fierce controversy among the experts who compared it to its equally beautiful replica in the Cleveland Museum, deserves to be singled out. The *Death of Dido*, also known from the copy in the Louvre from the Beistigui collection, reveals Rubens' equal ability in painting scenes of pathos and seems by contrast to flatter the splendour of the *Diana*.

Rembrandt's *St Bartholomew* (for a long time mistaken for a portrait of his cook) would do honour to any great museum. And the two Tintorettos, the *Toilet of Venus* and the *Allegory of Vanity*, in both of which the subject is a woman gazing at herself in a mirror, strikingly illustrate the Venetian master's sombre appeal and deserve to be considered among the origins of Expressionism.

However, the art lover who takes more pleasure in private discoveries than in visiting well-known museums will be delighted by Mr Getty's discernment in his purchase of

J. Paul Getty

less well-known, but no less magnificent works. The *Portrait of Gian Pietro Crivelli*, the goldsmith, by Lorenzo Lotto is both majestic and exquisite. The *Portrait of an Unknown Man* by Cariani, a melancholy and dandyish figure despite his ostentatious sword, is the perfect image of a seducer and speaks for itself.

Everyone will have his own preferences among the lesser works of art which set off the masterpieces in the Getty collection. He can never err, since Mr Getty has taken immense pains to be sure of the quality and authenticity of anything he acquires. In my opinion, the greatest reward for visitors to the collection is likely to be the *Rest on the Flight to Egypt* by Orazio Gentileschi, a Caravaggesque masterpiece by an artist who had learnt the lesson of realism.

Dr Held once remarked that the eighteenth century, in which Mr Getty so much admires the applied arts, is poorly represented on his walls. The century of Fragonard, Boucher and Watteau is represented only by two English painters, Gainsborough and Romney, both of them admittedly illustrious. There is Gainsborough's *Portrait of James Christie*, the celebrated auctioneer and founder of the London sale-room which still bears his name, as well as a very English *Portrait of Lady Chesterfield*. The Romney is a *Portrait of the Duchess of Cumberland*.

Finally, a strangely impressionistic painting by Gauguin, a Monet and a masterly Bonnard bring the collection to the beginning of this century.

There is certainly nothing very adventurous about this choice. Some of Mr Getty's friends have suggested that if he had thrown the weight of his patronage into the acquisition of contemporary works of art, he would have encouraged collectors who feel a certain hesitation about acquiring twentieth-century paintings. But Mr Getty would have been wrong to take their advice, since he is not moved by painting of this period, and has only succeeded as a collector because he liked what he bought. The prudence of this great collector is more akin to a simple integrity. Moreover in refusing to be guided by contemporary fashion, particularly if he does not fully understand it, there is less chance that a collector will be disappointed.

This is not a risk Mr Getty runs as a collector of French furniture, but those who can never go to California, and see for themselves the collection in the Getty Museum, do not know what they are missing, for even if it is possible to judge a picture by a photograph, the same cannot be said of a piece

NUDE *Pierre Bonnard (1867–1947)*
oil on canvas 54½ × 31½ *ins.* c *1912*

REST ON THE
FLIGHT INTO EGYPT
Orazio Gentileschi (1563–1639)
canvas 64 × 44¾ ins. c 1626

LANDSCAPE NEAR ROUEN
Paul Gauguin (1848–1903)
oil on canvas 22 × 33⅝ ins.
Signed and dated 1884

J. Paul Getty

Opposite top: *A roll-top desk in mahogany and ebony veneer, made for Louis XVI for the château at St Cloud in about 1787 and signed Bernard Molitor. Height 53½ ins.*
In the background on the right is a
drop-front secrétaire by Martin Carlin. Height 47½ ins.

Opposite bottom: *A magnificent Louis XIV*
Savonnerie carpet. 21 ft 11 ins. × 19 ft 5 ins.

Below: *A marble-topped commode with intricate diamond-shaped marquetry and decorated with bronze rosettes. It is the work of Gilles Joubert, cabinet-maker to Louis XV. Height 36½ ins. 1769*

of furniture. Mr Getty's flair can best be judged by his collection of furniture. Monsieur Pierre Verlet records: 'In the ground-floor drawing-room of Mrs Chester-Beatty's great house in Kensington, there was a commode which appeared, from its splendid design and diamond-shaped marquetry studded with bronze rosettes, to be a work by Joubert, the great cabinet-maker to Louis XV. On closer examination it proved to have the royal brand and number, which confirmed our identification. A few years later the piece was put up for sale. Many people, among them experts who should have recognized the work of the royal cabinet-maker, passed it by without suspecting anything unusual. Mr Getty saw it, liked it, guessed its noble origin, and bought it. When he learned that it had been made for Madame Louise's apartments at Versailles, it did not perhaps surprise him, but it was a fine reward for his perspicacity.'

This superb piece and, for example, the marvellous double writing-desk signed by Bernard van Risenburgh which is now at Malibu, make it easy to appreciate both the consummate craftsmanship of the French *ébénistes* and Mr Getty's own discernment. There is every reason to believe that this writing-desk, which was found in Scotland in the castle of the Dukes of Argyll, having been bought in Paris in 1760 by a Duchess of Argyll, was made for Madame Infante and her

*A double writing desk signed BvRB which
was almost certainly ordered
by Louis XV for his twin daughters.
Height 40 ins. c 1760*

Opposite: *A red lacquer writing cabinet
signed Jacques Dubois. Height 40 ins.*

J. Paul Getty

twin sister, Madame Henriette, when they were reunited at Versailles in 1749 after a long separation. Monsieur Verlet supposes that in order to give pleasure to the two princesses and to encourage their reviving affection for each other, Louis XV ordered this unusual piece so that his two daughters could write letters and arrange their papers without parting company.

Two other royal pieces of furniture in the Getty Museum bear witness to the splendour and originality of the French *ébénistes* of the period. The first, an almost-square table with three sliding leaves, is stamped, like the double writing desk, with the initials BvRB. Almost certainly, this is a work inspired by a table of the same type, but with mahogany veneer and fitted with a top of Italian *griotte* marble, ordered in 1752 by Madame de Pompadour from Lazare Duvaux for her Château de Bellevue.

The second piece is a great roll-top desk stamped Molitor, veneered in mahogany and ebony with a top of red *griotte* marble. Its very magnificence would suggest a royal origin and this is confirmed, according to Monsieur Verlet, by the fact that the bronze fittings are identical with those which the dealer Daguerre had made for the furniture designed for Louis XVI's château at St Cloud during the last years of the monarchy.

It would be tedious to list the carpets in the Getty collection. Nevertheless, one important piece should be mentioned, a Savonnerie carpet of an unfamiliar type acquired in London in 1938 at the Mortimer Schiff sale, which must be an early product of the factory dating from the beginning of Louis XIV's reign. Earlier in date than the carpets ordered by the King for the Gallery of Apollo or the Grande Galerie of the Louvre, it may well have been a royal commission, for

189

HUNT OF DIANA *Peter Paul Rubens (1577–1640)*
oil on canvas 92½ × 71 ins.

J. Paul Getty

it seems to correspond with this description: 'A big new Savonnerie carpet, brown background covered with big white scrolls and flowers in their natural colours, with an oval cartouche in the centre, containing a festoon of flowers with a sunflower in the middle, enclosed in a border which also has a brown background with baskets and vases of flowers.' The dimensions are different, but then we know that the Malibu carpet has been cut down at both ends.

It will not come as a surprise that so many pieces in this ambitious collection should have had royal origins. It should always be remembered that Mr Getty learned of these origins only after he had acquired the pieces, which is surely a remarkable fact.

Even more surprising is his relative detachment from his possessions. It is often said of collectors, and frequently with justification, that they are incapable of parting with a single item from their treasures, but Mr Getty has given the Museum of his home town, Los Angeles, the *Portrait of Marten Looten* by Rembrandt, a work which is all the more interesting because it dates from the painter's youth. Similarly, he has given the Louvre the gold box which Louis XV presented to the City of Geneva in 1727, and which is decorated with a miniature portrait of the king.

It is not impossible that one day he will offer to the Louvre some piece of sculpture or a painting as a symbol of his gratitude to the city where his favourite cabinet-makers were born. But it is inconceivable that he could ever disperse the treasures of Malibu amongst the museums of France or elsewhere. His own museum bears witness to a taste so exceptionally pure that it would be immensely sad to see it disappear into those enormous and often inhuman depositories, the national collections. To bring together masterpieces is in itself a form of art; to create a masterpiece with masterpieces is much rarer than one would imagine, even if a collector has the wealth to do it. The Getty collection should therefore be respected and admired for what it is: harmonious and sincere, in itself an expression of delight. GERALD MESSADIE

PORTRAIT OF MARTEN LOOTEN
Rembrandt van Rijn (1606–69) oil on canvas
35½ × 29½ ins. 1632

Paris Stavros Niarchos

French paintings, furniture and silver

THE NAME OF NIARCHOS has become world-famous in the last few years. Some people know him as the 'master of the seas'. Others know that he is also a master of the arts. Ship-owner and art-lover are two sides of a single personality: the first operates in the environment created by the second, with the money made by the first. Remarkable flair, swift decisions and scorn of the mediocre are characteristics common to both. In the field of art it is only right to associate the name of Madame Niarchos with that of Stavros S. Niarchos, who, although he began collecting only recently, is already renowned.

The purpose of his collection is in the first place entirely practical: to furnish his various homes. But his Mediterranean, even regal, sense of display demands the beautiful, the antique, the magnificent. Pictures led on to furniture, and carpets and porcelain to silverware. French art predominates but not exclusively. Since Niarchos, a great traveller, is obliged to move between his various homes in order to direct his empire, and as he likes to live and work surrounded by his works of art, he has dispersed and continually expanded his collection, but he has made his Parisian home, 'Chanaleilles', the centre of his collection of masterpieces; it represents all that he demands in a work of art.

The Hôtel de Chanaleilles is well-known today, and it was well-known to a number of people in the past. It stands on the corner of the rue Vaneau and the rue de Chanaleilles, an old house, a little dilapidated, but impregnated with the feeling of ancient France. It was once owned by the Chanaleilles family and later by a well-known journalist.

The arrival of Monsieur and Madame Niarchos and their children in 1956 was to give new life to this delightful house.

The restoration of this eighteenth-century folly by an enterprising owner, realistic businessman and eclectic art collector might have altered its appearance beyond recognition; but in fact Monsieur Niarchos' qualities combined to create unexpected magnificence in a building to which Madame Tallien, later Princesse de Chimay, had already given a character of splendour.

Since then the house and the collection have been closely linked. The house has been adapted to modern life without spoiling its architectural design, and in many ways has even improved on it. A recently added wing was demolished and rebuilt in good taste, and a courtyard was restored to its original level, both of which have recreated the nobility of the exterior and at the same time have provided rooms for the children. When the gardens had been redesigned and planted with large trees, lawns, boxwood and trellis-work, and indoors, floors had been repaired and modern comforts added, the house still had to be furnished and decorated. This was the purpose of the collection.

Since the collection was intended both for use and as a luxury, in a way of life in which family, business, friends, relaxation and the pleasures of an art patron all play their part, and since it had to serve this purpose in the framework

· ·

THE OLD CLOWN
Georges Rouault (1871–1958)
oil on cardboard 41 × 29½ *ins.* C1917

of the existing house, it is interesting to note its general composition; the origin of the pieces and the rapidity with which they have been assembled only partly explain their presence.

The framework, as a whole, is in Louis XVI style; additions and modifications were made by Madame Tallien, and more recently by the architect Emilio Terry, both fervent admirers of the art of the late eighteenth century. To match this unity of style there should have been a certain unity in the works of art. To assume this would be to underrate the eclecticism of the owner, whose personality we ought briefly to consider in its various aspects.

Greek art is represented. What could be more natural?

Above: 'PIETÀ' THE DESCENT FROM THE CROSS
El Greco (1541–1614)
oil on canvas 47¼ × 57⅛ ins. c 1585

Opposite: THE BLACK CLOCK
Paul Cézanne (1839–1906)
oil on canvas 21¾ × 29¼ ins. c 1871

Granted, the marble torso in the recess in the hall, or the piece of Attic pottery in the adjacent room, could have been there at the time of the *Directoire*. But the two pictures by El Greco, notably the one in the principal salon, the *Pietà* from the former La Béraudière collection which Monsieur Niarchos brought back from America, have been chosen because of his admiration for a painter of Greek origin.

The art lover reveals himself in the breadth of his selection: here a Goya, there a Corot and a Delacroix, but above all a famous collection of paintings by recent French masters, Degas, Renoir, Cézanne, Gauguin, Toulouse-Lautrec, Matisse, Rouault and several van Goghs. These pictures, exhibited in Zurich, Vienna, London and New York in the last few years, are too well-known to need description. But something must be said of the boldness with which they are hung in the midst of the old woodwork, spaced out on wall panels, above antique furniture, placed on tables, leaning on sofas; there is no suggestion of a gallery, no timidity about period; they strike you immediately and demand attention; décor and furnishing enhance and support them without detracting from them. What an astonishing place!

The owner's princely taste is evident not only in his superb disdain for chronology but also in his acquisitions of works of art of royal origin. One could find many examples of the excellence of his choice, among the pieces of furniture (such as the beautiful *secrétaire* in polychrome marquetry which

Above: HORSEMEN ON THE BEACH
Paul Gauguin (1848–1903)
oil on canvas
29 × 36¼ ins. 1902

Stavros Niarchos

Above: ARISTIDE BRUANT AUX AMBASSADEURS
Henri de Toulouse-Lautrec (1864–1901)
gouache and watercolour on paper mounted on canvas
54½ × 36½ ins. c 1892

Left: BEACH SCENE, TROUVILLE
Eugène Boudin (1824–98)
oil on wood 7½ × 12¾ ins. 1886

may have been part of the furniture ordered from Roentgen by Catherine II), or among the porcelain (notably the Vincennes and Sèvres porcelain, a close study of which would enable us to discover their original owners). We shall consider two Savonnerie carpets whose magnificence will not escape the perceptive visitor and whose distinguished origins can be proved by documents as yet unpublished.

The first of these carpets, probably the one sold in London in 1939 by Lord Rosebery, is in the 'grand salon'. It bears the arms of France on a spread eagle in the centre and it is said to have been given by Louis XV to his father-in-law, Stanislas Leczinski. Louis XV, who commissioned the design for this carpet from P. J. Perrot, had it woven, to my knowledge, three times: the first time in 1735 for the dining room of the Château de la Muette, the second in 1740 for his Château de Choisy, and the third in 1769 for his chapel at Fontainebleau, where it was to be used 'when His Majesty hears Divine Service' down below instead of in the upper tribune adjoining the lobby at the top of the horse-shoe staircase. A similar carpet is in the Cleveland Museum of Art.

The other Savonnerie carpet in the Hôtel de Chanaleilles is in the next salon and is also in the Louis XV style. It has an overall flower pattern, with neither coats of arms nor fleur-de-lys. To recognize its importance requires the intuition of really great connoisseurs and museum experts. It was put up for sale in London in 1955, at a time when there was much talk in France of refurnishing Versailles, in particular Louis XV's inner study. Countless people filed past this carpet without knowing it for what it was. It was said to have belonged to an Archduchess of Austria to whom it had been given by Marie-Antoinette. The pattern is based on a watercolour now in the print room of the Bibliothèque Nationale and the carpet itself, of which the Nissim de Camondo Museum owns a copy, was put on the loom at least three times: twice for the chapel of Versailles in 1760 and again, six years later, for Louis XV's study at Versailles.

A patron, according to Littré's definition, is a 'rich or powerful man who encourages the sciences, letters and the arts'. The Louvre owes an immense debt of gratitude to Monsieur and Madame Niarchos, as the display cabinets at the Hôtel de Chanaleilles prove, for the masterpieces of French silver which they own have now been generously bequeathed to the Louvre, subject to their keeping them for life. The room which houses this treasure is called the Salon Puiforcat, in homage to the great contemporary silversmith

Above: *Savonnerie carpet with a sepia ground and
a central cartouche of yellow, green, blue and
pink scrolls and leaves surrounded by a garland of flowers.
16 ft. 6 ins. × 11 ft. 18th century*

Left: *Plaque of Sèvres porcelain with a medallion
portrait of Louis XVI inset and bearing the inscription*
Du peuple à ton avènement, Louis, tu te montras le père
et, de son premier mouvement, il te nomma Louis le
Populaire. *7½ × 6⅜ ins. 1774*

Opposite: *The salon rouge of the Hôtel de Chanaleilles,
showing Goya's Portrait of* Donna Joaquina Candado
(*far wall*), *an ormolu and crystal chandelier (c 1810),
the famous savonnerie carpet bearing the arms of Louis XV
and some fine pieces from the collection of furniture*

Stavros Niarchos

Above: LA BOULANGERE
Pierre Auguste Renoir (1841–1919)
oil on canvas 21 × 25¾ ins. 1904

Opposite: *A corner of the* salon blanc
with van Gogh's Portrait of Père Tanguy
hanging over a Louis XVI *marquetry secrétaire.*
On either side are two
of a set of four Louis XVI *carved and gilt chairs*

Stavros Niarchos

Opposite: THE ZOUAVE
Amedeo Modigliani (1884–1920)
oil on canvas 24¾ × 19 ins. c 1918

Gold goblet of Anne of Austria.
Height 3¾ ins.
First half of the 17th century

who built up this unrivalled collection. Monsieur Niarchos saved the collection from dispersal by acquiring it in its entirety before the public sale. He stipulated, in one of the clauses of his deed of gift to the Louvre, that the collection should be placed on public exhibition every ten years, so that each generation of craftsmen, students and art-lovers should have the opportunity of seeing it in its entirety.

To describe the Niarchos collection in detail would take too long and would probably not be in the spirit of this great collector, who has not been restricted by any narrow historical limitations but has simply sought his own pleasure and that of others in creating his magnificent achievement at the Hôtel de Chanaleilles. We must, however, try to explain how such a busy man has obtained such complete success in a matter of scarcely ten years. The tactics of the shipowner do much to explain it. Certain objectives are defined; their importance, however real, is such that failure to achieve any one of them would not materially affect the venture as a whole. There are other decisions in which the risks taken might have transformed the Niarchos 'empire'. So it is with the collection.

Certain purchases, taken individually, add to the whole,

but their absence would not alter the general shape of the collection which they simply reinforce. El Greco's *Pietà* is an example, or the Berkeley silver dinner service or even the famous silver-gilt toilet set, which belonged to the Empress Josephine. This toilet set, which found no purchaser of sufficient stature for a period of thirty years, was put up for auction, and despite the assembled group of experts would probably still not have found one, had not Monsieur Niarchos suddenly acquired it and brought it back in triumph to Paris.

The acquisitions from which the rest followed and which give the collection its real character are the entire collections which surprise even connoisseurs by their richness and variety and have proved to be singularly well advised: the pictures from the Edward G. Robinson collection, the massive purchase of furniture including the Ricardo do Esperito Santo collection acquired at an auction at the Galerie de Charpentier and the Chester Beatty collection purchased privately, almost all Louis XVI and in harmony with the future Hôtel de Chanaleilles; or the collection of Puiforcat silver mentioned earlier. It is by gestures such as these that we recognize the master.   PIERRE VERLET 203

Oskar Reinhart

European drawings and paintings

IT IS NOT OFTEN THAT one encounters nowadays a *mécène*, but Dr Oskar Reinhart is such by instinct. I do not mean by this that he has been an active protector and patron of the significant artists of his own time, because in fact Dr Reinhart has not really concerned himself with the art of the twentieth century. What he has done, however, in the course of the last fifty years, is to assemble three major collections of works of art, and this not, as is so often the case, to satisfy some personal aspiration but out of a genuine desire to contribute something of his own to the already rich artistic patrimony of his native Switzerland.

Oskar Reinhart (b 1885) was able to begin his artistic education early, for his parents had many artistic and literary friends and he often accompanied his father on trips round Europe visiting the great museums and artistic centres. During those years he developed a special interest in drawings and prints, and when he began to buy works of art for himself, during the first decade of this century, he concentrated on graphic works. But Oskar Reinhart is not the sort of collector who allows personal taste alone to determine his artistic judgment. He knows how important it is to cultivate a true aesthetic sense and to be able to back up appreciation with knowledge. So he frequented the Print Rooms of London, Berlin, Dresden and Paris as a student, and as his knowledge increased over the years so did his collection. Mention is seldom made today of Oskar Reinhart's remarkable collection of prints – which is especially rich in examples of the sixteenth and seventeenth centuries – because it is overshadowed by his more famous private collection of paintings. Perhaps too it has been overlooked because it has never been publicly exhibited. Nevertheless, it can still be found in the library of his house, Am Römerholz, on the outskirts of Winterthur, and must be regarded as a significant appendage to the rest.

Oskar Reinhart's name is associated above all, and justifiably, with two great collections of paintings and drawings, which came into being after he gave up collecting prints. The most important of these, with which the present article is essentially concerned, is the very impressive group of paintings and drawings by European masters which cover the walls of his home and its two adjacent galleries. The second is a collection of works by German, Austrian and Swiss artists of the eighteenth to twentieth centuries, which became the *Stiftung Oskar Reinhart* when it was donated to the town of Winterthur in 1951 and set up independently as a museum in a specially reconstructed building.

Originally, Dr Reinhart had no intention of making two separate collections. He bought what he liked, and that was that. Then one day, after he had already acquired a considerable group of works by Old Masters and nineteenth-century French painters, his eye was caught by a painting by Max Liebermann, which he promptly added to the rest. Charmed and interested, Dr Reinhart began from that moment (c 1926) to enlarge his scope as a collector to take in

· ·

PORTRAIT OF DR JOHANNES CUSPINIAN
Lucas Cranach (1472–1553) oil on wood panel 23¼ × 17¾ ins.
Dr Cuspinian was born in Spiessheim in 1473 and died in 1529. The companion portrait of his first wife, Anna Putsch, is also in the Reinhart Collection

Oskar Reinhart

*Am Römerholz: View from the large gallery
into the smaller one beyond,
showing on the right of the doorway
Van Gogh's*
Interior of a Ward in the Hospital at Arles
and his Portrait of Madame Roulin,
and in the corner Toulouse-Lautrec's
La Clownesse Cha-U-Kao.

*On the wall of the small gallery,
shown in detail, is Manet's* Au Café
on the left and on the right Pissarro's
Un Coin de l'Hermitage, Pontoise

German, Austrian and Swiss painting of the eighteenth, nineteenth and twentieth centuries. The alacrity with which he collected, in the space of a few years, in this unfashionable field, was first revealed in 1932–33 when his collection was exhibited at Basle and Winterthur. But after that date he continued to buy Agasse, Blechen, Boecklin, Calame, Friedrich, Hodler, Kobell, Leibl, Menzel, Waldmüller, the Nazarenes and the like in such quantities that when the Reinhart Collection was shown again in Bern in the winter of 1939, it was seen that these later German, Austrian and Swiss schools accounted for roughly half of the paintings and drawings on view. And Dr Reinhart went on buying in this field until he was forced to recognize that he had created a secondary collection within the other. So, at the end of the 1940's, he decided that he had to make a division. Accordingly, he set aside some four hundred paintings and two hundred drawings and watercolours and founded a museum of Germano-Swiss art of the eighteenth to twentieth centuries in Winterthur. This part of Dr Reinhart's collection has been separately published in catalogue form by the museum authorities.

The more opulent part of Dr Reinhart's collection has remained as a personal possession on the walls of his house Am Römerholz. Here he lives as a private citizen among his treasures, and insists that his home should not be regarded as a museum, even though he has recently donated its entire contents to the Swiss Confederation. Dr Reinhart makes no loans to temporary exhibitions, and his private apartments and galleries are never open to the general public. These are, certainly, severe restrictions, but the collector must be allowed to consider his personal convenience. Dr Reinhart has neither forgotten the needs of specialists, nor the privileges due to serious art-lovers, nor has he overlooked the obligations of a *mécène* to the world at large. Those who have a valid reason for wishing to study the works of art in the Reinhart collection are usually received with great kindness at the Römerholz, while the collection as a whole has twice been placed on public exhibition in Swiss museums during the last twenty years. This occurred at Bern in November 1939, and again at Winterthur in the summer and autumn of 1955 on the occasion of Dr Reinhart's seventieth birthday. Each time, a good illustrated catalogue was published, and further information about the collection can be found in the pictorial repertoire *Aus der Sammlung Oskar Reinhart* by R. Seiffert-Wattenberg (Munich 1935). These are not, admittedly, scholarly publications, but for the researcher they are useful points of departure.

Dr Oskar Reinhart's private collection comprises today about one hundred and forty paintings, as well as some forty drawings and watercolours by European masters. These pictures have not been chosen with any preconceived purpose in mind. Dr Reinhart did not set out to prove a theory with his collection, nor to survey the work of any particular artist, school or period, nor yet has he specialized in pictures with

Left: WEEPING WOMAN WITH CLASPED HANDS
Matthias Grünewald (1470/80–1528) black crayon heightened with white 15¾ × 11¾ ins. c 1515

Right: THE HOLY FAMILY
Nicolas Poussin (1593/4–1665) oil on canvas 34⅝ × 26⅜ ins. c 1632

Oskar Reinhart

ADORATION OF THE KINGS
Pieter Brueghel the Elder (1528–69)
oil on wood panel 13¾ × 21⅝ *ins.*
Signed and dated 1567.
By introducing the 'realistic' note
of a snowstorm, appropriate to
the season, Brueghel created a new
conception of this scene

a specific subject. His choice has been governed by only one standard of judgement: technical mastery and perfect realization of a vision. Like all collectors, Oskar Reinhart has sometimes made mistakes, wearied of pictures that he has bought, or perhaps been able to find finer examples by the artist concerned, so that over the years he has occasionally made changes in his ensemble. Yet he has never got rid of any major work, and his collection has basically the same character and look today as it had twenty-five years ago, even though he has added some forty-five paintings and drawings since 1940. The explanation of this can be found in the constancy of Dr Reinhart's personal taste. For he has not been interested in expanding his collection through the introduction of works by other artists – though it must be admitted that Simon Marmion, Jan Provost, Claude, David, Fragonard, Chassériau and Picasso are among those artists who have appeared in the last twenty years – but has concentrated on expanding the existing groups of works by those artists who have most meaning and appeal for himself. There is nothing experimental or *avant-garde* about the Oskar Reinhart collection. Art historians will not find surprises hidden there, nor paintings whose unusual subject-matter or style merits the adjective 'exceptional'. This is a collection which can best be described as an ensemble of outstanding achievements in painting, selected by a man with great taste and knowledge, who happens also to be very rich. It is the impeccable quality and the magnificence of the ensemble that prove stunning.

Oskar Reinhart's private collection contains works by artists of the French, Spanish, Flemish, Dutch, German, Italian, English and Swiss schools from the fifteenth to the twentieth centuries. The earliest examples are a *Coronation of the Virgin* by a Florentine painter of the last years of the fourteenth century, and a charming small *Annunciation* (*c* 1420) by a German artist of the Upper Rhine School. The latest works are three fine drawings by Picasso (1919) in his classicistic manner (Zervos, Vol 3, Nos 369, 370, 372). Between these extremes the collection may be roughly divided into pre-nineteenth-century works and those of the nineteenth century, the former group (Goya included) numbering a bare sixty works, while the latter amounts to twice that number. Similarly, there is a great preponderance of works by artists of the French School, this too being in the proportion of two to one over all other schools combined. The Oskar Reinhart collection is thus dominated by French nineteenth-century art; indeed, the only non-French artists of the period represented are Eugenio Lucas (1), Constable (2), Jongkind (2) and van Gogh (6), the last two being nowadays generally regarded as French, like Constantin Guys (2).

Oskar Reinhart began by buying nineteenth-century paintings: his first purchases as a matter of fact were two small landscapes by Renoir (long since exchanged) bought in 1906. He did not venture into the field of the old masters (except, of course, for prints) until about 1922. Today they are most nobly represented on the walls of the Römerholz, though the choice of names and works has been determined by a strict sense of individual values. There is a small group of works of the late fifteenth and early sixteenth centuries, among which should be singled out a portrait of Philippe le Beau (c1498) by The Master of St Gilles and an *Adoration of the Kings* (c1490) by Geertgen tot Sint Jans, both great rarities. The only Swiss work in the collection is an altar diptych painted in 1515 by Niklaus Manuel Deutsch. The German School is, however, very strongly represented by a great, tragic drawing (c1515) of a *Weeping Woman with clasped hands* by Grünewald, as well as by two of the most beautiful portraits (c 1503) by Cranach of Dr Johannes Cuspinian, a historian at the University of Vienna, and his first wife Anna Putsch. These last were formerly in the collection of King Charles 1 of England.

The high-lights of the sixteenth century in the Reinhart collection are an *Adoration of the Kings* (1563) by the elder

Brueghel, whose snowstorm effect is painted with a lightness of touch such as one usually finds only in Impressionist painting; a fine early (c 1540) *Adoration of the Shepherds* by Jacopo Bassano; and a restrained but penetrating head and shoulders portrait (c 1576) of the Grand Inquisitor Cardinal Nino de Guevara by El Greco. This last must have been a preparatory study for the great full-length portrait in the Metropolitan Museum of New York and may have been done from life.

Among seventeenth-century works, the most memorable are the *Holy Family in a Landscape* (c1632) by Poussin, from the Lansdowne and Westminster collections, an unusually warm and tender picture in which the master has for once allowed a trace of humour to burst through in the antics of the *putti*; the group of three Rembrandts, a late painting of a *Man by a Furnace* (c 1660), and two fine drawings (c 1648 and c 1655); and the unusually subdued early Hals (c 1628) of a *Boy Reading*. The outstanding eighteenth-century contributions to the Reinhart collection are two groups: four paintings by Chardin, including a *Faiseur de Châteaux de Cartes* (c1740) and three appetizing still-lifes (1758–59), then six paintings by Goya, including two preparatory sketches for tapestries (1778–79), two late still-lifes which are direct anticipations of Manet, the sensitive and haunting *Portrait of an Unknown Young Man* (c 1796), and the artist's last portrait, that of Don José Pio de Molina (1828), which is unfinished.

For all that the school of painting most prominently represented in the Reinhart collection is the French nineteenth century, one must not expect to find the representation of it balanced or in any sense conventional. The paintings on the walls of the Römerholz make it quite explicit that while Dr Reinhart loves the work of some painters immoderately, others command no more than his respect and are therefore hardly to be seen, while others – Prud'hon, Barye, Théodore Rousseau, Daubigny, Bazille, Seurat and Signac, for example – do not appeal to him at all and are conspicuous by their absence.

Basically, Oskar Reinhart's nineteenth-century collection is composed of eight important groups of works by those artists nearest to his heart: Corot (twelve oils), Delacroix (nine oils), Daumier (eight oils, eleven drawings), Courbet

· ·

PORTRAIT OF AN UNKNOWN YOUNG MAN
Francisco de Goya y Lucientes (1747–1828)
oil on canvas 26⅜ × 21⅞ ins. c1796

209

Oskar Reinhart

(nine oils), Manet (four oils), Cézanne (seven oils, four watercolours), Renoir (fourteen oils) and van Gogh (four oils, two drawings). Admittedly this is no ordinary choice. Charm and *volupté* it seems are weighed against harsh reality, deep feeling and natural grandeur. Thus no one could maintain that Dr Reinhart favours one type of painting exclusively. Here sensuality is not allowed to obscure the tragedies of life; the sensuous delights of Impressionist painting do not rule out a look at the harsh realities of different social orders; equal allowance is made for visual pleasure and intellectual satisfaction; romantic upsurges do not rule out classical restraint; the earthy, peasant tones of Courbet and the bitter mocking voice of Daumier are not hushed to make room for the poetry of Corot and the humanism of Cézanne. But now let us look at the other side of the medal, at the art which has found little favour in Dr Reinhart's eyes. He has, for example, only one painting by Ingres, though it is a remarkable and unmannered portrait of his second wife (1859), which for once seems to have been painted out of sincere admiration and affection. Of the Barbizon painters, only the earthy Millet has found acceptance (one oil, three drawings), though he is not to be seen at his best. There is also only one work by Degas, though admittedly it is the splendid pastel *Danseuse dans sa Loge* (1879) which was shown at the fourth Impressionist Group Exhibition. This seems all the more surprising in that on the plane of taste a bond exists between Degas and Oskar Reinhart, for no less than four pictures at the Römerholz come from the Degas collection: Manet's *Départ du Bâteau de Folkestone*, Corot's *Châtaigneraie Rocheuse* and *Mantes, Une Amorce du Pont*, as well as Cézanne's small *Self-Portrait*. Three other major painters are represented in the Reinhart collection by only one work each: Monet (a *Débâcle* of 1882), Gauguin (a view of Rouen of 1884), and Toulouse-Lautrec (a superb *Clownesse* of 1895). On the other hand, Dr Reinhart has been more generous to Géricault, whose *Général Letellier sur son lit de mort* (1819) and *Fou Maniaque du Commandement Militaire* (*c*1822) show, in their respective ways, that this somewhat cold and overpowering artist was also capable of poignancy and human understanding. That there should be only two works each by Sisley and Pissarro also seems strange. But Dr Reinhart has selected in the former's *Canal St Martin* (1870) and the latter's *Un Coin de l'Hermitage, Pontoise* (1874), both acquired (with ten others) in the early 1920's from the great collection of the Danish ship-owner Wilhelm

Above: PORTRAIT OF MADAME INGRES *(Delphine Ramel)*
Jean Auguste Dominique Ingres (1780–1867)
oil on canvas 24⅝ × 22 ins. Signed and dated 1859

Hansen, two examples of Impressionist landscape painting of the vital years whose quality is unsurpassed in the work of either artist.

All of this provides a background for, and fills gaps between, the eight major groups of works. These may not show the full achievement of each artist, but they certainly show him at the top of his form. The Corots divide up into a good group of early (1830–45) landscapes – the pastoral *Châtaigneraie Rocheuse* (c 1830), the gentler and more lyrical *Rochefort-sur-Mer* (c 1840) and *Château-Thierry* (c 1845) – after which there is a leap to the very late *Dunkerque* (1873). Limpidly painted and elegiac in mood, this harbour scene is one of the collector's favourites. In between these landscapes, which are strangely akin, comes a group of melancholy late figure pieces, among which *La Petite Liseuse* (c 1850), an outdoor subject, and *Italienne assise jouant de la Mandoline*, an indoor scene, are outstanding. The group of

Delacroix's covers a much wider range of subjects and spans his lifetime. The series opens with three powerful tragic works of 1827: *Le Tasse dans la Maison des Fous*, a brilliant sketch for *La Grèce expirant sur les ruines de Missolonghi*, the masterpiece in the Museum of Bordeaux, and a spirited oriental battle-piece *Scène de la Guerre en Grèce*. This last prepares for the later and more masterly equestrian composition *Exercices militaires des Marocains* (1847) where the artist has articulated the impetuous movement more perfectly and used a fuller range of colour. Of the later works by Delacroix in Dr Reinhart's ensemble, a sketch for *Samson et Dalila* (1854) which once belonged to Daubigny, and a *Mort d'Ophélia* (1859), only purchased in 1960, are the most striking. Dr Reinhart's group of Courbets – which includes neither a portrait nor a hunting scene – is exceptionally varied and significant. *Le Hamac*, or *Un Rêve de Jeune Fille* (1844) as it used to be called, is an early masterpiece in the

Right: THE FUGITIVES *Honoré Daumier (1808–79)*
oil on paper laid on canvas 15⅛ × 27 ins. c 1849.
A recurrent theme in Daumier's work
immediately after the 1848 revolution
Below right: EXERCICES MILITAIRES DES MAROCAINS
Eugène Delacroix (1798–1863)
oil on canvas 26 × 32⅛ ins.
Signed and dated 1847
Opposite: STILL LIFE WITH PLUMS
Jean Baptiste Siméon Chardin (1699–1779)
oil on canvas 16½ × 18⅞ ins. Signed and dated 1759
Below: THE HAMMOCK *Gustave Courbet (1819–77)*
oil on canvas 27½ × 38¼ ins. Signed and dated 1844

AU CAFE
Edouard Manet (1832–83)
oil on canvas 30¾ × 33⅛ ins.
Signed and dated 1878.
In 1878 Manet painted a great
many brasserie *and*
café chantant *scenes*
such as this canvas.
The bearded man is
Henri Guérard and the girl
in the hat beside him
is the actress Ellen Andrée

DEPART DU BATEAU
DE FOLKESTONE
Edouard Manet (1832–83)
oil on canvas 24⅜ × 39¼ ins.
1869. Painted during a summer
holiday spent at Boulogne.
The incipient impressionism
in the handling reflects the
influence on Manet of his
friendship with Monet
and Berthe Morisot.
This canvas marks the
beginning of plein air
painting in Manet's work

Below: CHESTNUT TREES AND ROCKS
Jean Baptiste Camille Corot (1796–1875)
oil on canvas 21⅝ × 33 ins. c 1833

Bottom left: PENICHES SUR LE CANAL ST-MARTIN A PARIS
Alfred Sisley (1839–99)
oil on canvas 21⅜ × 29⅛ ins. Signed and dated 1870

Bottom right: LA GRENOUILLERE
Pierre Auguste Renoir (1841–1919)
oil on canvas 25⅝ × 36⅝ ins.
Signed. A scene painted several times
by Monet and Renoir in 1868–69

Oskar Reinhart

artist's tight Germanic manner of painting and in this setting forms an extraordinary counterpart to Delacroix's *Mort d'Ophélia*. In the same way, two of his other Courbets, *La Vendange à Ornans* (1849) and *Nature Morte aux Fleurs* (1863), have a special interest as fore-runners of paintings by artists of the following generation. Thus the former anticipates many a work by Pissarro and Monet, while the latter points directly to Renoir's *Fleurs* (1864), painted a year later, which now hangs on a wall nearby. The sketch for *Les Casseurs de Pierres* (1850) is the only *genre* subject of the group, while the big *La Vague* (1870), in a purple and green tonality, is one of the finest versions of the subject. The group of Daumiers is splendid, none of them being, as is so often the case with this painter, strained or banal. All are comparatively late works, except the composition *The Fugitives* (c 1849), a straggling procession of refugees whose plight is represented in such realistic terms as to arouse a sense of horror and pity such as one associates with Callot, Rembrandt or Goya. For the rest, there are three *Don Quixote* episodes (c 1866–1868), an *Amateur d'estampes*, a group of law-court subjects, and the usual theatrical and café *genre* pieces, notably *L'Entr'acte* (c 1858) and *La Politique des Buveurs de Bière* (c 1860). But the two *pièces de résistance*, both very different in style and mood, are the tightly drawn *Le Wagon*

Oskar Reinhart

COURTYARD OF
THE HOSPITAL IN ARLES
Vincent van Gogh (1855–90)
oil on canvas 28¾ × 36¼ ins. 1889
The courtyard of the hospital
in Arles, where Van Gogh was
treated several times between
24th December 1888, after cutting
the lobe of his ear,
and 8th May 1889, when he left
for the asylum at St-Rémy

de 3ème Classe (*c* 1862), dispassionate as reportage yet intensely human in feeling, and the amazingly free, romantic oil painting *Pierrot jouant de la Guitare* (*c* 1869).

So much for the four painters of the first half of the century; the other four belong to the second half. First of all Manet. Dr Reinhart's Manets may be few in number, but each represents a different aspect of a great artist and is superlative of its kind. This is as true of the less ambitious late *Bouquet de Fleurs* (1882) as it is of the enchanting and sensuous portrait of *Marguerite de Conflans* (1873), where the *bravura* of Manet's handling and the subtlety with which he paints flesh and silk reveal him as a true successor to Hals. On the other hand, the two *genre* subjects *Départ du bâteau de Folkestone* (1869) and *Au Café* (1878), painted almost ten years apart, show how personal Manet's pictorial vision was and how keenly he observed the easy bourgeois life of his period. The group of Renoirs, for all that it is much larger, contrasts sharply with the Manets, as much in character as in importance. Here virtuosity plays no part, and apart from *La Grenouillère* (1868–69), a masterpiece of early Impressionist *plein-air* painting, Dr Reinhart has been attracted to the charming rather than to the great works of the painter. Virtually all are of modest dimensions and the majority

are *genre* pieces and portraits – *M. Choquet* (1876) the collector, *Mlle Henriot* (*c* 1878) an actress at the Comédie Française, *Confidences* (*c* 1877) and *La Modiste* (*c* 1876) – or else opulent nudes – *La Dormeuse* (1897), *Grand Nu* (1913). Turning from Renoir to van Gogh one moves again into another world and is faced with a very different conception of painting. It is also difficult to think of two great van Goghs which are more sharply contrasted in mood than those in the Oskar Reinhart collection. For where the one is a radiant spring vision (April 1889) of the flower-bedecked *Courtyard of the Hospital in Arles*, the other is a haunting and melancholic canvas (April–October 1889) showing the interior of one of the wards in the same building. The painting in both canvases is unemphatic and calm; in neither does van Gogh 'hit the high yellow note' of which he had been so afraid a few months previously. Yet there is such intensity of feeling in both that their confrontation alone suffices to illuminate the drama of this spontaneous artist, who has been suddenly deprived of the possibility of feasting his eyes and nourishing his spirit on the spectacle of nature. To have picked out these two canvases, as well as the two magnificent Provençal drawings of the summer of 1888 which complement them, is one of Dr Reinhart's master-strokes.

STILL LIFE WITH A JUG
AND APPLES
(Nature Morte au
Pot de Faïence)
Paul Cézanne (1839–1906)
oil on canvas 28¾ × 39⅜ ins.
*c 1902. This still life must
have been painted after
Cézanne moved to his new
studio on the
Chemin des Lauves
on the edge of Aix*

Despite all these riches, the *clou* of the Reinhart collection is a carefully chosen group of works by Cézanne. Four are datable before 1880, that is to say they belong to the artist's first period, whereas the other seven are late works, having been executed after 1887. Again, Dr Reinhart has not attempted to cover the entire range: there are no great portraits, no great compositions of *Bathers*, no *genre* pieces, no views of L'Estaque or Bibémus. But he has selected telling examples. The *Portrait d'Homme* (c 1865), which once belonged to Monet, and the *Self-Portrait* (c 1879), which Oskar Reinhart bought at the Vente Degas in 1918, obviously do not represent Cézanne at his most monumental as a figure painter, yet they are finished and successful paintings which illustrate to perfection Cézanne's capacities at two important moments in his early stylistic evolution. Dr Reinhart's choice of landscapes centres particularly on late works. He has a fine watercolour, *Le Jas de Bouffan en Hiver* (c 1880), but his two most significant examples are the oil painting of *Le Château Noir* (c 1897) and a large late watercolour of *La Montagne Ste-Victoire* (c 1905) which has been taken further than most in its execution and glows with form-giving colours. Two of the most beautiful and solidly constructed of all Cézanne's still-lifes complete the group: the *Compotier et Pommes* of about 1877, which was painted in Paris, and the simple but sublime *Nature Morte au Pot de Faïence*, painted at Aix about 1902, which sets the seal on the works by Chardin, Goya, Manet and Renoir hanging around it.

It is impossible to do justice, in an article of this length, to a collection so full of treasures as that of Oskar Reinhart. But enough has been said to explain the history of its growth, to indicate its salient characteristics and to bring out its great interest. Oskar Reinhart has not looked for pictures which are extraordinary by any other standard than that of their artistic quality. His choice has not been at all affected by currents of fashion or by great names. But once one starts to look into the provenances of the paintings he has bought one is struck by the number which have belonged in the past to artists, writers or men of exceptional taste, such as Degas, Monet, Daubigny, Octave Mirbeau, Alexandre Dumas, Gauguin, Théodore Duret or Alexander Cassatt. This discovery at once throws the deeply artistic nature of his sensibility into relief. And then one begins to understand why, underneath its magnificence, his collection of works of art possesses a subtlety and distinction the like of which is not to be found in other collections of this sort made in our time.

DOUGLAS COOPER

215

Emil G. Bührle

French nineteenth-century painting

THE BÜHRLE COLLECTION is, after the Oskar Reinhart collection, the largest and most comprehensive in Switzerland. It is the creation of the industrialist Emil Georg Bührle (1890–1956), and is certainly not the product of a life of leisure. It was in fact put together by a man who held an important place in the business life of Switzerland, a man who, by committing his whole personality and by a combination of energy, personal gifts and luck, built out of nothing a highly successful industrial undertaking.

In his youth Emil Bührle had studied the history of art and literature, until the First World War gave a new direction to his life and, to use his own words, 'turned an aesthete and philosopher who was a stranger to reality, into a human being who became accustomed to looking brute facts calmly in the face, cultivated the habits of quick decision and effective action and learned how to accept responsibility for others.'

It is not for us to say whether it was the war that liberated his real gifts for action. We can only be sure of this, that Bührle, whose field of activity from 1924 onwards was Switzerland, Bührle the successful entrepreneur, who was shortly afterwards to make that country his home, remained true, despite all the changes of circumstance, to the dreams of his youth. He was an unusually active man, always planning for the future, but the other side of his nature was never wholly submerged; it flowed on like a subterranean river. This became plain when the pressures grew less, when success opened up the possibility of realizing the ambition of his early years. What could be more natural than that he should begin his collection with the masters who had delighted him in his school and university

years – the French Impressionists? What he had so much desired, the possession of a painting by one of the Impressionists – perhaps a Monet – now became a reality, and to an even greater degree than he had hoped. He has told us something of this in his lecture *Vom Werden meiner Sammlung* (How my collection began). 'In the autumn of 1913 I saw for the first time in the Nationalgalerie in Berlin those magnificent French paintings which, to the annoyance of the Kaiser, had been acquired by that Swiss man of genius, Hugo von Tschudi, the director of the gallery. The atmosphere of these pictures, above all the lyrical quality of a landscape by Monet of the country round Vetheuil, completely overwhelmed me. It was at that moment that I determined that, if I were ever in a position to do so, I would hang on my walls just such paintings by Manet, Monet, Renoir, Degas and Cézanne.'

The first pictures, acquired in the mid-thirties, have among them certain works that indicate the general trend of the collection and are a measure of its quality. These comprise Manet's *Rue de Berne Decorated with Flags, A Field of Poppies near Vetheuil* by Monet, *The Olive Grove* by Van Gogh and, particularly noteworthy, a late and quite perfect painting by Cézanne of the Montagne Sainte-Victoire. These

••

BOY WITH A RED WAISTCOAT
Paul Cézanne (1839–1906)
oil on canvas 31¼ × 25¼ *ins.* c1895

216

THE SOWER
Vincent van Gogh (1853–90)
oil on canvas 29 × 36⅝ ins.
Painted in Arles in October 1888

BORDEAUX HARBOUR
Edouard Manet (1832–83)
oil on canvas 26 × 39⅜ ins.
Manet spent a week in Bordeaux
during the Franco-Prussian War
and painted this picture in
February 1871 from the
window of a quayside café

Emil G. Bührle

CHATEAU D'ORNANS
Gustave Courbet (1819–77)
oil on canvas, 38 × 48 ins. 1853.
One of a number of paintings
of Ornans, where
Courbet was born

were the painters in whom Bührle had a special interest, and the most important part of the collection was formed from their works. It is significant that one of Monet's Vetheuil landscapes has a place here, for it was just such a landscape that had aroused Bührle's first enthusiasm for the Impressionists. The first of these landscapes was soon joined by another and even richer one, and there followed a whole succession of works from Monet's middle and essentially Impressionist period. Yet the collector had found at a comparatively early stage that, though the esteem in which they were held was at that time still inconsiderable, Monet's later works, in which the subject matter of the picture is dissolved in a lively harmony of colour, had something meaningful to say to him. A number of water-lily pictures in the collection bear testimony to this. However, the master's early period has by no means been neglected. It is impressively represented by a brilliant portrait of Camille Monet with

a little dog and an interior with artificial light, *Dinner at Sisley's*, a work that seems to foreshadow Bonnard and Vuillard. One of the most rounded and complete groups of paintings, is that formed by the Manets, for the intensely distinguished quality of Manet's art made a special appeal to the collector. Here the outstanding pictures are *Bordeaux Harbour*, painted in 1871, the grandiose *La Sultane*, which is a somewhat earlier work, the *Rue de Berne Decorated with Flags*, to which reference has already been made, *Still Life with Roses and Tulips in a Dragon Vase*, and the pastel portrait of the Viennese Irma Brunner. We must also mention a picture which has a unique place in Manet's work, *The Suicide*, a little masterpiece very reminiscent of Goya, on which – though its macabre theme might by some have been thought repellent – the collector set a very high value indeed. In the case of Degas, he refused to be limited in his choice to pastels of dancers with no great depth of meaning

219

Emil G. Bührle

THE DEATH OF HASSAN
Eugène Delacroix (1798–1863)
oil on canvas 13 × 16⅛ *ins.*
1826. An episode from
The Giaour *by Byron, who*
had a strong influence on the
work of Delacroix and
provided the subject matter for
a number of his paintings

or works deriving from the world of the racecourse, though these last must surely have had an attraction for the some-time cavalry officer. No, the most important items in this group of paintings are two portraits. That of *Madame Camus at the Piano* might well be called one of the most perfect portraits that Degas ever painted, and in it we are still conscious of the master's admiration for the severe elegance of Ingres; but in the later portrait of Count Lepic and his two little daughters, he approaches closer to the Impres-sionists both in his general style and in the way in which his composition catches the fleeting moment and seems to be almost fortuitous.

Compared with Degas, Manet and Monet, Renoir, Sisley and Pissarro occupy a rather subordinate place in the collec-tion. But they are not wholly absent. There is, for instance, Renoir's fine portrait of Mlle Irène Cahen d'Anvers, a work superbly characteristic of this delicate artist. There is also his landscape *The Harvest*, while special note should be taken of Sisley's *Regatta at Hampton Court* and of his *Land-scape at Port Marly*. One work of Pissarro's early period deserves particular mention. It is his *La Route de Versailles à Louveciennes*, which is not, as the title might suggest, a straightforward landscape, but also includes human figures, the artist's wife and daughter in the front garden of the house close to the road. How far the collector was conscious of the fact that he had given these three painters a place in his collection that was just perceptibly secondary and how far this is attributable to the circumstances that suitable offers did not happen to be forthcoming at the time, is difficult to say. Yet we shall not be wholly wrong in sus-pecting that there was an unconscious choice at work here, that the appeal of these gentler painters, which may have been much stronger in his youth before the First World War, was now less powerful. His interest now centred much more on those artists who may be regarded as having blazed the trail for modern painting, and who because of the strength of their personality measured up more closely to his own personal standard of values – Cézanne, Van Gogh, Gauguin and Toulouse-Lautrec. One of the strongest im-pressions that the collection makes upon the visitor is that produced by a kind of triptych of three of Cézanne's por-trait masterpieces, each entirely different from the others. These are *Self Portrait with Palette*, the best known version of *Boy with a Red Waistcoat*, and the portrait of Madame

PORTRAIT OF MONSIEUR DEVILLERS
Jean Auguste Dominique Ingres (1780–1867)
oil on canvas 38¼ × 30¾ ins. 1811
One of a number of portraits of the French colony
in Rome, where Ingres spent long periods of his life

Cézanne. Opposite this group, so notable for its superb discipline and classical restraint, are two early works full of passion and marked by a certain eccentricity, *The Temptation of St Anthony* and *Melting Snow at l'Estaque*. Cézanne is also well to the fore as a landscape painter, most typically in his Montagne Sainte-Victoire, already mentioned. He is less strongly represented in still life.

A number of outstanding works make it possible for us to follow Van Gogh's progress from his Dutch beginnings up till the last phase of his activity at Auvers. There is, for instance, that tremendous still life of 1884 with pumpkins and jugs, and the self-portrait from the Paris period. Above all, there is *The Sower*, painted at Arles, behind whose figure the mighty disc of the sun stands like an aureole. *The Sower* is the definitive formulation of a theme which had occupied the artist's mind for a considerable time. Something like a companion picture, which is also a contrast, to this painting, is *Les Sarcleuses (Weeders in the Snow)* which, making use of a composition of Millet's, gives expression, in a strangely etherealized blending of colours, to the artist's longing for the cool North. By the side of this picture we should place two others from Saint-Rémy: a view of the *Park of the Hospital* and the magnificent *Cornfield and Cypress Trees*, of which another version is in the Tate Gallery in London. From the earlier part of his stay in Auvers, and midway between a still life and a landscape, we have a blossoming chestnut branch, which does not show the despair visible in the later Auvers work.

It is natural enough that the collector should have been particularly attracted by Gauguin's South Sea paintings, and it is remarkable, considering how rarely they come upon the market, that he was able to acquire so many of them. From the early days in Tahiti there is *Pape Moe (Holy Water)*, and from his later sojourns in La Dominique *L'Offrande*, which represents a young mother next to a girl and is like a transposition of the Madonna theme into other terms. Both are pictures of rare beauty. Toulouse-Lautrec is another artist who is richly and worthily represented, his early period being illustrated by such works as *La Rousse*, the picture of a redhaired girl, one of those *plein air* studies which the artist painted between 1888 and 1890 and in which his sense of humanity was so happily combined with an Impressionist's sensitivity to atmosphere. There is a particularly beautiful picture from the period when the artist was painting the world of the *maisons closes*. It is the painting *Au Lit*, in which this delicate subject is treated with tact and human understanding, though wholly without sentimentality or meretricious embellishment, something that we can always take for granted in Toulouse-Lautrec's work. His later period, which in some respects already formed a link with

221

CAMILLE MONET IN THE GARDEN WITH HER SON AND HIS NURSE
Claude Monet (1840–1926)
oil on canvas 23½ × 32 ins. 1873

such artists as Rouault, is magnificently illustrated by a scene from the opera *Messalina* by Armand Silvestre and Isidore de Lara.

While the group of pictures with which we have dealt above form the heart of his collection, Emil Bührle was much too sensitive a devotee of the arts, too cultured a connoisseur and too impassioned a collector not to have reached out further. As a collector he could in the final analysis only accept as his guide that spark which leaps between a work of art and its beholder; and it was in the whole nature of the man to reach out rather than to draw in. It is easy to understand why he should not have come to a halt with the Impressionists proper, but should have extended his interest to Daumier, Courbet and Delacroix.

Courbet's simple but unerring power made a highly individual appeal to him and works by this artist appeared early in his collection, but he was also captured by the verve and pictorial magnificence of Delacroix, and the group of this master's paintings is one of the most important in the collection. The generation of French painters who followed the Impressionists also received due consideration, Bonnard and Vuillard being treated with special honour while the Neo-impressionists were not wholly neglected. Among Emil Bührle's earliest acquisitions, which he made while he was still young and had to use other resources than his own, are two watercolours by the German Expressionist Erich Heckel. This purchase dates back to 1920 when Bührle could not so much as think of acquiring a collection. When

222

Emil G. Bührle

Below: THE ROAD FROM VERSAILLES TO LOUVECIENNES
Camille Pissarro (1831–1903)
oil on canvas 40 × 32¼ ins. 1870.
The artist's wife and daughter
outside the house
where they lived from 1868 to 1870

Above: STILL LIFE WITH ROSES AND TULIPS
Edouard Manet (1832–83) oil on canvas 22 × 14⅛ ins.
One of a series of flower paintings
made in 1882–83

we reflect on this, it is not wholly surprising that, besides important works of Rouault, we should also encounter some of those of the Fauves, to say nothing of paintings by Corinth, Kokoschka, and Soutine. The admirer of Cézanne was quite ready – and such readiness was surely natural enough – to include Braque and Juan Gris. As to Picasso, he is represented by a number of early works, though special mention should be made of a classical painting *L'Italienne*, made in Rome in 1917.

Bührle the collector did not penetrate further into the present. This was not because he rejected the new; his interest in modern painting was proved by his work as President of the *Sammlungskommission* of the Kunsthaus Zürich and, in an even more profound and impressive manner, by

223

Emil G. Bührle

a remark of his to C. J. Burckhardt, 'Personally I am convinced that the ways of looking at the world are inexhaustible in their variety, and that all that is present within ourselves – and more than all – can be expressed within the changing forms which succeeding generations have evolved for this purpose.'

As against this, it was only natural that the man who had started out as an art-historian, and had the art-historian's width of horizon, should have reached back further in time. It was no mere chance that the first of the older pictures to be added to the collection should have been a Frans Hals,

a masterly picture of Christ from his later period. The rediscovery of the Haarlem master was one of the achievements of the artists and art lovers of the Impressionist generation. Bührle himself, however, was particularly fond of pointing out the relationship between Impressionism and Venetian painting. Certainly he had a warm place in his heart for Guardi, Tiepolo and Canaletto, and these artists were represented in his collection by fine examples of their work.

In later years he also concerned himself with works of a different kind. Thus he acquired a church interior by Saen-

CORNFIELD AND CYPRESSES
Vincent van Gogh (1853–90)
oil on canvas 28¾ × 36⅞ ins.
Painted at the sanatorium at St-Rémy in 1889

redam and he also discovered his affection for Ingres, a number of whose works was added to his collection in the years before his death. Among these, is the brilliant portrait of Monsieur Devillers, dating back to the painter's Roman period. There is also the portrait of Dr de France with its strange mixture of intensity and reserve.

One might almost believe that he was led to such works by the interest he developed at quite an early stage in the carving and sculpture of the Middle Ages. Here too the experiences of his youth played a part. Freiburg im Breisgau, where he studied as a young man, is full of works of mediaeval art; Strasbourg and Colmar are not far away. In addition to all this, the young student had the good fortune to have an excellent teacher in the person of Wilhelm Vege, a man with a real talent for arousing enthusiasm for the mediaeval plastic arts. It is thus not difficult to understand why in 1939 the first examples of the mediaeval plastic arts took their place next to French paintings of the nineteenth century, and that by the fifties the group of such mediaeval works of art had attained a considerable size. In a number of instances Bührle went even further back into the past; his pleasure in the art of antiquity, to quote but one example,

Emil G. Bührle

THE OFFERING
Paul Gauguin (1848–1903)
oil on canvas 27 × 31 ins. 1902.
One of a series of paintings
completed in Hiva-Oa (Marquesas Islands)
during the last year of Gauguin's life

is represented by a superb horse's head from Greece dating back to the fifth century BC.

'An art-historian is no more a predestined collector than a philologian is a predestined poet. I would much rather say that a true collector is an artist *manqué*. The work of the collector consists in very deliberate acts of choice and in the highly individual arrangement of certain works of art.' These were Bührle's own words, from a lecture delivered in 1954 on the origin of his collection. Certainly in choosing works of art, his own personal artistic experience was the determining factor. He would of course ask the opinion first of one person, then of another, and there were always the dealers, many of whom were his personal friends. But in the final analysis the decision was invariably his own and it was often quite different from what his advisers had suggested. He loved his pictures, and he had the ardent eye of the lover. When one stood beside him in front of his collection, he expressed by gesture rather than in words a direct and almost childlike pleasure in the beauty of these things. Those who were in his company at such a time knew very well that here was a man seeking a refuge from the spinning world, and that in these rooms, though they contained works of great price and of the highest quality, his purpose was a kind of inward self-communion and not any form of outward show.

'I have had to steal all the time I have spent with my pictures,' he once told a companion, 'yet their company has restored the stolen time many times over. All the moments I have spent here are moments of unlimited duration.' It was no doubt Bührle's intimate knowledge of every individual picture, his strange ability to see each divorced from its surroundings, that explained a fact which astonished many people who came prepared for an exhibition of showmanship or at least for some display of the ordinary curator's technique, for this collector cared nothing for the effect produced by his collection as a whole or for any effective arrangement of it. Part of his collection hung in the rooms of his home, but the greater part was placed in the empty rooms of a house not far away, and here they were hung quite close to one another. They might almost have been in the storage rooms of a museum. Later he often thought of putting up a special building to house his collection, but his death prevented his wish from being realized. Unfortunately he did not live to see the great exhibition which he planned to hold in the great new exhibition wing presented by him to the Kunsthaus Zürich. That exhibition, which was actually held in 1958, after his death, would have given the collector an opportunity for self-criticism and enabled him to hear the criticisms of others; it would thus have helped him in the selection of further purchases and in the planning of the final arrangement of his collection. After his death his family made over to the public the main part of the collection. By eliminating the less important pictures, they were able to arrange them suitably in the empty house which had already served the collector as a gallery.

RENÉ WEHRLI

Right: *The salon of Emil Bührle's house in Zurich, showing on the right of the door* Woman in a Red Shawl *by Degas, and Manet's* Bordeaux Harbour
Below: *A gallery in the adjacent house where the majority of the Bührle Collection is now housed, showing on the left Canaletto's* S. Maria della Salute, Venice *and over the mantelpiece* Procession in Valencia *attributed to Goya*

Nineteenth and twentieth-century paintings

A BLAZE OF MODERN COLOUR from Renoir to Matisse, against plain light walls, is salient in one's memory of the Lasker paintings, for this is a collection specifically of *paintings*, with the muted accompaniment of a few drawings. Of the several considerable, separate waves of American collectors concentrating upon the great modern revolution in French painting, 1850–1950, the Lasker Collection belongs to the very active and determinative second phase. It was preceded only by those, so to say, contemporary or near-contemporary collectors to whom the swan song of the Impressionists and early Post-Impressionists was actually a matter of personal experience. This group of early American admirers of Impressionism began collecting even before the sagest German pre-1914 collectors and was active from the last two decades of the nineteenth century to shortly after the end of the First World War. These collectors were considered as daring and eccentric in their own time as perhaps five years ago one might have thought collectors concentrating largely on Action Painting. The fact is that, although Europeans began collecting Impressionists and Post-Impressionists assiduously from about 1919 onwards, there was a relative gap in American activity after the first pioneers. It was not until about ten years later that many new, large collections were begun, and these were not fully established until the later 1930's. The most active of these new collectors were Chester Dale in New York, Robert Treat Paine in Boston, Duncan Phillips in Washington, and John Spaulding with Alvan Fuller in Boston, both of whom acquired Impressionists as well as Old Masters.

Near the chronological end of this procession, in fact during the Second World War, comes the beginning of the Lasker Collection. Indeed it presciently foreshadows the third or post-war phase of large scale American collecting in this field, which still heavily concentrates on living artists. The Lasker Collection stretches from Corot and Impressionist works by Renoir and Manet, through Toulouse-Lautrec and the late Monet waterlilies, to a series that runs from Vuillard, Rouault and Utrillo to Picasso, Matisse, Braque and even Salvador Dali, and finally on to the American Abstract-Expressionists acquired in recent years.

Such a sweep was less the result of planned eclecticism than of the curiously personal combination of Albert Davis Lasker, who started the collection, and of Mary Woodard Lasker, who helped him with it and has enlarged it interestingly since her husband's death in 1951. Albert Lasker himself came to art, like many American millionaire collectors, utterly untutored; yet unlike these other collectors, he approached it with an eye by no means untutored. He had spent a long life in the advertising business which he had conducted with such originality and talent that he is still regarded as the founder and shaper of modern advertising – in its vast, lucrative transformation from a haphazard profession into an organized marketing technique. As the head of the largest American advertising agency, he often had

· ·

INTERIOR AT NICE
Henri Matisse (1869–1954)
oil on canvas 30¾ × 31½ ins. 1924.
The artist's distant reflection can be seen
in a mirror to the left of the window

Albert and Mary Lasker

Opposite: WHITE ROSES
Vincent van Gogh (1855–90)
oil on canvas 36⅝ × 28⅜ ins. 1890.
Painted in May 1890 at St-Rémy, on the eve of his
departure for Auvers, where he died two months later

WOMAN IN RED
Henri de Toulouse-Lautrec (1864–1901)
gouache 28½ × 16 ins. 1890

to approve the illustrations and layouts for advertisements varying from magazine pages to large billboard posters. Daily application to these tasks made him rudimentarily, if informally, familiar with some idea of composition and colour, although commercial art has always lagged a good generation behind advanced artistic concepts. Years later, as an energetic collector, Albert Lasker used to say he had now finally succeeded in tracing to their origins the visual and stylistic principles he had, in his youth, only vaguely felt at work behind all applied art.

On the other hand Mary Lasker had both a professionally trained and a practical approach to art. She had studied at the University of Wisconsin and art history at Radcliffe College. After her graduation she worked for some years as an art dealer and organized – among other distinguished exhibitions – several of the best of the rare exhibitions of modern art in New York during the 1920's and 30's. Later, after her marriage to Albert Lasker, when she had long since ceased to have any connection with art, she did little or nothing to interest him in collecting (he had never bought a picture of importance for himself); she felt that a strong personality like his would better enjoy an activity he had found entirely for himself. The catalytic moment arrived when he set out to purchase a picture for a member of his family; he instantly became fascinated with the pictures he was shown in the course of this project, and needed only a few words of encouragement to go soon after to buy for himself the two best pictures he had seen – the two superb Renoirs that are still masterpieces of the present collection: *Flowers and Cats* (1881) and the *Young Girl in a Boat* (1877).

Soon the combination of Albert Lasker's naïve flair with Mary Lasker's well-educated eye began to function at a great rate. Between 1944, when the two Renoirs were purchased, and 1951, the year Albert Lasker died, they purchased over one hundred and forty pictures – some of them of course no more than small watercolours and drawings, yet including also no less than eleven Picasso oils and nine important oils by Henri Matisse. This was, however, not the wholesale buying as beloved of satirists or cinema scripts. It proceeded gradually out of a genuine enthusiasm to which was given considerable time and study. Albert Lasker had retired from business shortly after his marriage, and now he had discovered an avocation to which he and his wife gave a great deal of their time and energy.

The developing operation of their taste is interesting. Although the Manet *Portrait of Méry Laurent*, with its wonderful 'snapshot-blurred' face and Impressionist-blurred blue and beige colours, the Cézanne *Vase of Flowers*, monumental as a Venetian High Renaissance mural, and the Sisley *Seine at Bougival*, a fiery canvas which is a perfect high-key

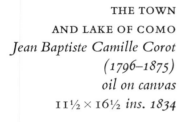

232

Albert and Mary Lasker

WOMAN IN WHITE MANTILLA
Pablo Picasso (b 1881)
oil on canvas 20 × 24 ins. 1905

chronological sequence, now runs from the Blue period up to several important works of the late 1940's. Three of the four important Braques are in what might be termed his own 'Synthetic Cubist' (to use the label usually applied to Picasso) style of the 1930's.

In continuing along this direction within the School of Paris, Albert Lasker began to echo his own lifelong interest in the theatre by somehow seeking for immortal 'stars' among the great painters who were his own contemporaries. He used to say, 'If Renoir and his contemporaries really formed taste for the next half century, I want to know the man painting today who will influence the future.' Probably his own affinity for brilliant colour added to Mary Lasker's early interest in Matisse combined to elect Matisse to that position of eminence in the minds of both the Laskers. To this may also be credited the resultant personal friendship between Matisse and the Laskers, which began with a visit of the latter to the Chapel at Vence just before it was publicly opened to the public, and which continued until Albert Lasker's death. Indeed shortly before Albert Lasker died Matisse sent him a letter illustrated with drawings and watercolours to cheer him in his hospital bed. One of the last pictures Albert Lasker purchased was Matisse's *Plum Blossoms* (1948). The faceless figure in this painting mystified the art public when it was exhibited in 1950, though now its recognition as a masterpiece seems assured.

The warm relationship that was to grow up within a brief time between the ageing Albert Lasker and the octogenarian Matisse symbolizes in many ways the intensely personal basis of this collection. The nine significant paintings by Matisse are not only a tribute to this friendship and to the Laskers' understanding of Matisse that had preceded it, but they constitute, as the major strength of their collection, one of the finest representations in any private hands of this modern master, whose free, expressionistic form and bold colour has influenced the current direction of abstraction more than any other artist. Beginning with the 1924 *Interior at Nice*, which almost hides the artist's self-portrait in the left middle-ground and prophetically proclaims the Matisse tonalities for many years to come, the chronological survey goes on through the *Spanish Woman with Flowers* (1924–25), a classic amongst the young women painted by Matisse in the 1920's and 1930's (for which the original drawing in pen and Chinese ink was also bought by the Laskers), to *The Idol* (1942), presaging the darker, more vibrant colour of the later war

plein-air painting even to its heat mists, closely followed the initial purchase of the two Renoirs, these seem to have quite early satisfied the need for Impressionist painting. The next steps are clearly seen as the result of both Albert and Mary Lasker's joint fascination with brilliant, joyous colour. Although they seem to have skipped over the perhaps all too obvious brilliance of the pure Fauves, they quickly went on to Soutine, Modigliani and the later works of Dufy, along with Chagall and Odilon Redon for more typically twentieth-century tonal expressions.

A keen awareness of the actual currents of thought of the day may well have been responsible for the rapid shifting of the Laskers' artistic focus from a period of several generations before, straight into the present. The great living personalities of the School of Paris became their next goal. Both Picasso and Braque engaged them at first and the representation of the former, although not actually acquired in

time and post-war Matisse. Nearby hang several paintings in the same manner: *Woman with Anemones* (1937), the famous *Pineapple with Anemones* (1940), and finally on to the *Plum Blossoms*, which can claim to have that final resolution and economy of means of a late Titian or a late Goya.

Still, the Laskers were no slavish followers of collectors' and museum fashion and they often made acquisitions outside the School of Paris. Their sympathy with *joie de vivre* – that quality keenly expressed by Matisse himself, who had used the same phrase as the title of one of his important early paintings – also ranged far and wide along less well-travelled routes. The three flower paintings by Fantin-Latour in the collection came perhaps less out of a purely artistic taste than as an echo of both Laskers' consuming interest in flowers.

THE MAUVE CLOTH
Georges Braque (b 1882)
oil on canvas 33½ × 35 ins. 1936

Right: STILL LIFE WITH FISHES
Pablo Picasso (b 1881)
oil on canvas 51 × 38½ ins. 1923

235

Ten works by Raoul Dufy and twenty-four watercolours by Salvador Dali seem to have captivated both collectors' feeling for brilliant colour and vivacity of subject matter, just as the four Utrillos clearly supplied a nostalgic charm to complete the diverse impression made by the collection as a whole. Along with such sophisticated decorative painting, there was also a taste for the simple bright colours of *naïfs* like Buachant, Bombois, Jean Eve and Foujita. These give vivacity and colour to the sunny walls of the Lasker house in the country where they now hang, and provide a foil to the more serious nineteenth-century works, which were added later, as important examples became available in the growing seller's market in this field. They include distinguished works by Cézanne, Boudin and Toulouse-Lautrec. The greatest triumphs in this rarefied area, however, were the two magnificent paintings by Van Gogh, which were acquired against ardent competition at astronomical prices, as the development of the collection was passing its halfway mark: the famous vehemently present *Zouave* (August 1888), the full-length portrait of the artist's Arles friend and bugler in the Zouave regiment; and the still more famous *White Roses*, painted at Saint Rémy in May 1890 – the often reproduced upright composition of the great tumbling cascade of roses. To come upon these in the Lasker drawing room is a little like the moment of one's very first glance at the *Mona Lisa*, accompanied by that strange feeling of not being quite sure that one is actually looking at the original of the pictures so long familiar through countless large facsimile reproductions.

In our day when fashionable taste has concentrated on expensive works by the Impressionists and Post-Impressionists alone, it was perhaps more individual to have bought in a wide range of schools. The truth simply is that the Lasker pictures were acquired out of deep affection for works of art rather than along any pre-dictated lines – the true result of a combination of the natural flair of one partner with the educated eye of the other.

The additions which Mary Lasker has made to the collection since her husband's death echo the same degree of real artistic involvement. Her first purchase alone happens to have been an exceptionally handsome Ingres portrait drawing. Then after a long interim she has recently become interested in American painters of the 1950's and 1960's who are mature exponents of the Abstract Expressionist School which developed in post-war New York, as well as in a few Europeans like Soulages and Mathieu, who are stylistically related. These newest acquisitions include two important works by the late Franz Kline, two large canvases by Mark Rothko, as well as two large-scale works by Adolph Gottlieb and a half dozen by other artists – all characteristically

Albert and Mary Lasker

MERY LAURENT IN A VEIL
Edouard Manet (1832–83)
pastel, gouache and oil 22 × 13½ ins. c 1882

Right: PLUM BLOSSOMS
Henri Matisse (1869–1954)
oil on canvas 45⅝ × 35 ins. 1948

236

huge canvases. Originally they were purchased to hang, not in the already-filled houses in New York City and in the country, but in Mary Lasker's office where she deals with her philanthropic affairs and those of the Lasker Foundation, initiated by Albert and Mary Lasker mainly for medical research. However, the enormous scale of these paintings turned out to be too great for these offices and they now hang either as long-term loans to several American museums or as a special loan at the United States Mission to the United Nations where they have become international representatives of contemporary American art.

In the New York town house on Beekman Place which overlooks the East River with a half-marine, half-industrial view, the major paintings of the Lasker Collection fill the house almost as they did when Albert and Mary Lasker had together completed the collection. Although the walls are filled there is no sense of crowding. The furnishing of each room is relatively simple and has been kept to an extremely light, quite pale colour scheme, even to the walls, so that the brilliance of the paintings really becomes the chief motif of the interior architecture. The same scheme has been kept in the country house ninety miles north of New York City in the Berkshire Hills. To allow the paintings to speak boldly for themselves without any accents of 'interior decoration' has been the consistent rule.

Not the least interesting aspect of Albert Lasker's collecting has been the continuity which it engendered. Like many recent converts, he became a relentless, even aggressive proselytizer for the art which had given him so much pleasure in the later years of his life. As a man long influential in the business, social and political life of the entire United States, he had friends far and wide across the American continent, and he influenced many of them to begin to collect with fervour, achieving a success that a Duveen might have envied had he been in the least interested in modern painting.

But the most immediate beneficiaries of Albert Lasker's collector's zeal were his own family. One of his sisters began to collect quite late in life and she has since bequeathed distinguished works by, of course, Matisse and by his contemporaries to American museums and to institutions in Israel. His children, notably his two daughters, have by now accumulated outstanding American collections and are very active in the affairs of their local museums, in Chicago and Los Angeles. Their collections are continually growing and being improved on by exchanges and substitutions. Thus, as was the case with older European collections, but is rare nowadays, a real sense of continuity has been established, and the artistic ideas put into effect when Albert Lasker bought his first painting scarcely twenty years ago continue to exert their influence.   ALFRED FRANKFURTER

OPHELIA *Odilon Redon (1840–1916)*
pastel 25 × 36 ins. c1905.
One of a number of 'dream' pictures by Redon,
who was a leading Symbolist painter

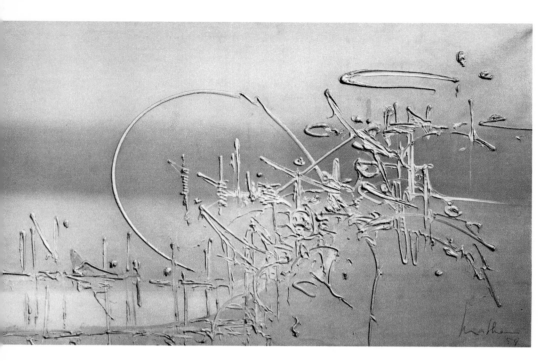

Albert and Mary Lasker

VINAYA
Georges Mathieu (b 1921)
oil on canvas 58 × 36 ins.
1958

Below: THREE SUNS
Adolph Gottlieb (b 1903)
oil on canvas 72 × 90 ins. 1960

Objets d'art by Fabergé

A SEASONED COLLECTOR may have gathered around him the furnishings, silver and porcelain he most admires. The shelves of his library may support volume after volume of his favourite literature, and the walls of his home may be hung with paintings by the artists that lie nearest to his heart. Yet with all this, he may still hunger for some small, precious and light-hearted objets d'art with which to ornament his home. It is exactly this need for which the creations of Carl Fabergé have so often supplied an answer, and they are superbly represented in the collection belonging to Helen and Lansdell Christie. They are unselfconscious objects of luxury never losing their sense of informality, off-duty pieces which reconcile the wealthy to their wealth in a relaxed, good-natured manner, with never a hint of moral accusation to cause discomfiture and there is nothing about them of arrogance or ostentation.

The materials used by Carl Fabergé and his craftsmen were chosen entirely on grounds of their suitability for the particular task in hand; their intrinsic worth was their least interesting attribute. One of the loveliest pieces in this extraordinary collection, a dandelion plant, illustrates the point most eloquently. The 'seed clock' is made of asbestos fibre sprinkled with tiny rose diamonds and the gossamer effect is quite enchanting and completely naturalistic.

The Christies have built up this glittering array of art objects in the short space of about five years, for, once they had been fired with admiration for the brilliance of Fabergé's objects, their curiosity and interest grew rapidly. Lansdell Christie himself, an outstandingly relaxed and amiable character, never appears unduly concerned about the outcome of any of his operations, whether concerned with some

matter of business or the purchase of a Fabergé Easter Egg. But it becomes increasingly clear with personal acquaintance that once he has taken a firm decision in either field his efforts are generally crowned with dramatic success. He has charmed some of the finest pieces in the collection, which would not normally have come on the market, from dealers and private collectors, not merely by financial negotiation, but by his infectious personality allied to a quiet determination. It was entirely characteristic that the Christies should have made the opening ceremony of the Fabergé exhibition at the Metropolitan Museum in New York a festive occasion, and the present writer, upon whom fell the honour of lecturing about the St Petersburg goldsmith, recalls the real pleasure they had in discussing the merits of their favourite pieces with their many friends.

It is hardly necessary to set down a detailed history of the house of Fabergé. The outlines are well known: how the Huguenot family, victims of savage religious persecution, were obliged to abandon their home in Picardy after the revocation of the Edict of Nantes in 1685. Eventually, after years of wandering as refugees through Europe and the Baltic States, Carl Fabergé's father, Gustav, was able to set himself up in a small goldsmith's and jeweller's shop in St Petersburg in 1842.

Four years later Carl Gustavovitch was born, and after a thorough general education, embarked on an elaborate pilgrimage around the museums and palaces of Europe to supplement his recent training as a goldsmith by studying works of earlier periods. When he was only twenty-four, he took over control in 1870 of his father's humdrum but flourishing business and revolutionized it. He turned away

Left: *Chanticleer Egg probably presented to the Dowager Empress Marie Feodorovna by Nicholas II. The diamond-set cockerel rises from the interior of the egg automatically at each hour, flaps its wings and crows. When it has announced the time it disappears inside the grille which closes down over the top of the egg. Height 11 ins. c 1903*

Spring Flowers Egg presented to Marie Feodorovna by her husband Alexander III. The enamelled egg parts to reveal the delicately carved flower basket. Height of egg 3 ins. Height of basket 1 5/16 ins. 1885–90

Lansdell K. Christie

Opposite: Top left: *Basket of lilies of the valley in gold, oriental pearls and nephrite. Height 3 ¼ ins.*

Top right: *Small strawberry-coloured Easter egg in translucent enamel. The yolk conceals a gold hen, which in turn contains a tiny folding easel, with a portrait diamond. Height 2 ¼ ins. 1898*

Bottom: *A group of Fabergé fruit and flower studies with a Siberian nephrite watering can in the centre*

Right: *Gold musical box presented to the Prince and Princess Youssoupoff on their twenty-fifth wedding anniversary. Height 2 ⅝ ins.*

more and more from the manufacture and sale of jewellery, hitherto the mainstay of the firm, and started designing decorative objects which offered far more scope for his adventurous imagination. This was the greatest gamble of Fabergé's career, but it came off, and it was a gamble that paid handsome dividends both artistically and materially. Art objects, he contended, should be judged by the beauty of their craftsmanship, not by the value of their ingredients. To this end he exploited the natural hardstones that were mined principally in the Urals, the Caucasus and Siberia, and he exulted in the technical skill of his craftsmen, who by fusing different alloys were able to produce gold of varying shades. Fabergé's greatest achievement was probably his revival of the complicated eighteenth-century craft of translucent enamelling over a previously engine-turned surface. He gathered around him the finest lapidaries, chasers, setters, engravers, gilders, and enamellers, as well as designers, to help him carry out his ambitious and highly imaginative projects.

After the first Imperial Easter Egg was designed and presented to the Tsarina in 1884, the Tsar Alexander III, a man quick to recognize an original talent, granted Fabergé his Imperial Warrant of Appointment. From then on it was a story of unbroken success, of prizes at International Exhibitions, world-wide acclaim and an increasing number of commissions from eager patrons in countries as widely spread as Great Britain, India and China.

Fabergé acquired generously designed premises in St Petersburg's fashionable Morskaya Street, where he could accommodate under one roof all the separate small workshops, each of which was controlled by its own master. The advantages of this arrangement were enormous, allowing the craftsmen to consult among themselves during the execution, for example, of some complicated project demanding the skills of several technicians, while preserving a sense of independence and personal achievement within each workshop. Carl Fabergé himself presided over this hive of activity, designing, surveying, checking and finally judging each object before it was entitled to bear the housemark and be offered for sale in the ground floor showroom.

Fabergé was obsessed by a love of the miniature, and his toys, apart from their miraculous delicacy of fashion, provide a fascinating comment on his epoch. The exquisitely enamelled sedan chair in the Christie Collection and the watering can carved in dark green Siberian jade, are two splendid and original examples of this taste for the minuscule, and the world is the richer for the presence of these completely original masterpieces of applied art.

As in all good anthologies, there is in this beautiful collection a distinct and readily discernible bias. Helen and Lansdell Christie favour those objects which have been fired with the translucent enamels for which the House of Fabergé was so justly famed. Works in other media are, however, also well represented; indeed, one of the rarest treasures in the collection is the celebrated model of Vara Panina, the gypsy singer, realistically executed in semi-precious stones.

243

In spite of her extreme ugliness, this luckless entertainer could keep audiences entranced nightly at Moscow's *tzigane* restaurant Yar by the extraordinary range and beauty of her voice. When her love for a member of the Imperial Guard was unrequited, she took poison and died at his feet singing 'My heart is breaking'. Another particularly attractive figure among the treasures owned by the Christies is the little coachman which is quite simply designed as a cone in lapis lazuli of superb colour.

Among several splendid gold presentation boxes, one supreme example is of translucent chartreuse-yellow enamel encased in a coloured gold trellis with black-enamelled diamond-set double-headed Romanoff eagles. The sheer cloth-of-gold *richesse* of the box must have caused Nicholas II to catch his breath when he received it as a coronation gift from the hand of his Tsarina, Alexandra Feodorovna.

The collection is rich in these specially commissioned gold presentation boxes, which were designed more to impress and dazzle by their pomp than merely to delight by their charm. Two examples in particular deserve special mention. One is the magnificent *bleu-de-roi* box, set with a lattice of diamonds, which was made for the lovely Elisabeth Balletta of the Imperial Michel Theatre, an *innamorata* of both the Grand Duke Alexis and his nephew, the Tsar Nicholas II. Another important piece, the Youssoupoff Box, which contains a musical movement set snugly in the interior, is superbly enamelled *en grisaille* in the best Louis XVI manner. An entrancing jade box, set with diamond 'frost' mounts, was once, without doubt, a gift to a lady at one of Doctor Emanuel Nobel's famous dinner parties. This gentleman, a nephew of Alfred Nobel, loved this particular *motif* and insisted that it be incorporated in some form in all of the many presents he gave. Other boxes in the Christie Collection are enamelled in subtle shades of pink, mauve, grey and blue over different patterns of machine-engraving which we call engine turning.

The fan illustrated here must surely be accounted a technical triumph of a very high order. It is composed of many delicately balanced elements harmonizing felicitously together: opalescent oyster and pale blue enamels, four shades of gold on the stick and inlaid in the iridescent mother of pearl ribs, intricately worked Brussels lace and here and there the occasional flash of an individually set diamond.

Fabergé's studies of flowers, like the dandelion, set casually in a clear rock crystal pot carved in the round to give the illusion of being partially filled with water, are often highly naturalistic. Yet they are also selective, and by their crystalline simplicity and clarity of design they escape the banality of photographic representations. In conception more conventionalized, the little basket of lilies-of-the-valley is a charming essay in various materials; the basket is plaited in gold wire and is filled with granulated gold moss from which rise engraved gold stalks bearing lily flowers of oriental pearls and leaves of delicately reeded Siberian jade. Fabergé carried this use of the pearl one stage further away from naturalism in the jewelled swan. This exploitation of the intriguing form and lustrous quality of a large baroque pearl is a tour-de-force in pure Renaissance taste.

Fabergé's feeling for *matière* is to be seen again and again in his entrancing stone animals and birds, notably in the obsidian bison so tenderly carved, with its muzzle, horns and hooves brightly polished. The use of obsidian for this carving is characteristic of Fabergé's unerring instinct for the most suitable material for a particular project; this volcanic glass, when polished, imparts a wonderfully soft silver-grey translucence which gives an added sense of liveliness to the carving as a whole. But, above all, this bison is a superb illustration of the Russian craftsman at his most naturalistic.

His animal sculptures fall into two distinct manners. His

Gold whistle. Length 1¼ *ins.*

Opposite: Top: *A group of enamelled cigarette cases shown with examples in dark green nephrite and pink rhodenite on the left*

Opposite: Bottom left: *Coronation presentation box given by the Tsarina to her husband Nicholas II on Easter Day 1897. The lid is decorated with black enamelled Romanoff double-headed eagles and the Imperial cypher. Height* 1 15/16 *ins.*

Opposite: Bottom right: *Enamelled and decorated snuff-box, the lid painted with an allegorical scene. Height* 1 5/16 *ins.*

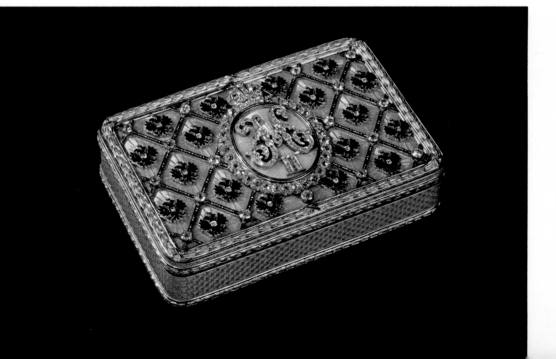

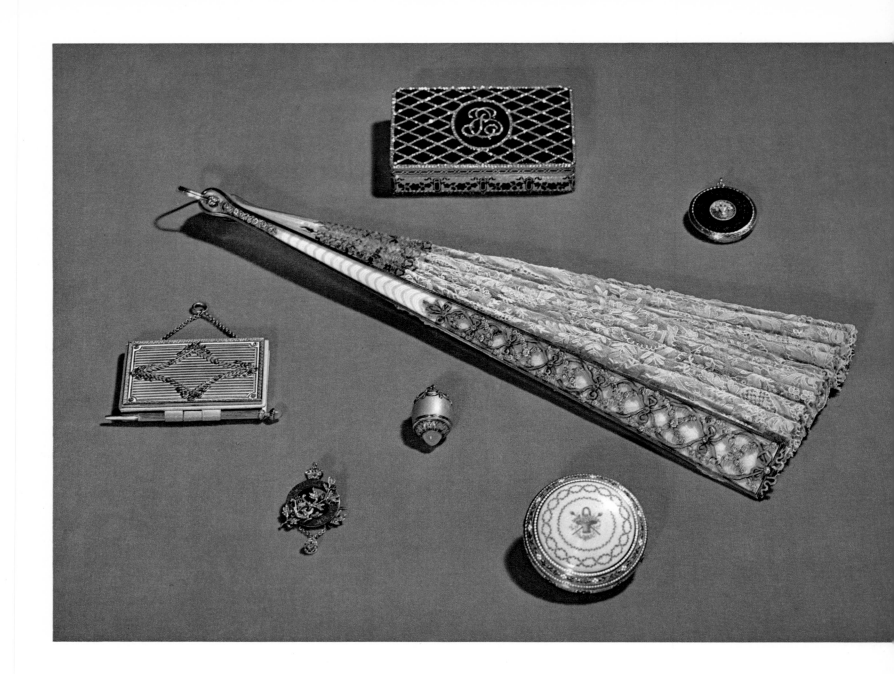

Lansdell K. Christie

Opposite: top: *Gold fan decorated with translucent enamels
and coloured golds, with above it a vanity box given
to Madame Balletta and a small circular powder box.
Below it, a carnet, an Imperial brooch, an Easter egg pendant set
with a moonstone and a domed* bonbonnière *decorated in opalescent enamel*

Opposite: bottom left: *A pair of swivel seals, the one on the left
in cornelian and gold and the one on the right an Imperial
seal in nephrite and gold. Height 2⅛ and 1⅜ ins.*

Opposite: bottom right: *A carved obsidian bison,
with a matt surface, except for the brightly polished muzzle,
horns and hooves. Height 3 ins.*

Above: *A group of animal sculptures*
Below: *A goose carved in bowenite
with ruby eyes. Height 4⅞ ins.*

Lansdell K. Christie

Top right: *A crouching frog carved in jadeite with gold-set rose diamond eyes. Height 3 9/16 ins.*

Right: *A cigarette case in Siberian nephrite with diamond mounts. Height 1 1/16 ins. Beside it a carved figured agate boar's head box mounted in gold, set with diamond eyes and thumb piece and gold tusks. Length 3 1/4 ins.*

Below left: *Enamelled* bonbonnière, *hand seal and gum pot. The handle of the seal is set with a moonstone finial and the white chalcedony sealing stone is engraved with the initials of Queen Victoria of Spain*

Below right: *An ibis carved in agate with gold legs and bill. Height 2 3/4 ins.*

uncompromisingly realistic studies live in an entirely different world from that of his more freely and imaginatively expressed 'cartoon' animals, which are stylized in much the same way as the Japanese treat their *netsuké,* or the delightful highly finished watercolour studies of parrots made by the young Edward Lear, humorous, sympathetic and intensely personal utterances. The carved bowenite goose, with its bell and low-slung undercarriage, its inquisitive backward look and beady ruby eye, epitomizes very well the special quality of engaging good-natured charm that Fabergé's carvers were able to wrest from small pieces of semi-precious hardstone.

For sheer majesty it would be difficult to surpass the Chanticleer Egg, an Imperial gift conceived on truly noble lines in the Sèvres manner; regularly on the hour, a grille on the top flies open and a brightly enamelled cockerel slowly rises, flaps its wings and crows the time. The tiny Spring-flowers Easter Egg, also an ornament of the Christie Collection, is in complete contrast, with its prettiness and delicacy.

Another Easter Egg of strawberry-coloured translucent enamel over a *guilloché* field, was designed in 1898 for Alexander Ferdinandovitch Kelch to present to his wife, a lady, it seems, who fancied herself as a sort of Tsarina in her own right. This ingenious confection opens to reveal the egg-white and yolk and, opened again, a hen inside, which in turn contains an easel supporting a portrait diamond.

The Christie Collection, an extraordinary group of unashamedly costly *objets-de-luxe,* is fully representative of the great Russian goldsmith's craft, and has the distinction of being the first to have been the subject of exhibitions in major museums, initially in the Corcoran Gallery of Art, Washington, in 1961 and then in 1962 in the Metropolitan Museum, New York. In an age dedicated to the mediocre, they have an instantaneous and welcome tonic effect on those fortunate enough to see them in the beautiful home of Lansdell Christie and his charming wife.

A. KENNETH SNOWMAN

Antiquities, paintings and furniture

I FEEL A CERTAIN HESITATION in introducing this collection, since nothing has so far been published about it and in many ways it lies outside my own particular field. Many people collect works of art as a form of social ostentation, guided by changes of fashion and the advice of experts, but the true art lover trusts his own instincts and is naturally inclined to be secretive, for he cannot display his treasures without giving something of himself away; his collection is to him a living thing, a tangible expression of his own personality. The slightest sign of qualified approval, or, worse, indifference on the part of other people towards something with which he has identified himself absolutely, wounds him deeply and increases his aversion to the society of those who do not share his tastes. 'L'objet d'art,' wrote Edmond de Goncourt, 'dégoûte du forum. Il se fait en vous un égoisme spirituel et idéal.'

A collection is often focussed on some obsessive interest and is confined to a specialised field in which it becomes imperative to fill the gaps. The collector who suffers from an 'objective' fixation of this kind is prey to an obsession that will not let him rest. But there is a higher form of collecting, which could be called 'subjective'. In this case the owner remains master of his collection, since it evolves and changes at the same time as himself, reflecting the development of his own tastes and interests, or rather of his inner personality with its constant factors, its anxieties and its changing attitudes. It is fascinating to trace the origin, direction and development of a collection of this kind.

In the world of Jean Davray's social origins, collecting was considered something of a status symbol. He retains active control of his business affairs, but devotes a large part of his time to prolific activity as a novelist, essayist and dramatist. As an adolescent, when his precocious literary gift was already evident, he began to collect rare books and autographs, manuscripts of past writers, soon adding to them those of contemporary authors whom he admired and with whom he came increasingly into contact. He became equally interested in painting and the plastic arts and in 1937 wrote a biography of Michelangelo, in which he expressed his ardent love of beauty.

After the upheavals of the war years the need to gather works of art round him became for him a matter of immense importance and was not simply an idle wish to impress society. It was then that he found an appropriate setting for his collection, one which combined intimacy with magnificence – an apartment once inhabited by *fermiers-généraux*, which he had restored with enormous care by craftsmen from Versailles. In this setting the fine pieces of furniture with which Jean Davray loves to surround himself, found their right place and their justification. In the principal salon the beauty of each individual object is enhanced by the harmony of their arrangement – something which he considers to be of the first importance.

One of the most valuable pieces, which stands in a group

· ·

WOMAN AND BOY STANDING BY A SAILING BOAT
Pablo Picasso (b1881)
pen and ink 11 × 7¼ *ins. 1903*

251

Jean Davray

DANS LE JARDIN
Edouard Vuillard (1868–1940)
oil on canvas 18⅞ × 15⅜ *ins.* c 1900

CAUSERIE
Edgar Degas (1834–1917)
oil on canvas 23⅝ × 19⅝ ins. c 1885

with four armchairs made by Louis Delanois, all with their original upholstery, is a *guéridon* bearing the stamp of Carlin and coming from the Dubois-Chefdebien collection. An almost identical piece, with curved feet, a basket top and a band of plaques in soft paste Sèvres, is in the Louvre. A limited number of such pieces were made between 1770 and 1780 – four or five are to be found in private collections – and they are among the outstanding achievements of French cabinetmaking. The salon also contains some fine and rare pieces of porcelain, including some Louis XV wall-brackets with parrots in Mennecy china, several objects with bronze and gold mounts in *porcelaine de Saxe*, including a small *jardinière* with flowers from Vincennes, which may have once belonged to Madame de Pompadour. The splendour of this stately salon, with its *Régence* chairs and painted cupboard by Tuard, reveals Monsieur Davray's understanding of the art of furnishing a room to be used for social gatherings. At one end, and setting the tone, is an admirable late

canvas (*c*1635) by Rubens, a portrait of a fair-haired young woman, haughty, distinguished, full of life but somewhat mysterious. Rubens is painting incarnate, summing up all its ancient magic and anticipating future trends.

Jean Davray's choice in the field of painting is singularly consistent and reveals his uncompromising taste. He picks only works of exceptional freshness, which have been jealously preserved, and sheltered from exhibitions and changes of ownership, and which, however daring their innovations, still show a classic mastery. Thus Impressionism is represented by two Renoirs: a landscape (1873) and a portrait (1878); Cubism by two canvases by Juan Gris, its purest interpreter: a moving *Maternity* (1922) and an accomplished *Still Life* (1926). Renoir, heir to Rubens and the French eighteenth century, brought Impressionism to its full flowering, relating form to light and involving his figures in the full play of sunlight. The sensitive and finely-chiselled features of Lestringuez, the hypnotist and cabbalist, one of

Jean Davray

Above: LA MAJA GALANTEADA
and LA LECTURA DE LA CARTA
Francisco de Goya y Lucientes (1746–1828)
3½ × 3½ ins. Two from a series of forty
miniatures. Painted on ivory by Goya
during the winter of 1824–25

Opposite: LA RÉSISTANCE INUTILE
Jean Honoré Fragonard (1732–1806)
sepia wash over charcoal heightened with watercolour
13¾ × 9⅛ ins.

Renoir's most intimate friends in his youth, who went with him to Algeria in 1881, are portrayed with great verve and sympathy. The brushwork, flexible and light as in a water-colour, catches both the play of light and the movement of life itself. This masterpiece came straight from the Lestringuez family.

Degas, temperamentally the very reverse of Renoir, was the most complex and exciting personality among the Im-pressionists, with his unrelenting quest for a synthesis be-tween line and colour, between the classical tradition and the most advanced modernism. Dissatisfied with a first ver-sion of his painting entitled *Bouderie* or *Causerie* (1873–75), now in the Metropolitan Museum in New York, Degas painted it again some time later (about 1885) in a larger ver-sion with a more natural and intimate composition. When the contents of Degas' studio were sold, this painting was ac-quired by Georges Viau and now it belongs to Jean Davray. It displays the essential qualities of Degas' art, boldness of treatment and a search for visual truth. His friend the sculp-tor Bartholomé is said to have posed for the brooding father, a figure which is contrasted with the delightful young girl.

A tiny yet monumental still life of apples (about 1877) by Cézanne has all the richness of colour and density of con-struction that mark the peak of his maturity. This painting comes from the former Durand-Ruel collection.

Gauguin, as is well known, was a great admirer of Cé-zanne, Renoir and Degas, and was a source of inspiration to the Nabi painters. In October 1888 Serusier showed his astonished fellow students at the Académie Julian the famous Pont-Aven 'talisman' and after the exhibition at the Café Volpini in the spring of 1889, during the Universal Exhibi-tion, Maurice Denis hailed Gauguin as the 'unchallenged leader' of the new movement. According to Thadée Natan-son, the Nabis then decided to buy between them a painting by Gauguin which they could enjoy in turns. The fine *Breton Landscape*, dated 1889, by Gauguin of which Jean Davray is justly proud, comes directly from the Vuillard estate, and because, unlike many others, it has never been cleaned, it still has a decorative luxuriance and nostalgic charm all its own. No less fascinating is Vuillard's *In the Gar-den* (c 1900), which shows Missia Sert with Cipa Godebski. The southern clarity and classicism of Bazille fits in well with the character of the collection. Before either Cézanne, Seurat or Renoir, he took up the male nude, which had been neglected since David, and set it in the open air – for in-stance in his studies of bathers. *Le Pêcheur à l'Epervier*, dated July 1868, is a vigorous painting which succeeds in render-ing both the brilliance of light and the plastic majesty of the human body. Besides these major canvases, there are in the Davray collection some fine *Fauve* paintings by

255

Above: A MAN WEARING A WIG AND A
TRICORN HAT; TWO SKETCHES OF A HAND
Antoine Watteau (1684–1721) black and red chalk
9½ × 6¾ ins.

Right: PORTRAIT OF A WOMAN
Peter Paul Rubens (1577–1640)
oil on canvas 25¼ × 19⅝ ins. c 1635

257

Jean Davray

Above: *Silver plate, inlaid with gold,*
representing a royal horseman in a lion hunt.
Diameter 8⅞ ins.
Iran, Sassanian Empire, 4th century AD

Head of an Achemenid king or prince
in turquoise, originating from Persepolis.
Sculpture in the round
is rare in Achemenid art.
Height 4¾ ins. Iran. 5th century BC

Opposite left: *Gold goblet from Amlach*
depicting lions attacking rams.
The design is set in two panels
between lines of decorative work. Height 4¾ ins.
Iran. 10th century BC

Opposite right: *Protome of a crouching ibex*
in solid gold. Height 4½ ins. Southern Iran.
Late 6th century BC

Vlaminck, and works by Utrillo and Modigliani. Of contemporary painters, only Nicolas de Staël is accepted without reservation.

Jean Davray's choice of drawings is no less strict. 'A taste for fine drawings,' Foçillon said, 'is one of the higher refinements of the mind.' It is also a distinguishing mark of great art lovers that they can appreciate both the directness and the infinite nuances of drawing. Watteau's use of red and black chalk, a technique which goes back to Fouquet and became more current with Bellange, gives his drawings a flawless grace and precision. The *Head of a Man Wearing a Wig and Tricorn Hat*, with its slightly blurred profile, is set between two studies of hands – one open and the other holding a walking-stick – the sort of study which, whether done in realistic terms or a more inspired vein, proclaims the authorship of Watteau. The man, who also appears in a drawing in the Musée Jacquemart-André in Paris, may well be Julienne. Fragonard used red chalk only for landscapes; for his witty *genre* scenes he drew in black chalk first, then added a sepia wash and some touches of watercolour. Monsieur Davray's *La Résistance Inutile* is a brilliant and famous drawing which belonged in turn to F. Villot, curator at the Louvre and a friend of Delacroix, to A. Michel-Lévy and then to David-Weill.

In a letter of May 1825, Goya, then in his eighties, wrote to his friend Ferrer that during the previous winter, when he had moved to Bordeaux, he had painted some forty miniatures on ivory – not portraits, as usual, but fantastic scenes,

more original efforts, 'closer to Velasquez than to Mengs', as he says. The two miniatures belonging to Jean Davray must form part of this strange and little known series, now dispersed, which was contemporary with the Tauromachia lithographs and with the last drawings, which are so striking because of their freedom. In the same proud tradition as Goya is Picasso, who is represented here by some fine drawings, together with Seurat, Renoir, Modigliani, Suzanne Valadon and many other masters, old and modern.

In December 1961 Jean Davray disposed of the magnificent collection of books and autographs which he had assembled with such enthusiasm over the years, and of which there is an impressive catalogue. He retained for himself only two or three exceptionally rare pieces, such as Molière's autograph, while the Bibliothèque Nationale received the only established portrait of Pascal – the red chalk drawing by Domat, which once belonged to Barrès. What was the reason for this decision? With age and experience Jean Davray judges men more severely and has come to look on literary fame as something fragile and over-valued. On the other hand, his growing love of beautiful objects has led to an unexpected expansion of his collection. In the face of the spiritual and social confusion today, Jean Davray felt the need for order and discipline and so decided to go back to the sources of classicism which are fundamental to Western culture. Abandoning Impressionism and the eighteenth century, Monsieur Davray went back to the Renaissance (Limoges enamels, a bust by Rizzo, centaurs by Giovanni da Bologna),

Jean Davray

A Louis XVI cupboard signed Tuard,
with painted decoration, attributed to Rousseau.
Height 69 ins.

to the Classical and pre-Classical art of Greece (head from Olympia, Attic head of a horse, Mycenaean gems), and finally to Persia, whose role of assimilation and humanisation in the Eastern world was very similar to that of Greece for the West. In a few years he has assembled a fabulous collection of Iranian objects in gold and other precious materials, ranging from the Medes to the Sassanids, a collection unparallelled outside the museums of Teheran and New York. Amongst his most outstanding pieces is the head of an Achemenid king or prince from the region of Persepolis, carved in turquoise, which apart from its aesthetic appeal has the rare distinction of being carved in the round instead of, as is usual, in relief. Two heads of tigers with open jaws, one in turquoise and the other in hard stone, still show Assyrian characteristics. The gold objects, on the contrary – the protome of a lion, the sparrow-hawk's head, the two magnificent ibexes, one crouching like a wild beast and the other stretched out like an insect – are classic examples of Achemenid art, that is to say, specifically Iranian. The barbaric violence of most primitive portrayals of animals is restrained here by the decorative sumptuousness of the material and the technical mastery of the goldsmiths. The three gold goblets, decorated with lions and deer, with plaited bands or the tree of life, and the gold protome of a tiger, are examples of the earlier, mysterious art of Amlach (provisionally dated as ninth or tenth century BC), which has only recently been discovered, and was first shown en masse at the Exhibition of Iranian Art in Paris in the winter of 1961–62. Amlach was a community of farmers and cattle breeders in the mountainous region south-west of the Caspian Sea, away from the main trading routes. This accounts for the unique quality of the art of this region, which has an amazingly 'modern' feeling and, as with the bronzes from Luristan, shows the influence of the steppes rather than that of Mesopotamia.

A collector's taste is revealed as much by what he rejects as by what he selects. Jean Davray excludes the art of the Middle Ages and the Far East, and all the currently fashionable, baroque, expressionistic, naïve or exotic forms of expression which reflect the crisis in the history of that Western classicism to which he remains unswervingly faithful. True, his collection is still in the making and therefore liable to new and unforeseeable extensions, but its tendency is already strongly marked, for it centres upon the Mediterranean, from pre-Sumerian civilization to Picasso. JEAN LEYMARIE

The study in Jean Davray's Paris apartment.
From left to right: Pêcheur à l'Epervier *by* Frédéric Bazille;
in the corner cupboard, three sixteenth-century Limoges
enamel plates; Causerie *by Degas and* Dans le Jardin
by Vuillard; above the mantelpiece, Breton Landscape
by Gauguin and Apples *by Cézanne; on the mantelpiece*
a 5th-century BC *marble head of an ephebe from Olympia,*
standing between two centaurs by Jean de Bologne;
in the hearth, two pigeons in painted ceramic by Picasso;
on the right, Portrait of M. Lestringuez
and Le Petit Bras de la Seine *by Renoir*

Head of a horse in patinated bronze.
Height 7½ ins. Attic.
5th century BC

James Hooper

The art of primitive peoples

THE HOOPER COLLECTION began with a spear given to James Hooper by his father in 1908. The schoolboy was fascinated, as we all have been, with the romantic stories of the great prairies, the wild bush of Africa, and the islands of the wide ocean. Who were the people who inhabited these lands? What were the weapons which the intrepid adventurers of the story books had to face? Here was the first one to come to the hands of one of the most discriminating collectors of our time.

It was not so many years later that the boy was handling weapons himself, as a teen-age soldier on the Western Front in the First World War. Amid the mud and horror, the world of the primitive heroes suddenly came alive. The young man found himself in a world where men had to rely on each other in closely knit units of soldierly comradeship for their safety and success. Even more than in primitive tribal society, man was surrounded by imminent danger at the hands of other men. Suddenly a new link was forged between present and past. The little collection of primitive weapons seemed very modern when home on leave from the Front.

Then came the new peace, peace in a world which was never to go back to its old ideas. Already in 1906, the artists had discovered primitive art. This held an excitement of form and rhythm which had not been shared by the world of convention around them. Quite apart from the coteries of the young painters there were an increasing number of ethnologists following the path of General Pitt Rivers, who collected ethnological specimens a generation earlier. They looked at the art of primitive peoples as an expression of a human culture. To them these works were not art, but rather the objects of everyday life belonging to peoples whose culture must reflect that of our ancestors as they progressed from the age of stone tools, to the use of metals, and on to Western civilisation as we know it. It was this aspect of mankind which really inspired the development of the Hooper Collection. What were these objects? How were they used? By 1930 gods, demons, and children's dolls were standing among the spears and war drums. The collection had begun to reflect more than arms and the excitements of youth. In the objects of belief and love the collector began to discern the other values which we simply describe as Art.

Mr Hooper was now a professional man. He was deeply absorbed in his work and when at home found an equal absorption in gathering together his collection. Even the simplest object changes its nuances as its story is being revealed. Half a coconut, polished smooth, has a beauty of its own. The modern abstract painter would delight in the surface with its differing grain and subtle interplay of soft colour. But when it has a lining of opaque amber colour showing it was once used for drinking kava, and then on one side is sewn a fibre fringe for wiping the mouth of the drinker, one is taken into another world of formal ceremony. This is a drinking cup from Fiji. It is something beautiful and something rare, something also, of which we have knowledge.

The interplay of cultural and aesthetic considerations is for most of us a process which develops apart from consciousness. The meaning of these objects grows through study, but eventually one becomes aware that there are other values on the aesthetic plane. This shows itself in the

mind of the collector as a selective judgement, which usually takes the form of a question: Shall I, or shall I not, retain this particular piece in my already fast growing collection? If it fills a gap in a developmental series, well and good, but if two specimens of equal importance in the series present themselves the one having superior aesthetic value is chosen. This matter of aesthetic value is not often expressed in intellectual terms, quite rightly because it is not a matter of the intellect, but of a subjective judgement. But what is important is that in the final analysis many of these judgements will concur. Although fashions change there remains a select group of objects of all or any period which the great majority of people will accept as beautiful and pleasing to them.

Such considered selection over half a century of collecting has worked in freedom on the Hooper Collection. It was very much a personal collection entirely the work of one man, not attempting to follow a fashion or copy a museum. It found its own way through the personality of the collector. In sales and exchanges, searches often covering hundreds of miles, and the unexpected discovery next door, the collection was brought together entirely from British sources. None of it was fresh from the field, but all of it had been originally acquired by explorers and collectors while the artists of that particular region were actively producing work unspoiled by the infiltration of the fashionable standards of Europe.

More and more the collection came to represent the truly native arts of the lands which gave them birth. Older pieces were sought after, and as they were found it became clear that they were fresher and more natural than the sophisticated works of the period of culture contact. Man in a state of independence had been free to express his tribal ideals.

Often the research of the collector led to rescue operations. Too often the result of a search for the family of some old-time voyager resulted in 'Oh that old stuff. There's some of it left in the lumber room, but we burnt most of it. Nobody was interested after great-grandfather died.' In one case the sole survivor of a well-known Arctic collection was a pair of Eskimo boots which a young lady had rescued because they would be useful when she was washing the car. In assembling the collection there was constant excitement

....

Yoruba epa mask of a goddess with a child on her back, carrying a gourd in her right hand and a carving of Eshu, the god of uncertainty, in her left. This was said by the original collector to have been a 'God of Smallpox'. Height 54 ins. Nigeria

263

Above: *A painted wooden mask from the North West Coast of America, used in the winter ceremonies. The eyes are movable by the actor from the inside. Height 9½ ins.*

Extreme left: *A rare early sixteenth-century bronze head of a young prince. Height 8 ins. Benin, Southern Nigeria*

Left: *A double-faced wooden mask used by the Yoruba Gelede Society. It was only when a rusted nail was removed that the second face was discovered below. Height 9 ins. Nigeria*

264

James Hooper

A carved wooden rattle used by shamans, *depicting the legend of a young noble carried through the sky on the back of a thunderbird. Length 14 ins. Queen Charlotte Islands*

and enjoyment. Can one imagine the feeling of the expert who found that the beautiful drums of the Austral Islands had been covered with a skin of elaborately plaited strips of cane, and then discovered less than ten years ago what seems to be the last surviving drum with its original adornment? Curious ethnographically, no doubt, but also of great aesthetic value. All at once we knew that the curiously plain body of the drum was not an anomaly, that it had once been as richly decorated as its carved pedestal. An aesthetic judgement of a primitive Polynesian had been revealed. It needed no explanation, because it was right in itself.

The private devotion of the collector eventually found unity with the more official world of art. Aesthetic judgements became less and less based on traditional art of western Europe. The artists had revolted and discovered that the civilisation which had disgraced itself in wars and cruelties was not the sole arbiter of taste. The savages had something to say for themselves. The message seems to have been mostly taken as simplification of form, and, once the *Demoiselles d'Avignon* had donned their pink-powdered African masks in 1907, the world of artists and connoisseurs became sharply aware that there were new fields of form and rhythm to be explored. The impact was more theoretical than ethnographical. Rightly the artist felt that what mattered was the object itself. Once a strange mask had been seen as a work of art, it was a kind of *objet trouvé*. It no longer reflected the ritual dance to the artist, it spoke directly to his unconscious. It awakened all kinds of archetypal images and made him tear at his own heart, for here was a new kind of direct strength independent of the simulation of nature.

In a world longing for direct expression and escape from the traditions which had reached a dead end, the impact of 'primitive art' was tremendous. It canalized much that had been foreshadowed by the discoveries of Kandinsky, and joined forces with the young artists just at the magical moment when they were prepared to accept the revelation.

Since that time they have taught us to look for strength, beauty and pathos with new eyes. We can face a rock or a piece of driftwood and see beauty in it as our fathers could not. This is a triumph of the personality over the demands of scientific consciousness, but it is no surrender to the depths within us. Instead it is a mark of the widening of consciousness. We can now accept the strange images, and the natural patterns which reflect our unconscious knowing. They are an extension of our personality, not a shocking secret to be hidden in the darkest closet. We have even discovered with the savages that sex can be decent, holy and elegant. It was all there, but the gay Edwardians performed some kind of erotodectomy on art; which unpleasant operation was not forgotten, or forgiven, without the intervention of Freud at the time, and later of the delicate healing of Jung to make us understand the wonderful sources of our life and of art.

It is its unity within the world of the Common Unconscious which justifies a mixed collection of Primitive Art. These things, be they Zulu or Eskimo, all speak straight from the heart of man. The strange deities of Polynesia and the little Kachina dolls of the Pueblo Indians are alike manifestations of the spirit. They are literally 'the stuff which dreams are made of'. In fact they are expressions of the artist's only true stock in trade. Not all can be called works of art. As with us, only one in ten thousand can make a work which has true power as art. But the discriminating collector, who has become sensitive to these things, selects and disposes until he has achieved a quintessence of the work of man.

It would not do to assume that the primitive artist has any great freedom of expression. He did not have to face the boisterous vituperation which greeted the 'Greenery-yallery Grosvenor Gallery' in Victorian times. If his work was unconventional in the eyes of his fellow tribes-people, disgrace or death awaited him. There was little mercy for the heretic who had made the images of the gods in novel forms.

265

a   b   c   d

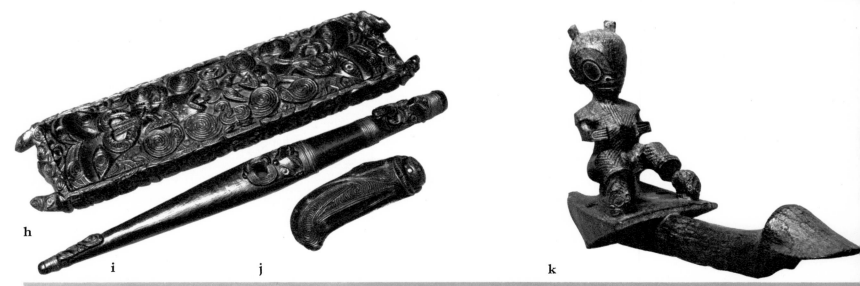

h   i   j   k

James Hooper

Hence we have to regard primitive art as the expression of the soul, through the straitjacket of tribal traditions. The existence of a tradition was valuable. It ensured that a continuous tradition of the representation of an archetypal form was not broken. However, it will easily be seen that in almost any historical series an evolutionary development in style can in fact be observed. Individuals display little idiosyncrasies in their work. Fashion gradually changes, not to

a   *Female figure in toro miro wood.
Height 22 ins. Easter Island*

b   *Male figure of an ancestor.
Height 16 ins. Lake Sentani, New Guinea*

c   *Eshu, the Yoruba god of uncertainty. This carved wooden figure bears symbols of sexual insecurity and also a spear and medicine gourd referring to the union of opposites in one deity. The cape is embroidered with beadwork in a special pattern. Height 15¾ ins. Southern Nigeria*

d   *A carved double figure made from toro miro wood, with eyes of obsidian set in ivory. Height 15½ ins. Easter Island*

e   *Carved figures from the gable front of a Maori house representing the protective power of the ancestors of the family living there. Height 38 ins. New Zealand*

f   *Carved wooden figure of a boy. Height 8 ins.
BaKongo, Angola*

g   *Mother and child. Height 13 ins. BaKongo, Angola*

h   *Maori feather box used to preserve the* huia *feathers worn by a high-ranking chief. The carving represents the ancestors in the act of creation. Length 18 ins. New Zealand*

i   *Maori wooden flute with carvings of symbolic ancestral faces. Length 18½ ins. New Zealand*

j   *Maori wooden ocarina played by blowing across the narrow end. Length 6 ins. New Zealand*

k   *Carved wooden figure of a guardian spirit, once forming part of the prow of a war canoe, as can be seen from the heads beneath his feet and the hair which is done in two tufts in the style of a warrior. Height 12 ins. Marquesas Islands*

l   *Ancient soapstone head,* nomolli, *used in recent times as a fertility charm in the rice fields. Length 10½ ins. Sierra Leone*

m   *Haida Indian wooden mask with movable eyes, used in the winter ceremonies. The designs in very low relief represent face paint. Height 8¼ ins. Queen Charlotte Islands*

Eskimo carvings in bone and ivory.
Left to right:
Walrus, height 2¼ ins.;
Box with 'scrimshaw' work, length 3½ ins. Alaska;
Bear, length 2½ ins. North Canadian coasts;
Seal, height 2½ ins.

*A unique carved wooden drum which still retains
its original decoration of plaited strips of fibre.
Height 4 ft 5 ins. Raivavae, Austral Islands*

the extent of total alteration, but in the varying amount of emphasis put on portions of the total design. Art is not static in any environment without text books.

The great importance of the Hooper Collection is that it covers the whole world of primitive art. There are remarkable objects of the most diverse cultures. The complex symbolism of the mythological carvings from the Haida of Queen Charlotte Islands is matched by the fantastic ancestral symbols in the works of the New Zealand Maori. Zulu and Eskimo vie in simplifications. Bambala figures from the Congo are to be matched with Indonesian carvings of sheer human elegance. The materials are more restricted, mostly because the technical abilities of the primitive artists are limited. The only good metal work in this collection was produced by Africans. The other peoples worked in wood and ivory, in clay and fibre, to make simple things which held beauty within themselves.

The African collection contains some of the best bronzes and ivories which we know from the ancient city of Benin; in particular, one of the finest cast bronze heads from a royal Altar, thin, and four centuries old. The great Yoruba people of Southern Nigeria have contributed wonderful cult masks of their gods, and of their great mother goddess; there is strange beauty and some terror here. From the Congo come ivories, including some deep brown ivory from the Waregga people, and beautiful little initiation masks once worn by the young men of the BaPende. Bambala figures show by their sheer beauty that once this was the leading tribe within the great Bushongo nation.

From America there are the exquisite ivory implements and model animals of the Eskimo, carved from narwhal tusks and whale teeth. From North West Coast tribes there is the totemic art of a warrior people expressed in wonderful

James Hooper

Chilkat blankets, storage chests, oil dishes and ceremonial rattles. There are kachinas and jewellery from the Pueblo Indians, war bonnets and painted shields from the warrior tribes of the untamed prairie. Then from South America there is a very special wood carving done by a tribe of the north west Amazon forests, one of a dozen or so survivors of an almost forgotten art. All this American art is remarkable for its use of colour and insistence on linear design, in contrast to the African use of more directly sculptural qualities.

From the great Pacific Ocean, perhaps the truest wealth of the Hooper Collection, come many things. There is the unique drum from Raivavae and the best collection in the world of carved wooden clubs from the Marquesas Islands. From mysterious Easter Island there are the finely carved figures of ancestors, and small images of the spirits carved from hard, cross-grained, toro-miro wood. The elegant fans and sacred whisk handles from Tahiti are matched by the genealogical staff figures and the adze gods from the Herveys. There is a feather cloak and helmet from Hawaii in beautiful condition, splendid in red and yellow. The Maori of New Zealand are honoured in the feather-boxes, house panels, whistles and pendants of wood, all showing their beautiful and complex art styles. There are sacred heirlooms in the form of *hei tiki*, the first ancestor, and adze blades and fighting meres, all ground out from amphibole jade.

Also from the Pacific, but from the huge Melanesian Islands and New Guinea, come further collections of fantastic painted carvings, shell money, forehead ornaments for young warriors, and, of course, the carvings from great canoes and the sacred club houses for young men.

The Indonesian Islands are represented by some very good carvings and engraving from the Iban and Klemantan peoples of Borneo.

This is a rich collection of great beauty which is still being developed. It was brought together out of an interest in humanity combined with a love of good workmanship.

COTTIE BURLAND

....

A carved wooden house board collected by a former
Earl of Jersey when Governor of New South Wales.
It was retrieved from the debris of a bombed orangery
attached to an old estate near London.
Height 7 ft 4 ins. New Caledonia

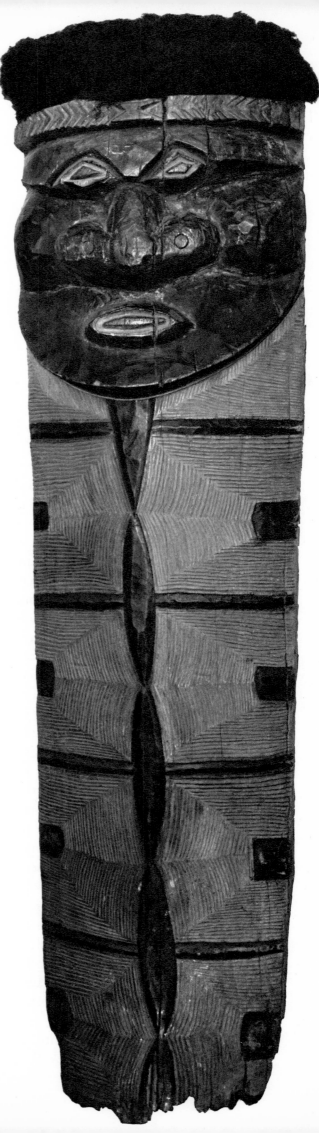

Primitive art and the twentieth-century

WERE THE TOTAL COLLECTION of Nelson A. Rockefeller to be put on view, it would produce an extraordinary impact of breadth, variety, and the movement of one man's taste. To do it even partial justice a very considerable and diverse selection would be needed. It is an inductive, pragmatic gathering, the product of many and apparently various aesthetic interests pursued with equal energy. If one reviews it as one might in an exhibition, it strikes one as built from a continuing series of immediate, whole-hearted responses to individual works of art, unconcerned with a limiting consistency, unworried by confining rules, free of any predetermined notions of static perfection. Unlike many other collectors, Governor Rockefeller has had no set image of his collection. He has made it much as the artists have made the works that are in it – through intuitive choices in a continuous present, out of the conviction that quality can only enhance other quality. Its over-all style is in its attitude of reflective immediacy and constantly renewed response – a style of growth and enthusiasm.

Yet as one returns to the collection and studies it, certain areas of concentration emerge. Evidently certain themes and periods are constantly present in the mind's eye of the collector. Primitive art is one of these. It is in fact more than one, since the works that represent it reflect the five continents, the long centuries, and the almost infinite variety of styles which have all come to be designated by a single term. Modern art is the collection's other great theme, and out of its enormous wealth certain subjects have been stressed. Classical Cubism plays an important role, with significant works by Picasso, Braque, Gris, and Léger. Voluminous, but less conspicuous are the prints, of all styles and media, and the

fine book illustrations. Numerically, the folk arts of Mexico and South America probably outweigh all the rest, although they are seldom to be seen. American painting of the post-war period is very considerably represented, given prominence by the large, bold canvases of the abstract expressionists. And the sculpture of our own time from its fauve and cubist beginnings up to the present – naturalistic and stylized, abstract and representational – makes up in itself a major collection within the whole.

The arts of the twentieth century and of the primitive, which are the foci of this collection, can be seen either as sympathetic or contrasting. What the collection omits suggests that they are looked upon as more related than opposed: there are no old masters, either of the Renaissance or the nineteenth century. With a fondness for sculpture, nothing would have been more natural than to include works of the classic Mediterranean, or the Orient; but with an occasional exception, such as the seventh-century Bodhisattva from Ling Yen Ssu, these are hardly represented. With a sympathy for the modern movement, it would have been more than reasonable to document its immediate sources in Impressionism and Post-impressionism, which would have lent historical perspective to the more recent works. Nelson

••

WHITE AND GREENS IN BLUE
Mark Rothko (b 1903)
oil on canvas 102 × 82 *ins.* 1957

Governor Rockefeller

Below: CLARINET *Georges Braque (b 1882)*
pasted paper, charcoal, chalk and oil on canvas
37½ × 47⅜ ins. 1913

Above: PENDANT: *Anthropomorphic bird figures. Panama:*
Veraguas. Height 3 ins. 1000–1530 AD. Large bird figure pendants
of gold, probably portrayals of forgotten gods, are mentioned
in the early Spanish accounts of voyages to Central America

FINIAL: BIRD *Colombia: Sinu. Gold, height 4⅜ ins.*
1000–1500 AD. A symbol of rank made to fit the end
of a baton or sceptre

Rockefeller has often been tempted, and his friends remember instances when he almost acquired important Post-impressionist canvases; yet each time he has decided that he must stay within his chosen area of the twentieth century, that the flexible character of the collection must not be stretched too far. Besides, in the long run he finds these nineteenth-century works unsatisfying, since for him they have a quality of softness, a kind of passivity, unequal to the demands of modern life.

It would be a mistake to suppose that Nelson Rockefeller's double fondness for the primitive and the modern has anything to do with historical influences, or even with those superficial parallels that over-simplified aesthetics too often remarks. One suspects rather that there is in each a range of style that appeals to him. They are both recent arrivals in the arena of taste (the one perforce, the other through historical accident), and so they may be approached with an independence and a self-reliance of judgement that is at once challenge and refreshment. He says, 'What I like about them is that they are both immediately and fully expressive.'

Nelson Rockefeller's parents were both passionate collectors and he grew up in an atmosphere of concern for the arts. But, of course, environment is not enough. Nelson Rockefeller is himself a born collector. He gathers wherever he is, with decisiveness and promptness – the applied arts as well as the fine arts – in Mexico, or Peru or Persia, as well as in Manhattan. While he was still at college, he furnished a country house with American antiques sought out in New England barns and attics. He has always had an interest in weaving and materials, whether pre-Columbian or oriental or modern. In the bazaars in Isfahan, studying the block prints offered in the markets, and finding their five colours

garish, he traced their manufacture to its source, and convinced their makers to let him have them with only two colours applied. Folk art of all times and places has held a continuing fascination.

The modern and primitive facets of the collection began to form equally early. A trip around the world in 1930 aroused an interest in the arts of the Pacific and of Indonesia. In the thirties, too, there were visits to Mexico, and friendship with contemporary artists whose work had roots in the pre-Columbian past. In 1937 Matisse was commissioned to execute an over-mantel decoration. The artist studied the location in New York and executed the mural on his return to Nice. In the following years (1939–41) Léger was asked to carry out another over-mantel design and also a large staircase and hall mural. In addition, both these painters are represented in the collection by important works: Matisse by two sculptures, *Nude Reclining* (1907), and *Grand Nue Assise* (1925), and two oils, *Collioure* (1911), and *Italian Woman* (about 1915), as well as drawings and lithographs; and Léger by the *Woman with a Book* (1923), *Armistice* (1918), a study for the *Divers* (1940), as well as a large group of sketches and colour lithographs.

These commissions were occasions seized, a fruitful rapport established with the artist, an interest in him and his work that continued into other purchases. There had been a similar opportunity in 1935 when, after years of obscurity and poverty, Gaston Lachaise was given his first exhibition at The Museum of Modern Art. At that time Nelson Rockefeller acquired a whole group of his sculptures, including the characteristic *Torso* (1932), which although small, has all the fertile power of the sculptor's most monumental conceptions.

Nor was the earlier American tradition neglected during this period. Nineteenth-century prints, and a few oils, some of them gifts from his mother, were added to the collection. In 1939 three works of William Harnett were acquired, two of which later turned out to be Peto's. In another sense, however, these pictures are exceptions in the collection. The appreciation of such artists, whose entire conscious intention was certainly in the direction of realism, was largely due to a new vision, educated in Surrealism, which perceived unsuspected overtones in their carefully articulated arrangements. But Surrealism itself (and its modulation into Neo-romanticism, so important to the taste of many New York collectors during this decade), is largely absent from the Rockefeller collection. There is a single de Chirico, *Song of Love* (1913–14). The three Miró oils, including a 1933 *Abstraction* and the large and beautiful *L'hirondelle d'amour* (1934), or the brilliant Giacometti, *The Spoon Woman* (1926–27), *The Slaughtered Woman* (1932), *Headless*

273

Governor Rockefeller

Above: MATERNITY FIGURE *Nigeria: Yoruba.*
Painted wood, height 28½ ins.
Identified by the double axe-shaped headdress, this
nineteenth-century fertility figure is known to be
a priestess or devotee of Shango, god of Thunder
Above right: MASK: DEAD MAN *United States, Alaska:*
Tlingit. Wood, paint, leather, metal and rawhide,
height 13⅝ ins. This nineteenth-century mask of a dead man,
indicated by the closed eyes, was found in a shaman's box

Woman (1932–34), which are pivotal works in the history of modern sculpture, while peripherally related, are both more abstract and more meaningful than what was then thought of as characteristic Surrealism. These, together with the Kurt Schwitters, are as much a part of Cubism as of Dada.

During most of the decade of the forties the collection quite naturally grew slowly. Even before Pearl Harbor, and then during the war years and afterward, Nelson Rockefeller was occupied with matters of government. But his post as Co-ordinator of Inter-American affairs increased his interest in the pre-Columbian history and the arts of South America, and this was reflected in his later collecting.

Beginning in 1949, however, all the major facets of the collection grew rapidly. These years marked the emergence of the new American painting, a style of abstraction best described by its most neutral designation: the New York School. This was a new kind of painting, based upon all that had gone before in Paris – Cubism, Surrealism, and constructive abstraction, but with an inflection all its own, an art born of an international tongue that spoke with a peculiarly local accent. Its courage, its determined fusion of subtlety and energy, these appealed to him. He was one of the first to acquire works of the New York School, at a time when few would grant it any merit. As early as 1949 he bought de Kooning's *The Mail Box* (1948), and two years later *Asheville*; in 1950 he purchased Gorky's *Calendars* (1946–47), one of the artist's most important paintings, which along with the fine *No. 12, 1952* of Jackson Pollock was tragically injured in the fire of 1961 that almost razed the Governor's Mansion in Albany. Works by Rothko, Brooks, Guston, Kline and others of the New York School were added later, rounding out a significant group of contemporary paintings.

These same years saw the collection augmented by key

WOMAN WITH A BOOK
Fernand Léger (1881–1955)
oil on canvas 45½ × 32 ins. 1923

compositions of the modern Europeans: in 1949, the three canvases of the *States of Mind* by Boccioni, works in which the futurist programme has been given a satisfying visual embodiment; in 1950 Picasso's *Interior with Girl Drawing*, one of the finest of that style of the thirties whose combined sympathetic pathos and monumentality already foreshadow the *Guernica*, and a characteristically meticulous and coherent Juan Gris, *The Buffet*; in 1951 Braque's *Clarinet* (1913), a picture whose fusion of absolute clarity and absolute mystery makes it one of Cubism's greatest works. Kandinsky's *Street in Murnau* (1908) and Klee's *Sharp Profile*, also acquired in 1951, added the rare aspect of Expressionism to the collection. With the additional canvases of Matisse, Léger, Braque and Picasso that found their way into the collection in the following few years, the School of Paris was brilliantly represented.

At the same time the sculpture grew apace. The sculptors' names are now familiar to us, and it is an international roster: Lehmbruck, Lachaise and Nadelman, Picasso and Matisse, Calder and Lipchitz, and numerous others all have more than one work in the collection. Now that we have had a 'sculpture revival' and a revival of interest in sculpture, this would not be exceptional. Nelson Rockefeller, however, was acquiring sculptures at a time when painting still dominated the thought of most collectors. He was setting it out of doors as the most natural thing before 'sculpture gardens' had become the commonplace they are now. Not only did he seem to have a natural affinity for sculpture, but the directness of his approach brought works of art usually kept at distance into an ambience of which they at once became a part. This is perhaps why he sees no conflict between the representational and the abstract; in the right setting each is equally at home and leads its own life.

His trip around the world first interested Nelson Rockefeller in the primitive arts, especially those of the western Pacific. Then in the late thirties, after he had been to Peru and brought back two mummy bundles as museum gifts, he and William Harkness tried without success to interest the Metropolitan Museum in a programme of joint expeditions with the American Museum of Natural History. But it was too early for such ventures into areas still unexplored by traditional aesthetics. Even in 1950 there were few collectors of primitive art. There was a vague sense of a relation to contemporary sensibility, and the knowledge that modern artists had found stimulation in the figures and masks of Africa, Polynesia, Mexico and elsewhere. But the Rockefeller Collection was one of the first to include the primitive arts on their own terms, and accept their achievements as the equal of the more conventionally recognized cultures. In such figures as the Mangareva *Man*, the Yoruba

275

MAIL BOX
Willem de Kooning (b 1904)
oil on canvas 23⅛ × 30 ins. 1948

276

Governor Rockefeller

CORINTHIAN II
Franz Kline (1910–62)
oil on canvas 79¾ × 107 ins. 1961

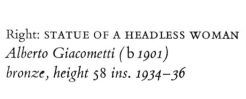

THE ITALIAN WOMAN
Henri Matisse (1869–1954)
oil on canvas 35¼ × 45¾ ins. 1915

Right: STATUE OF A HEADLESS WOMAN
Alberto Giacometti (b 1901)
bronze, height 58 ins. 1934–36

278

Governor Rockefeller

STATES OF MIND III THOSE WHO STAY
Umberto Boccioni (1882–1916)
oil on canvas 27¾ × 37¾ ins. 1911

Above: TORSO *Gaston Lachaise (1882–1935)*
brass, height 7¾ ins. c 1932

Right: MONKEY EATING FRUIT *Peru: Chimu. Wood,*
height 11⅝ ins. Most of the rare pre-Columbian wood
sculpture that has survived, such as this fifteenth-century piece,
has been found in the high dry climate of coastal Peru

Mother and Child he found a sensitivity and an expressiveness to which he responded as he did to contemporary art, while in Meso-American stone work and gold he discovered a strength that delighted him. He did not stop to question the pleasure these objects gave him, or to wonder if they fitted into any accepted canons. For him they were unmatched, and he proceeded to collect them enthusiastically in quantity, but with an eye that soon became most discriminating – even though on one famous occasion some forty important objects were selected in the twelve hours that lay between two overnight plane trips.

It was in this spirit of unhesitating discovery that works as different as the Tennessee *Figure* and Tlingit *Dead Man's Mask* were acquired, and the well-known Baule *Girl* and the Lake Sentani *Double Figure*, the Panamanian *Metate* and the Celtic *Janus Head*; the Colima *Bound Prisoner* and the Peruvian *Monkey Eating Fruit*.

In fact, the number of works of primitive art of all kinds increased so rapidly from 1950 onwards that in a characteristically spontaneous fashion its owner began to see it as something more than a private possession. He felt that what these works meant to him they could also mean to others: it was time for the so-called primitive arts to join the arts of the world. This was the origin of The Museum of Primitive Art, which was founded by Nelson Rockefeller in 1954, and opened to the public in February, 1957. That in the midst of all his public duties he is still its president is some

indication of his devotion to this particular area of the arts.

Any busy man who forms a collection in this energetic manner, and who has been the president of two museums has, of course, had professional co-workers. Alfred H. Barr, Jr, and Dorothy Miller have been long-standing advisers in the modern field; René d'Harnoncourt has given counsel for the folk arts and the wide range of the primitive. But anyone who has worked with Governor Rockefeller knows that his response, his judgement, and his decision are unhesitatingly his own.

The Rockefeller Collection is large and varied. It is an important collection – in the double sense of that adjective. The spirit which has inspired its making may be best suggested by the intense activity in the halls and public rooms of the Governor's Mansion in Albany, on the last day of 1958, just before Mr Rockefeller's inauguration. He had arrived in the early afternoon; an official dinner was scheduled for seven-thirty that evening. The hours between were spent hanging pictures and placing sculpture, works of contemporary and primitive art such as had never been seen before in the old Victorian house, brought together in such profusion that its walls were obscured. The Governor directed and helped execute that installation, insisting that it must and could be ready, even as the dinner party assembled. He wished to receive his first official guests in a setting which expressed his personal taste.

ROBERT GOLDWATER

L'HIRONDELLE D'AMOUR
Joan Miró (b 1893)
oil on canvas 78½×97½ ins. 1934

STILL LIFE WITH PLASTER ARM
Pablo Picasso (b 1881)
oil on canvas 38 × 50½ ins. 1925

Chicago Samuel Marx

Twentieth-century European painting

THE COLLECTION OF Florene and Samuel Marx represents a point of view in collecting perhaps more European than American: the aim of acquiring a discreet, small collection of material of the highest quality. This collection consists in thirty-nine pictures, of which there are one each by Bonnard, Chirico, Derain, Dufy, de la Fresnaye, Modigliani, and Soutine; two each by Gris, Léger, and Rouault; three by Miró; six each by Braque and Matisse; and eleven by Picasso. There is also a small handful of sculpture. The element common to these works – and the motivating consideration for the Marxes – is an understated, austere beauty of form, enhanced and expressed through glamour of colour, beauty of texture, and the utmost probity of drawing and placement. These elements are combined in each case to achieve works of extreme subtlety which emerge to be seen suffused with the hard-to-define qualities of nobility and grandeur. In retrospect the collection stays in memory as a larger one than it actually is, so intense is its impact upon the beholder.

The collection was begun, a bit haphazardly perhaps, when shortly after their marriage the Marxes installed in their new Chicago apartment a fine reproduction of an oil by Rouault only to discover, because of its handsome frame and presentation, any number of people (who might have known better) took it to be a real one. With this as a shock to their sensibilities the Marxes found that they wished to own paintings. Their first purchase was Braque's *Yellow Tablecloth*, 1935, which they saw when it was exhibited at the San Francisco World's Fair in 1939. This celebrated work had previously won the first prize at a Carnegie International Exhibition, and though its classic serenity and

ordering seem today to be the essence of calm – even old-fashioned – clarity, many people of a Philistine bent looked to jeer while the Marxes sat spell-bound in front of it. They soon discovered they could not live without it, and it became their first purchase. Once they discovered the pleasure of acquisition and possession they continued to buy for a generation, with only an occasional refining when a picture did not wear well and was withdrawn.

Most impressive is the Braque *Mantelpiece*; 1922. This is a capital performance which integrates form, colour, and textures (which are ambiguous in their function in that the patterning and marbleizing have a life of their own beyond their functions of reference). The piling up of forms and shapes in this canvas achieves the serenity and lucidity which epitomize the French classical tradition in painting.

The Bonnard *Nude* must be esteemed one of the painter's half-dozen finest figure pieces. Colour and form are expressed in terms of texture and pattern, and the process achieves not only a statement of form and the concomitant space about it, but it also is a comment about place and person at a particular moment in time, with full implications about the life experienced. Bonnard has so concentrated his world that the canvas grows in one's recollection, and it is a shock to discover it is not life-sized.

Chirico's *Ariadne* (1913) ranks as one of his incomparable and inimitable fantasies about both Greco-Roman antiquities and Renaissance Italy which are used as means to communicate the hallucinatory world of the dream.

The Modigliani is one of the master's superlative works, one in which he demonstrated, among other things, how much he must be counted part of the great Italian tradition.

Samuel Marx

Above: SEATED WOMAN
Amedeo Modigliani (1884–1920)
oil on canvas 45¼ × 28½ ins. 1915–16

Left: WOMAN ON A HIGH STOOL
Henri Matisse (1869–1954)
oil on canvas 57 × 37 ins. 1915–16

Opposite: GIRL READING
Pablo Picasso (b 1881)
oil on canvas 63½ × 51 ins. 1934

285

Whatever other elements are present as remembered influences, the fact is that the picture contains aspects which parallel Sienese *trecento* painting as well as a tonality out of *ottocento* Italian art. Modigliani achieved his ends through the combining of earth colours and textures with a concept of line and form which is as recognizably elegant as that of Ingres or Raphael himself.

Léger's *The City* (1919) is one of his maturest works. It is the final study only for the great painting in the Philadelphia Museum. On a relatively slight format, it illustrates that grandeur lies in concept and apposite scale. This was a moment in Léger's career in which he was equipped to make grand even the slightest inventions, so that the impact of forms and of space itself becomes almost unbearably intense, and the colour assumes a subtlety which in fact the raw pigments do not possess.

The humour and wit involved in Miró's *Portrait* (1917) do not conceal either the personal awareness or the aplomb which combined van Gogh-like *matière* with the technique of *collage*. These references to other art underscore how much had happened after 1890, but it is the direct and simple statement which counts and registers as an expression of real power.

It is with the group of Matisses that one discovers how the quiet exercise of impeccable taste can achieve a group to epitomize some of the triumphs of pictorial invention in the twentieth century. The group is limited to a few years in the artist's career, but those were the crucial years not only for his career, but also for this century's art. The *Seated Woman on a High Stool* (1915–16) like the Bonnard, looms as large as life in memory, but is relatively not a large canvas. It is one of the painter's most severely architectonic works. Here the artist has achieved a synthesis of line and form in both two and three dimensions to convey the sense of the hollowness of space and paradoxically emphasizes the flatness of the canvas itself. This is done with painful

Samuel Marx

Above: NUDE
Pablo Picasso (b 1881)
oil on canvas 49 × 35 ins. 1906

Opposite: WOMAN AT HER TOILET
Pierre Bonnard (1867–1947)
oil on canvas 46 × 47 ins. c 1930

intensity and demonstrates, *multum in parvo*, the real meaning and substance of half of the great Western pictures of the first half of this century. The reworking of a still life by de Heem is both witty and pictorially brilliant. The history of great artists' copies of other masters' work is a fascinating one. This time the painter has achieved more than a free invention with a life of its own; he has actually painted a far better picture than his model. The *Goldfish Bowl* (1915–16) is yet another of Matisse's monumental renderings of bits of his rooms in terms to parallel not only those of the mural painter but also those of the architect. But it was the architect of Poincaré's world and not of the present, so that the humanistic element, always present in Matisse, is paramount in this picture. This recounts radiantly aspects of the visible world of the *maison française* and the life within it, then a most comfortable world. It is not for nothing that Sam Marx is by profession an architect whose long speciality has been comfort and suitability mounted in elegant terms. Nor is it surprising that he should react with intuitive sympathy to those works of Matisse which embody the French genius for architectural distinction in the world which used to be.

The *Moroccans* (1916) is one of Matisse's noblest canvases and was one of his own favourites. Its colours and pattern make it more than ordinarily compelling, a vision of the Moslem world in its outer aspects.

Matisse overwhelms the visitor to the Marx collection with spatial grandeurs of an almost baroque magnificence, but it is Picasso who flattens him by sheer genius of invention and power of statement. The rose period draped *Nude* is gracious and lovely in its evocations of feminine suppleness, or even female softness. But there are austere undertones, and the face reflects an awareness, unconscious or not, of old Iberian sculpture, and the full face with implicit profile lives to recur hundreds of times again in the painter's work. One of the surprises in the collection is the head of an *Old Gardener* (1906) which is electric in intensity and catholic in evocations of other worlds and other art. Yet it is in no wise eclectic, for the experience is entirely Picasso's own. It is part of his genius to make the spectator share some of his own private reactions to the art of the past, whether it be Italian Renaissance portraits, heads by Cézanne, or Roman portrait busts. In the end it is the presence of this old man which compels, and the compulsion is achieved merely through the placement of scumbles of

Samuel Marx

PORTRAIT OF E.C.RICHERT
Joan Miró (b 1893)
oil and collage on canvas 33 × 26½ ins. 1917

THE CITY
Fernand Léger (1881–1955)
oil on canvas 38 × 51 ins. 1919

THE MOROCCANS
Henri Matisse (1869–1954)
oil on canvas 46 × 32 ins.
1916

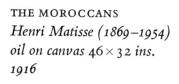

Above: YELLOW TABLECLOTH
Georges Braque (b 1882)
oil on canvas 45½ × 58 ins. 1935

Left: ARIADNE
Giorgio de Chirico (b 1888)
oil on canvas 52¾ × 70½ ins. 1913

Samuel Marx

colour, patchy brushstrokes, and fragmented lines which define ambiguously – yet lucidly – the reality of the working-man's head and shoulders, jacket, and collarless shirt. The heroic, early cubist *Head of a Woman with Pears* (1909) (with the Cézanne-like still-life of a napkin and fruit in the far distance) is wonderful in its sombre and rich colours which owe much to seventeenth-century painting. It is the *Plaster Arm* (1925) and the *Reading Girl* (1934) which demonstrate to the fullest the awesome intensity and real majesty of Picasso's art. The former is one of the grandest of his synthetic cubist still-lifes and belongs to that small group of works in which one can see the cruel truth of Willa Cather's remark that about the year 1922 the world broke into two parts. The subject is old-fashioned and many times familiar. The technique is that of a sophisticated and brilliant man in the prime of his early middle years, virile and tender. The statement is of the utmost clarity and of a deceptive simplicity which suggests the world of a wise child who remembers Punch and Judy; yet the composition and drawing are incredibly subtle and restrained, and the colours, on examination, are far from primary. The subject matter belongs on the far side of 1922, but the presentation and the real content (which concerns the reality and unreality of the visible world) belong on this side. Perhaps the most touching, awesome, and hallucinatorily intense work of the whole collection is the *Reading Girl*. Never was the truth of middle-class French wallpapered interiors, of all the split-leaf philodendrons outside of the jungle, or of the lamp with the shade made of *crêpe-de-chine* more devastatingly presented. Perhaps it is because Picasso is a southern Spaniard that he makes these household gods so much more terrifying than either Bonnard or Matisse made them; or, more probably, it is quite simply that he is entirely prepared to express his formidable sense of humour in visual terms. Whether or not school-girls of the French 1930's went about with garlands to suggest blessed damozels is arguable, but the idea of such a practice can be disconcerting, and never did a hot night seem more depressing. This picture was startling over a generation ago, and it still is so. By now it is unquestionably to be seen and accepted as one of the masterpieces of twentieth-century painting, completely *sui generis*. The means are entirely and simply those of the painter who, with colour, paint texture, line, and pattern, achieved the patterns of visible reality from which the psychic reality may be deduced.   JOHN MAXON

Top and centre: *Two views of the living room of Samuel Marx's Chicago apartment: the first shows* The Moroccans *by Matisse over the mantelpiece; the second shows on the left,* The Mantelpiece *by Braque and a Noguchi sculpture, and on the right,* Studio v *by Braque. In the centre, looking through to the dining room, Matisse's* Still Life After De Heem

Bottom: *Part of the library with de la Fresnaye's* The Artillery *over the mantelpiece, hanging between two pieces of Bakuba sculpture. Modigliani's* Seated Woman *can be seen in the right-hand corner*

Harry Lewis Winston

Futurist and other twentieth-century art

LIKE ALL GOOD PRIVATE COLLECTIONS, that of Mr and Mrs Harry Lewis Winston has a character quite its own. Covering in surprising detail many of the tendencies in art of the twentieth century, it is, however, not a dealers' choice, not a disinterestedly assembled group of works representing a few major painters. Instead it is a collection that invites exploration and promises surprise at every turn. Not only are there important representative examples of work by the well known and acknowledged great, but less familiar works that throw new light upon their accomplishment; and there is an impressive collection of painting and sculpture by less well known artists whose quality amazes and delights. Rather than swiftly confirming one's opinions about the nature of twentieth century art and its growth, the Winston Collection has a way of making one rethink the material, discovering new relationships, new possibilities in movements and in artists supposedly known and historically typed. Although as a group, works by the Italian Futurists outnumber those of other tendencies, the collection is by no means restricted to Futurist painting. The inclination of the Winstons has been, quite clearly, not to document a particular movement but to underscore the essential vitality, the innovating freshness of the art of the past fifty years.

The Winston Collection, which has been built up with care and sincere affection over the past twenty years, can be divided into three closely related parts. First of all are the paintings, ranging from early works by Picasso, Léger, and Boccioni to works by Pollock, De Staël, and Baj. There is no simple common denominator for the works chosen other than that of excellence. They do not tend towards some one general type, towards formal decorativeness, for example, or

towards the provocative gadgetry of the Neo-Dada. They remind one, instead, of the extraordinary gamut of experience available to the modern eye and mind. The poignant clutter of a Schwitters collage, the disarming evocativeness of an assemblage by Prampolini, serve as contrast to the pure formality of a carefully poised Mondrian and the geometric rhythms of the synchromist Macdonald-Wright.

The second part of the collection is the sculpture which ranges in style from Henri Laurens' jaunty cubist *Man with the Mustache* of 1917 and the complexly woven *Figure* by Antoine Pevsner (1925) to more recent evocative works by Hoflehner and Paolozzi. Here, too, the variety is great, the one continuing factor being creative vitality.

A third important part of the collection is made up of drawings and prints. Aside from the extensive collection relating to the Futurists, this carefully organized body of work presents a comprehensive view of trends in modern art. In building this part of the collection, the Winstons have thought not only of their own pleasure but also of the pleasure they might give to others by making available to them through exhibitions a coordinated presentation of twentieth century sensibility in art.

Cutting across these divisions is the rich collection of works

••

PORTRAIT OF DORA MAAR *Pablo Picasso (*b *1881)*
oil on canvas 16⅛ × 13⅛ *ins.* 1941.
One of a long series of portraits
of the artist's companion painted between 1936 and 1946

Right: STREET PAVERS *Umberto Boccioni*
(1882–1916) oil on canvas 39⅜ × 39⅜ ins.
This study of light and action probably dates from
1911 when Boccioni was first experimenting
with cubist forms

Below: THE INJECTION OF FUTURISM
Giacomo Balla (1871–1958)
oil on canvas 31¾ × 45¼ ins. c 1918

Harry Lewis Winston

DEVELOPMENT OF A BOTTLE IN SPACE
Umberto Boccioni (1882–1916)
bronze 15 × 24 ins. 1912

pertaining to the first Italian Futurists. When the Winstons began to investigate the movement of Futurism, it was a tendency in twentieth century art neither well understood nor prized. Since the second generation of Futurists were entangled with a political movement that must be condemned, the works of art themselves, even by those painters whose productive lives did not survive the First World War, were looked upon as politically suspect. But no misapplied political strictures can obscure the lyrical charm of Gino Severini or the irresistible vitality of Umberto Boccioni. Once they had purchased their first Severini in the early 1950's and had talked with that gentle artist about his Futurist experience, the Winstons, almost before they knew it, were on the way to the rediscovery of a vital and essential movement in modern art.

Certainly among the Futurist artists, Umberto Boccioni was the strongest and most genuinely creative. Nowhere is there a better chance to follow the development of his work or to appreciate the full force of his dynamic personality than in the Winston Collection. Boccioni wrote once to his friend Vico Baer that he felt that he had been forced to re-create the whole history of modern art in his own lifetime. Complaining of the backward attitude toward changes in art that characterized the Italian environment early in the century, he believed that in a few short years he had of necessity fought his way from the middle of the nineteenth century to his own time. Boccioni, of course, was not alone in this;

it is the fate of the modern artist that he is forced always to begin anew. But what the modern vision in art has meant to the creative spirit is particularly clear and telling in the work of Boccioni.

The over two hundred and fifty drawings by Boccioni in the Winston Collection most of which, until their acquisition by the Winstons, in 1956 and 1958, remained in the possession of the artist's sister, Signora Rafaella Callegari-Boccioni of Verona, trace his career from the early days in Rome and in Venice, from as early as 1902, to his discovery of the modern city, in Milan, and the gradual evolution of a formal language suitable to the dynamic principles of Futurism enunciated by Marinetti. There was nothing mechanistic in the thinking and feeling of Boccioni. A sensitive, self-questioning man, he desired none the less to feel at one with the new and exciting modern environment. The move towards Futurism was by no means an easy one for him, and it is evident that Boccioni sometimes privately doubted the virtues of action and noise. There was a side of Boccioni, well documented by his many drawings of fields and grazing animals, that led him towards the quiet country scene, towards the bucolic and rustic. And in the city he saw first the people, then the crowds, and only at last the might of the entire community personified as a tremendous overpowering force, greater than any man or group of men. These intimate glimpses of the artist reflecting, rather than the artist acting, are afforded both by this large collection of drawings and

295

STUDY FOR THE PORTRAIT OF MADAME S
Gino Severini (b 1883)
pastel 19¼ × 13⅞ ins. 1912

STUDY FOR 'MOURNING'
Umberto Boccioni (1882–1916)
charcoal, pencil and coloured pencils
with grey wash on paper 9⅛ × 18½ ins. 1910
One of a number of preliminary studies
owned by the Winstons showing how the form
of this painting developed

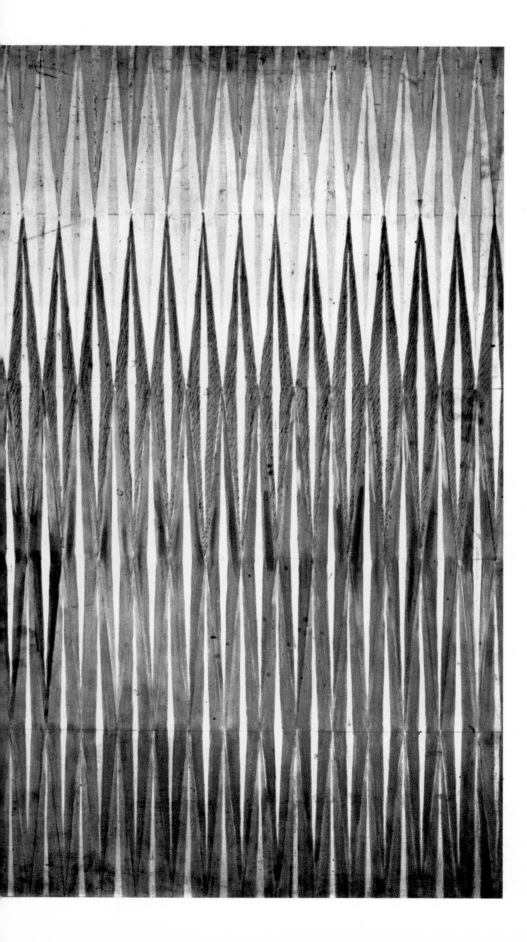

by Boccioni's little known but expert graphic works, all of which are represented by at least one impression in the collection. Most of Boccioni's etchings were done prior to 1910. They are not, in consequence, influenced by his ideas of Futurism. Instead they betray that particular sensitivity that shows Boccioni – and this was true even when he was most engrossed with formal problems and the impersonal intensity of modern life – to be a warm, responsive human being.

From late in 1910 through 1911 the work of Boccioni underwent a remarkable change, well documented in the Winston Collection by his lyrical painting of *Street Pavers*, executed probably in the summer of 1911. In this, early intimations of a contact with the Paris Cubists are mingled with a bold treatment of his divisionist colour to create a lively, rhythmic environment. Rather than being a study of human action, it tends to expand the action of the individual figure until it permeates the entire visual universe of the painting. Background, foreground, and figures are one in the vibrant experience. It is interesting to turn from Boccioni's colourful painting to Fernand Léger's *Woman in an Armchair* of 1912 in which the expanding rhythms of the forms seem to fill the space with true Futurist exuberance. Léger, not the Futurists, was to celebrate machine-like forms in his paintings. He seems Futurist here because of his exuberance, not because of his mechanical shapes.

The next phase of Boccioni's work, a phase reflecting his full knowledge of Cubism and the maturing of his own theories of space and perception, is best exemplified in the Winston Collection by his sculpture. First of all there is the *Development of a Bottle in Space* (1912), an analytical work in which Cubist analysis of form is subjected to the dynamic intensity of the Futurist regard for continuity. The fact that Boccioni should choose to model an unmoving, lifeless object in sculpture, generally regarded until then as a static medium, is significant. He was clearly establishing the fact that the sense of dynamism most treasured by the mind is not that deriving from physical action, but that which is instinct

· ·

IRIDESCENT INTERPENETRATION
Giacomo Balla (1871–1958)
oil on canvas 39¾ × 23⅝ ins.
One of several paintings executed in 1912
exploring the dynamic properties of light

Harry Lewis Winston

in perception itself. The active rhythms of Boccioni's *Bottle* do not give the object life so much as they restore to the observer a consciousness of his own alert, perceiving mind.

More characteristic of Boccioni, however, is the vigorously modelled, intricate head of his mother, which he chose to call an *anti-grazioso,* an 'anti-pretty' work. Here Boccioni's strong sense of empathy infuses the analytical forms of Cubism with an unwonted, pulsating vitality and flow of human warmth. But his great work, the work that remains one of the finest of modern sculpture, is his *Unique Forms of Continuity in Space*, the last in a series of striding figures and the only one to survive. Facing a flood of light from large windows overlooking an open expanse of garden, the flowing bronze form radiates a vitality and ebullience not to be resisted. It is both active and serene, continuous and unchanging. This is Boccioni's great proof that the transient experience of time in space can be transfixed, to be savoured in the synthetic image of a work of art.

Futurism was not a style but a driving force that expressed itself in quite different ways. At the opposite pole from Boccioni's empathetic involvement is the work of Giacomo Balla which demands contemplation rather than the memory of muscular action in its flight towards an expanding universe. His *Iridescent Interpenetration*, painted in 1912, the same year as his better known studies of action such as the charming little scampering dog, *The Leash in Motion*, holds the attention through the dynamic interplay within light itself. His painting is not a depiction of light as manifested by light and shade on an object, but a depiction of light seen as the product of dynamically interacting components. It is as if he had looked at an Impressionist painting until subject matter had disappeared and there remained only the active 'interpenetration' of the spectrum hues, neatly refined in interlocking shapes. It does not overwhelm by force but attracts by its complexity and its promise of an infinitely expandable space. In a very different way, yet not wholly unrelated, Brancusi's nearby *Blond Negress* disciplines the

• •

ABSTRACT SCULPTURE
Henry Moore (b 1898) height 20 ins.
Sculpture in Hopton Wood stone executed in 1937

EXAMINER 2861 MERZ *Kurt Schwitters (1887–1948)*
collage 8½ × 6⅝ ins. 1947.
In 1917 Schwitters founded the 'Merz' movement
which advocated the use of unconventional materials in order
to achieve contrasts impossible when using line and colour alone

298

complexity of light within a simple form: the reflexions catch the eye and hold the mind in a shredded fantasy world of light and space.

Balla's fascination for the persuasive vortex that holds the mind suspended in a luminous and spacious atmosphere – sometimes by a speed that seems to transcend motion – preceded his formal interest in Futurism. His strange, evocative *Stairway of Farewells* of 1908 is hauntingly memorable. Quite contrary in effect to Futurism, one might say. Yet the direction of Futurism was inward as well as outward. The 'state of mind' was no less a concern for Balla or Boccioni than the sense of speed. 'We choose to concentrate our attention on things in motion,' wrote Severini in 1913, 'because our modern sensibility is particularly qualified to grasp the idea of speed.' But the ultimate significance of motion for the Futurists was in the activity of the mind and imagination. Carra's quick shift in 1916 from Futurism to the still, airless spaces of the *Scuola Metafisica* was not so great as at first it seems. A trace can be seen already existing in Balla's lonely, evocative *Work* of 1902.

Balla was the only one of the original Futurists to continue faithfully according to the programme after the war. His work became more synthetic in the war years, more distilled, but was based always on the study of process, whether of moving crowds surging around the square in a patriotic demonstration or the driving force idealistically embodied in the symbol of *Boccioni's Fist*. This extraordinary work of sculpture, constructed from cardboard and painted red, was a kind of memorial to the vitality that early Futurism had stood for, and became the insignia of the post-war Marinetti movement. Balla had begun to make sculptural constructions at least as early as 1913, but most were made from impermanent materials and have been lost. The delightful apartment he decorated for himself and family in Rome, however, burgeoned with colourful constructions, and two of its constructed *Flowers* carry some of the sunny spirit of his studio into the Winston Collection.

The true lyricist of the Futurists was Severini, one of whose kaleidoscopic portraits of *Madame S.* dominates a wall in the Winston Collection. His bespangled *Dancer Beside the Sea* of 1913 was the Winstons' first Futurist acquisition. Its planes move in and out rhythmically, interchangeably miming the action of waves or dancer, inviting, in fact demanding, our participation. But the participation is neither the physical involvement required by Boccioni nor the serious concentration of Balla. It is a light and pleasurable diversion;

FAUNA OF THE OCEAN *Antoine Pevsner (1884–1962)*
brass and oxidized tin 20¾ × 28 ins.
In the Realist Manifesto of 1920, Pevsner and his brother
Naum Gabo, set forth the theory of Constructivism which
proclaimed the need to create new forms on a dynamic principle
using the materials of twentieth-century technology

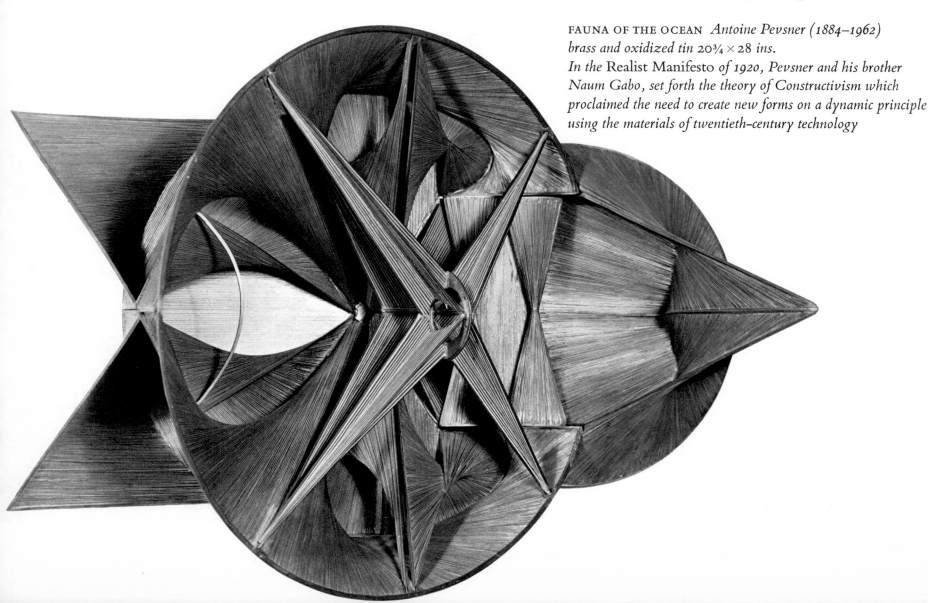

Harry Lewis Winston

MOON VESSEL
Jackson Pollock (1912–56)
oil on canvas 34⅛ × 18⅛ ins.
This work, executed in 1945,
was bought by the Winstons
in the same year, as part of their policy
of encouraging younger painters

Opposite: LINEAR CONSTRUCTION IN SPACE NO 2
Naum Gabo (b 1890)
height 17 ins.
A delicate sculpture
in plastic and a single nylon thread
executed in 1950

Harry Lewis Winston

Above: UNIQUE FORMS OF CONTINUITY IN SPACE
Umberto Boccioni (1882–1916)
bronze 48½ (including base) × 34 ins. 1913.
On Boccioni's death this figure existed in plaster only.
This bronze is one of four cast subsequently

Left: STAIRWAY OF FAREWELLS *Giacomo Balla (1871–1958)*
oil on canvas 41½ × 41½ ins. 1908

the translation of all aspects of perception into dance. Unless it is simply an illusion brought about by seeing the works together, there is something of this quality in the work of Antoine Pevsner when he is not too absorbed by geometry. His construction, *Figure*, of 1925 is closer to the rhythmic images of the Futurists than to the architectural constructions of the Cubists. His later work, with its transparent planes and smooth, continuous rhythms in space, is even closer to the Futurist ideal, an ideal that found life only in the continuous dynamic interplay of forces, forces not limited to the simple kinetic possibilities of massive bodies. It was Boccioni who first pointed out in 1912 that various new materials could be combined in sculpture and that light (a quality he admired in the work of his countryman Medardo Rosso, who is represented in the Winston Collection by a fine head) was a positive element at the command of the sculptor. It is a curious fact, that after he has looked at such disarming works by the original Futurist artists, a visitor to the Winston Collection begins to see Futurism, newly defined, manifest in almost everything, as if his eyes were freshly attuned to a new wave length.

In their choice of recent works, the Winstons have shown their usual sympathy for many points of view. Wherever possible they have searched out the artist to talk with him about his ideas and his goals, always looking towards broadening their own knowledge of art. In most of their recent acquisitions they have tended away from the purely non-objective and analytical – although one of their very beautiful recent accessions is Antoine Pevsner's sensitive construction, *Sea Fauna,* of 1944. Two aggressive paintings by the restless Italian painter, Baj, *Grand Uniform* and *Erano tutti e tre sulla buona strada*, bring the disruptive spirit of Dada noisily into the present. The Austrian sculptor Rudolf Hoflehner's dignified *Mediterranean Goddess* (1958) communicates a classical dignity through the heavy ingot language of massive cast and severed forms. Alberto Burri's large and brooding *Grand Ferro* prods a mystery untouched by the Futurists. These and many other works by provocative painters and sculptors, famous or unrecognized, become associates of the continually expanding collection of Futurist art.

The theme of Boccioni, that the modern artist must find his own way and realize his statement with methods and materials unmistakably of his time, is precisely the theme that radiates clearly through the collection of Lydia and Harry Winston. The fresh, positive expression of searching minds and vital creativity, not the 'representative work' of a style or a movement, dominates. For this reason it seems an assembly of art in action, a monument to creative expansion rather than to past accomplishment. It is, in other words, pervaded by the searching spirit of the first Futurists, whose works form the cornerstone of this lively and growing collection. JOSHUA C. TAYLOR

*The garden room and the south living room of the Winstons' house in Birmingham, Michigan.
The height of the walls and the use of natural and artificial light were carefully planned
for the display of the collection*